VOLUME 3

CIVIC LITERACY

VOLUME 3

CIVIC LITERACY

BUILDING CIVIC FUTURES IN TEACHER EDUCATION

EDITORS
Lakisha Odlum, Queens College, City University of New York
Nicole Mirra, Rutgers University
Antero Garcia, Stanford University

NCTE National Council of Teachers of English®

Copy editor: Michael Ryan
Staff editor: Cynthia Gomez
Cover design: Pat Mayer
Interior design: Ash Goodwin

ISBN 978-0-8141-0242-8
eISBN 978-0-8141-0243-5
PDF ISBN 978-0-8141-0244-2

It is the policy of NCTE in its journals and other publications to provide a forum for the open discussion of ideas concerning the content and the teaching of English and the language arts. Publicity accorded to any particular point of view does not imply endorsement by the Executive Committee, the Board of Directors, or the membership at large, except in announcements of policy, where such endorsement is clearly specified.

NCTE provides equal employment opportunity to all staff members and applicants for employment without regard to race, color, religion, sex, national origin, age, physical, mental or perceived handicap/disability, sexual orientation including gender identity or expression, ancestry, genetic information, marital status, military status, unfavorable discharge from military service, pregnancy, citizenship status, personal appearance, matriculation or political affiliation, or any other protected status under applicable federal, state, and local laws.

Every effort has been made to provide current URLs and email addresses, but, because of the rapidly changing nature of the web, some sites and addresses may no longer be accessible.

Library of Congress Control Number: 2025931661

VOLUME 3 | BUILDING CIVIC FUTURES IN TEACHER EDUCATION

CONTENTS

Introduction

LAKISHA ODLUM, NICOLE MIRRA
& ANTERO GARCIA

Lakisha's Story

The year 2014 marked a pivotal moment in my development as an English educator. At the time, I was teaching seventh-grade English language arts at an all-boys, predominantly Black and Latinx public school in New York City. I was also newly enrolled in a doctoral program in English education. It was the first time in my career as a secondary English teacher that I saw a connection between my pedagogy and the theory that I was learning in school. I was fortunate to have a professor who introduced me to educational theories and concepts such as critical media pedagogy (Morrell et al. 2013), sociocultural theory (Vygotsky, 1978), funds of knowledge (Moll et al., 1992), literacy practices and literacy events (Barton & Hamilton, 2000; Heath, 1982), culturally relevant pedagogy (Ladson-Billings, 1995; Kinloch, 2009; Tatum, 2009; Kirkland, 2013) and multiliteracies (New London Group, 1996). These mentor texts expanded my understanding of the myriad ways in which I could better understand my students and develop curricula that were affirming and humanizing. My students were always excited about learning, and I knew that they were the perfect group to begin implementing some of the theories that I learned in this course.

My first attempt at taking my practice to the next level occurred on October 20, 2014, which was the National Council of Teachers of English's (NCTE) National Day on Writing. The purpose of the event is to honor and celebrate "the remarkable variety of writing Americans engage in and to help make writers from all walks of life aware of their craft" (NCTE, 2024). The collective hashtag for the day was #WriteMyCommunity, and I asked my students to respond to the following prompt: If you could tell the world one positive thing about your community and one thing that could be improved, what would it be? Their responses exceeded my expectations and revealed to me that my students had a deep love for their communities and were civically minded and engaged in ways that I was unaware of. When reflecting on the day, students shared that participating in the National Day on Writing made them feel empowered and hopeful about improving their communities.

Without the guidance of a teacher educator who encouraged me to dream big and to espouse a Freirean pedagogy, I would not have been brave enough to implement that type of activity in my classroom. The negative perspectives about adolescents and social media and "woke" pedagogy could have easily deterred me from providing my students with a life-changing learning experience. Many of those students are now college graduates who are leaders in their churches, fraternities, classrooms, and home communities. When I see the work they are doing, I hope that my teaching was critical to their development as civically engaged citizens. As a teacher educator, I encourage my university students to create similar spaces in their secondary English classrooms, despite the vitriol they are facing as teachers in this political moment.

Nicole's Story

I was assigned to teach ninth-grade English language arts my first year in the classroom. As my new assistant principal showed me the part of the book room reserved for ninth-grade texts and directed me to the ninth-grade standards and curriculum guide, I felt that I could understand clear parameters for my role. My duty was to focus on my particular piece of the jigsaw puzzle of ELA content and skills; as a newbie, I was too overwhelmed to think in any broader terms about my purpose as an educator or my responsibility to my students. My job was to teach my students the ninth-grade content as well as I could and to send them on to the tenth-grade ELA teacher.

And then, the next year, as often happens in small schools, a colleague left. Suddenly, I found that I was the tenth-grade ELA teacher. In ways large and small, the continuity of time allowed me to see my students growing up—one getting a bit taller, one advancing in analytical ability, one finding new tastes in independent reading. The boundaries between ninth- and tenth-grade content became more flexible as I reminded students of what we had done together previously and bridged to new ideas, new skills. Instead of thinking within the confines of grade levels, I began thinking longer term.

This continued as, for a variety of reasons, I was able to loop with many of my students all the way through the twelfth grade—to see the entire cycle of a student's high school ELA experience. At the end of that year, I was pondering goals as a teacher in a way I couldn't have imagined when I was a first-year newbie; my students were about to head out into the world, and I was about to head to graduate school to search for the answers to my questions about the purpose of literacy education. I thought about what to write in their yearbooks—what I wanted them to remember about our time together playing with language. It was only through our years together that I was able to realize that I didn't care so much if my students could recall the plot of every text we read or the structure of every essay we wrote; rather, I wanted them to hold on to the power of reading, writing, listening, and speaking to advocate for themselves, their communities, and the issues they cared about to build the equitable future they deserved.

I would eventually find more language to articulate this desire when I got to graduate school—Paulo Freire's words helped me understand that we teachers are cultural workers rather than transmitters of content. But it was breaking out of the traditional boundaries that structure teachers' work—boundaries of grade levels, school years, relationships to students—that first helped me learn expansively that teaching is really about preparing young people to understand the world as it is and to build new worlds that could be.

Antero's Story

Several years into my high school teaching career, we'd received word of our umpteenth new principal coming—for real this time—to switch up how things had been progressing at our high school. At initial faculty meetings, I crossed my arms in skepticism as the new principal outlined a vision of student achievement that was—for real this time—going to change the culture and academic performance at our school. I, and my colleagues, had heard it all before.

Except this time, the principal didn't switch things up right away (and also didn't leave within months of arriving). Something was different.

At a smaller meeting late in the school year, the principal outlined a vision of focusing on ninth-grade students and creating small academies that would foster positive youth-adult relationships in these groups as well as harness a collaborative spirit. Having spent months visiting classrooms and listening to students, the principal was asking a group of us to pilot the academy. Even though I'd spent much of my previous years teaching eleventh and twelfth graders, I signed on to what would become some of my most rewarding years in the classroom. Looking back, it was the opportunity to spend time with research on the delicate year of ninth grade as well as the intentional relationship-driven nature of the principal's vision that led me to switch things up (for real this time). It's been rare, in my years as a teacher, to feel trusted, heard by administrative leaders. Learning was not tied to just the work happening in my classroom but to the ways school systems can open up and close off opportunities for collaboration, learning, and risk-taking.

Expanding Horizons of Possibility in Teacher Learning

All three of us had moments while learning to teach when the possible horizons of what it meant to be an educator expanded exponentially—when we realized that we were not there to simply pass on knowledge of what came before but rather to connect with our students and colleagues to build what could be next. We realized that:

- ELA is a uniquely powerful site of civic learning.
- Civics is not just about learning how systems currently work but how society could and should be.
- As teachers, we have the enormous power and responsibility to open those doors for students.

But it's tough—as a society, we're stuck in a lot of ways. We'll describe the stuck places but then remember that we have models to light the way toward a different vision of teacher learning. And then the authors of these essays will show us pathways forward.

Where We Are—The Stuck Places

"As a public good, universities have a rare and critical role to play. While we educate leaders for the future, we also address important societal issues of the day."

—Nancy Cantor

Throughout her career, world-renowned university educator and leader Nancy Cantor (2004) has declared that universities are public goods whose mission should include the combination of liberal learning and civic engagement. She asserts that "[i]n so doing, we will be able to educate socially responsible citizens who will not be complacent in the face of entrenched social norms, but will take the initiative in shaping our diverse democracy and its global interconnections" (p. 18). Twenty years later, universities in the United States are too often straying away from this mission. We are living in a time when politicians are calling for attacks on the university, and professors have even been called the "enemy." The Supreme Court has reversed affirmative action, and state legislators are passing laws to dismantle diversity, equity, and inclusion (DEI) efforts in universities. Free speech is being attacked through massive university book bans (Lavietes, 2024), and when students demonstrate "socially responsible" citizenship such as peaceful campus protests, university administrators have called law enforcement on them (NPR, 2024).

Moreover, the field of education and teacher preparation is suffering its own challenges. The research and curricula that teacher educators create in order to dismantle white supremacy in education is being portrayed as frivolous by the far right (Reichman, 2021). Furthermore, enrollment in teacher preparation programs continues to dwindle. A Pew Research study (Schaeffer, 2022) revealed that the amount of bachelor's degrees in education that were conferred in 2019–2020 was down by 19 percent, compared to the number of bachelor's degrees in education conferred between 2000–2001. More surprisingly, the study also revealed that women, the dominant teacher demographic, "have become much less likely to choose education as their field of study. More than a third (36%) of all bachelor's degrees conferred to women were in education in 1970–71." One factor that has contributed to the decline in enrollment is the "political and ideological arguments surrounding classroom curriculums." All of this leads us to ask: How should teacher educators respond to this current historical moment? What is the role of the teacher educator in fostering civic engagement and shaping "socially responsible citizens"?

Remembering Where We Can Go—Thinkers Lighting Our Way

We argue that a reexamination of Gloria Ladson-Billings's (1995) groundbreaking research on culturally relevant pedagogy is useful in beginning to unpack these questions. Ladson-Billings's theory of culturally relevant pedagogy was born out of a need for educational researchers to reimagine what teacher preparation should look like. Ladson-Billings believed that in order to reform teacher preparation, especially in the programs that trained teachers of African American students, it was important to study the pedagogy of exemplary teachers. Operating within Freirean (1970) and Black feminist (Collins, 2000) traditions, Ladson-Billings studied the pedagogical practices of classroom teachers and concluded that "effective pedagogical practice" incorporates students' cultural identities, provides them with skills to critically critique systemic oppression, and focuses on student achievement. These findings led to her steadfast belief about how to prepare prospective teachers:

> Although I agree with Haberman's assertion that teacher educators are unlikely to make much of a difference in the preparation of teachers to work with students in urban poverty unless they are able to recruit "better" teacher candidates, I still believe researchers are obligated to re-educate the candidates we currently attract toward a more expansive view of pedagogy. This can be accomplished partly by helping prospective teachers understand culture

> (their own and others) and the ways it functions in education. . . . The implication of continuing this work means that research grounded in the practice of exemplary teachers will form a significant part of the knowledge base on which we build teacher preparation. (p. 483)

Ladson-Billings's charge to teacher educators is twofold—first, she emphasizes the necessity for teacher educators to commit to expanding the ways that *all* of our teacher candidates view our most vulnerable student populations. Second, she believes that more of our research should be grounded in the practice of excellent teachers. Recent scholarship by Detra Price-Dennis and Yolanda Sealey-Ruiz (2021) as well as Nicole and Antero (2020) serve as contemporary models of the type of research that Ladson-Billings advocated for.

In *Advancing Racial Literacies in Teacher Education: Activism for Equity in Digital Spaces*, Price-Dennis and Sealey-Ruiz (2021) provide teacher educators with a racial literacy framework that empowers students to actively resist white supremacist ideology in their schools and in their teaching. They contend that "[r]acial literacy can be seen as a 'movement' that views educational spaces as grassroots organizing sites that prepare individuals for the 'racial battles' they will fight for equity and equality in schools and society" (p. 25). The racial literacy framework helps to prepare students for these "racial battles" by asking them to question their assumptions, having them engage in critical conversations, and providing them with opportunities to practice reflexivity.

Nicole and Antero's (2020) work with the Digital Democratic Dialogue (3D) Project, presented in "'I Hesitate but I Do Have Hope': Youth Speculative Civic Literacies for Troubled Times," is a model of how educational researchers can directly engage classroom teachers and students in the work that Ladson-Billings, Price-Dennis, and Sealey-Ruiz propose. Through the 3D Project, Nicole and Antero were able to collaborate with students and teachers from across the United States in an attempt to center youth voices in discussions about civic engagement—what they refer to as a speculative literacy approach. They assert that ". . . a speculative literacies approach supports [students] in restorying public life in ways that honor their experiences, relationships, and dreams for the future" (p. 297). With the support of Nicole, Antero, and ELA teachers who were committed to connecting literacy with democratic education, students were able to engage in authentic and nuanced discussions about their "civic present and possible civic futures" (p. 315).

Taking the Next Step: Where We're Going

The research presented by the authors in this book contributes to the burgeoning body of research on civic futures in higher education and the K–12 classroom. Each of the essays serves as a joyful provocation aimed at broadening our horizons just a bit further about what is possible in teacher learning—they remind us of the humbling responsibility we have to our students to support them to build a better world than the one we have bequeathed to them.

In the first essay, "Learning from Their Voices: Educators' Strategies for Teaching Social Justice in Turbulent Times," Kornbluh et al. explore the challenges and opportunities of teaching civics with a social justice approach in today's political climate. Despite difficulties, students are eager to discuss social issues and connect learning to advocacy. Based on interviews with eighty-three educators and focus groups in Oregon, the authors highlight actionable strategies for engaging in civics education. These include partnering with evidence-based organizations, building supportive networks, using student-driven pedagogy, and involving parents. The essay also provides links to resources for lesson planning, evidence-based practices, and networking for educators.

Next, in "Crip Your Civics: A Disability-Informed Approach to More Democratic Learning," Andrea Avery, a disabled educator, provides an approach to disability-informed curriculum and pedagogy in civics education. The author establishes both the overarching purpose of civic education and its particular relevance and responsibility to disability and provides a theoretical basis rooted in principles of disability justice and inclusive pedagogy, including the concept of "cripping." She provides a practical example of a way to revise a civics lesson to include disability. The example includes self-reflection questions teachers can use to assess their own practice and to generate possibilities for making it more disability informed.

In "'It's on a Banned Book List': Moving through a Landscape of Book Censorship in Literacy Classrooms," Murdter-Atkinson et al. address the complex dynamics of book banning and censorship in literacy classrooms as legislative measures in the United States have increasingly restricted educational content. The authors explore how these trends affect preservice teachers, who may feel pressured to avoid specific texts to prevent controversy. Drawing from legislative analysis, media critique, and insights from their own teaching experiences, the authors highlight the consequences of book banning on literacy education. They advocate for strategies that empower educators to take civic action in their classrooms by managing literature selections that reflect diverse identities, asking layered questions with mandated texts to promote critical analysis, and connecting to larger networks to advocate for intellectual freedom and shape students' civic futures.

In the fourth essay, "High School English Teachers Advancing Civic Possibilities through Assessment," Moore and Ho share the stories of English teachers advancing civic possibilities through the lens of assessment. It describes one professional learning community (PLC) of teachers striving to "reclaim assessment" in their classrooms. This group—the Alternative Assessment Collective (AAC)—interrogated the status quo of high-stakes testing and traditional forms of assessment while building toward literacy assessment "as it should be." Over one school year, the teachers applied principles of culturally sustaining and liberatory assessment as they designed, implemented, and received feedback on new assessments. This essay spotlights three assessment stories to showcase how teachers in the AAC engaged in "civic world building" by putting these principles into action. One developed a civic engagement capstone assessment; another created a map-based autoethnography assessment; a third designed a global issue speech and dialogue assessment. These teachers moved from imagining a different assessment future to actually advocating for it and experimenting with it in their classrooms. We hope their work may be useful to other educators who are building toward justice.

In "Teachers of Writing and Their Experiences: *Cuentos* from a Community Writing Workshop," Baldonado-Ruiz et al. explore the design and implementation of a professional development writing workshop for secondary ELA and history teachers working in the US/Mexico borderlands. The essay focuses on the experiences of two humanities teachers who participated in the workshop, in which they wrote their own testimonios and developed curriculum for their classrooms. The workshop brought together preservice, early career, and experienced teachers who all lived and worked in the borderland region. Grounded in testimonio pedagogy and community cultural wealth, the workshop provided strategies for teaching writing to adolescents, encouraging students to share their lived experiences and family histories. The essay highlights teacher voices, offers insights from the workshop, and discusses how the teachers implemented writing curricula inspired by the experience.

Next up, in "'You're Letting the Kids Really Go There': Practices of Novice Teachers Mentored by Experienced and Innovative Educators," Bonner and Seglem examine the intersection of civic education and English language arts (ELA) classrooms, emphasizing the potential to develop informed and engaged citizens through critical engagement with social issues. The authors highlight the importance of addressing fascism, racism, homophobia, climate change, and economic inequality, while calling for teachers to rethink traditional practices. Reimagining the ELA classroom allows students to not only explore their curiosities but also learn how to take action against injustice. The authors explore the impact of an experienced, civic-minded mentor teacher on novice educators, demonstrating how this influence can shape socially just practices during their formative teaching years.

In "Equipping Educators to Nurture Student Civic Advocates through Social Justice Pedagogy," Underwood et al. explore the challenges and opportunities within civics education, critiquing the traditional method of presenting sanitized historical narratives that celebrate individuals in isolation while neglecting systemic injustices and marginalized voices. The authors advocate for an antiracist curriculum and social justice pedagogy (SJP), defining SJP through the principles of equity, social literacy, and activism. The essay provides a research-based framework for educators to integrate SJP into literacy instruction, encouraging students to critically analyze and challenge social injustices. It highlights the use of project-based learning and performance tasks to foster civic engagement and advocacy skills. Additionally, the essay underscores the need for professional development and support for teachers to address challenges in teaching for social justice, concluding with practical guidance for developing thematic unit plans aligned with SJP principles to create inclusive and socially just learning environments.

In "ELA Teacher Educators and Activism: Concepts, Curricula, Barriers, and Possibilities," Cook and Sams draw on multiyear research into how ELA teacher educators incorporate activism into their preparation of future teachers and highlight four key themes identified through their study. The authors describe how educators conceptualize activism, provide examples of their activist teaching practices, and explore the barriers they face and strategies for overcoming them. The essay also includes examples of how students engage in activism as a result of these courses. Each theme is accompanied by practical connections for readers and reflections on future directions for advancing activism in teacher education.

In "Of Loyalty, Freedom, and Agency: Framing Our Roles as Citizens in Literacy Teaching and Teacher Education," DePascal and Rice frame their work through theoretical conceptions of freedom as discussed by various educational scholars. They present a specific example from ELA teacher education that involves questioning the daily practice of reciting the Pledge of Allegiance. The essay connects this examination of loyalty and civic activity to a roleplaying activity used in teacher practice. It concludes with reflections on the need to expand ELA teaching for civics to address the full range of challenges teachers face, including pressures to conform to injustices.

The tenth essay, "Educators Writing to Change the World," features contributions from participants in the Chicago Area Writing Project's (CAWP) EdWrite Collab, a group of twenty-one educators dedicated to "writing to change the world." It addresses the contemporary challenges faced by teachers, including issues of underpayment, undervaluation, and intense scrutiny. The authors, Wilber et al., discuss the pervasive lack of self-determination and the disrespect faced from elected officials and the media. The essay also highlights the gender imbalance in key forums influencing public policy and opinion, emphasizing the need for more educators to bring their identities, experiences, and aspirations into these spaces to help shape improved educational systems.

Next, "Participatory Action in Higher Education: Empowering a Collective of Education Majors as Partners in Institutional Change" by Douglas and Dove details strategies implemented by the school of education at a prominent Historically Black College or University (HBCU) in Atlanta, Georgia, to foster civic engagement among education majors. The authors begin by sharing their counterstories as Black men in academia—one as a teacher educator and the other as a preservice teacher. They then explore the social justice and activist work initiated by students, which was driven by the critical literacy learned in their teacher preparation coursework. The essay highlights how these students became leaders in promoting change within their university community.

In the last essay, "Cultivating a Pedagogy of *Comunidad* through Youth Participatory Action Research (YPAR) in Classrooms and Schools in Cleveland," Buckley-Marudas et al. share the ongoing work of an Ohio-based *comunidad* of teachers, university researchers, high school students, and graduate students who collaborate to design and implement Youth Participatory Action Research (YPAR) in Cleveland public high schools. The teachers, part of Project HighKEY, have integrated YPAR into their schools through various approaches—whether in their content areas, as electives, or as extracurricular programs. Focusing on the evolving collaboration between two YPAR teachers, the authors illustrate how individual agency is used to support collective goals. They introduce *pedagogies of comunidad* as a framework for understanding how these relationships are nurtured over time.

As you enjoy the pages to come, we invite you to consider what the next point on the horizon might be that you could push us toward in the struggle for an equitable tomorrow.

Works Cited

Barton, D., & Hamilton, M. (2000). Literacy practices. In D. Barton, M. Hamilton, & R. Ivanič (Eds.), *Situated literacies: Reading and writing in context* (pp. 7–14). Routledge. https://doi.org/10.4324/9780203984963

Cantor, N. (2004). Civic engagement: The university as public good. *Liberal Education, 90*(2), 18–25.

Collins, P. H. (2000). *Black feminist thought: Knowledge, consciousness, and the politics of Empowerment* (2nd ed.). Routledge. https://doi.org/10.4324/9780203900055

Fadel, L., & Martínez, A. (Hosts). (2024, April 19). A pro-Palestinian protest at Columbia University is broken up by NYPD officers [Audio podcast transcript]. In *Morning Edition*. NPR. https://www.npr.org/2024/04/19/1245810462/a-pro-palestinian-protest-at-columbia-university-is-broken-up-by-nypd-officers

Freire, P. (1970). *Pedagogy of the oppressed* (M. B. Ramos, Trans.). Continuum.

Heath, S. B. (2001). Protean shapes in literacy events: Ever-shifting oral and literate traditions. In E. Cushman, E. R. Kingten, B. M. Kroll, & M. Rose (Eds.), *Literacy: A critical sourcebook* (pp. 443–466). Bedford/St. Martin's. (Reprinted from *Spoken and written language: Exploring orality and literacy*, pp. 91–117, by D. Tannen, Ed., 1982, Ablex Publishing Corporation)

Kinloch, V. (2009). Literacy, community, and youth acts of place-making. *English Education*, *41*(4), 316–336. https://doi.org/10.58680/ee20097234

Kirkland, D. E. (2013). *A search past silence: The literacy of young black men*. Teachers College Press.

Ladson-Billings, G. (1995). But that's just good teaching! The case for culturally relevant pedagogy. *Theory Into Practice*, *34*(3), 159–165. https://doi.org/10.1080/00405849509543675

Lavietes, M. (2024, August 16). *Florida college dumps hundreds of books, many on sexuality, race and feminism*. NBC News. https://www.nbcnews.com/nbc-out/out-news/florida-new-college-books-removed-lgbtq-race-women-rcna166912

Mirra, N., & Garcia, A. (2020). "I hesitate but I do have hope": Youth speculative civic literacies for troubled times. *Harvard Educational Review*, *90*(2), 295–321. https://doi.org/10.17763/1943-5045-90.2.295

Moll, L. C., Amanti, C., Neff, D., & Gonzalez, N. (1992). Funds of knowledge for teaching: Using a qualitative approach to connect homes and classrooms. *Theory into Practice*, *31*(2), 132–141. https://doi.org/10.1080/00405849209543534

Morrell, E., Dueñas, R., Garcia, V., & López, J. (2013). *Critical media pedagogy: Teaching for achievement in city schools*. Teachers College Press.

National Council of Teachers of English. (2024). *National day on writing*. https://ncte.org/national-day-writing/

The New London Group. (1996). A pedagogy of multiliteracies: Designing social futures. *Harvard Educational Review*, *66*(1), 60–92. https://doi.org/10.17763/haer.66.1.17370n67v22j160u

Price-Dennis, D., & Sealey-Ruiz, Y. (2021). *Advancing racial literacies in teacher education: Activism for equity in digital spaces*. Teachers College Press.

Reichman, H. (2021, December 14). "The professors are the enemy": Right-wing attacks on academic freedom have real repercussions. *The Chronicle of Higher Education*.

Schaeffer, K. (2022, September 27). A dwindling number of new US college graduates have a degree in education. *Pew Research Center*.

Tatum, A. W. (2009). *Reading for their life: (Re) building the textual lineages of African American adolescent males*. Heinemann.

Vygotsky, L. S. (1978). Interaction between learning and development. In M. Cole, V. John-Steiner, S. Scribner, & E. Souberman (Eds.), *Mind in society: The development of higher psychological processes* (pp. 79–91). Harvard University Press.

Learning from Their Voices: Educators' Strategies for Teaching Social Justice in Turbulent Times

MARIAH KORNBLUH, SHERRY BELL, RAQUEL AMADOR & AUDREY LUCERO

Brock is a seasoned teacher with seventeen years of experience. He works at an alternative public high school, meant for students identified as being "at risk" for not obtaining a high school diploma, located in a suburban city within the state of Montana. His passion for teaching comes from a desire to inspire students to be their own civic actors. Like many educators, Brock is worried about his profession in the current political climate:

> I try to help students understand the importance of being engaged, especially in the past few years. And they see that. They understand what's on the line. I would say the biggest challenge is our state government. It's controlled by a governor who really doesn't care about education. Just yesterday, he was speaking to a group of middle school students. He told these middle school students that school was pointless for him and that he learned much more on the football field than he ever did in school.

English language arts (ELA) classrooms are essential spaces for fostering the health, wellness, civic imaginations, and the critical literacy skills of students (Mirra et al., 2018). Yet our civic landscape is ever changing. Youth today must combat the spread of misinformation, look beyond online echo chambers, and rebuild institutions that have systematically disadvantaged our most vulnerable communities. Teachers are navigating turbulent times as they work to meet the civic needs, hopes, and aspirations of their students. On top of politics, accessing high-quality civics curriculum is challenging. At its best, civics curriculum is designed to prepare K–12 students to be agentic actors by examining specific subject areas (i.e., labor movement history) as well as key skills (i.e., discourse, organizing, and advocacy).

ELA scholars stress the importance of facilitating students' *sociocritical literacy* (Guiterrez, 2008; Mirra et al., 2018). Sociocritical literacy views citizenship and literacy as dynamic social acts that are influenced by cultural, political, and historical contexts with an orientation toward social change and justice. Yet resources to support such pedagogical practices are often underfunded. Furthermore, civics curriculum in general is often siloed within specific content areas (i.e., social studies), at times lacking research evidence to support it, and failing to connect to students' lives.

In this essay, we focus on sharing actionable co-created strategies from stakeholders themselves invested in civics education and social justice. In doing so, we aspire to uplift and center the voices of educators from eighty-three interviews and two focus groups across the United States.

Research Project

From 2023 to 2024, the first three authors conducted over eighty-three interviews with teachers, superintendents, subject coordinators at the district level, state officials, community organizations, and youth activists from diverse geographic states, communities, and regions. Partnering with an advisory board (composed of teachers, youth activists, community organizations, and school administrators), we collectively identified key pathways for both accessing and delivering civics curriculum with a focus on social justice education and liberation. Lastly, Drs. Kornbluh and Lucero partnered in conducting two focus groups on a critical literacy pedagogy course (developed by Dr. Lucero) for ELA educators within the state of Oregon. Findings are shared across projects with an emphasis on the first.

We begin the essay by unpacking how educators accessed civics curricula, and then we highlight strategies shared by the educators themselves. We discuss these strategies at the intersections of ELA teaching and constructs.

Part One: What Strategies Are Being Used to Access Civics Curriculum with a Focus on Social Justice Education?

For over twenty-three years, James served in various school administration roles. During the last seven, he has been the District Superintendent within the California Central Valley. Using a social justice framework discussed by ELA scholars (see Dover 2015; Mirra et al., 2018), James envisions civic literacy intersecting with aspects of cultural and community pride. Yet he couldn't do the work alone. Specifically, he discusses his district's partnership with a local nonprofit, which provides multicultural educational resources:

> Our city is a Latino story. So, having like-minded partners who help kids understand their own value, those are things that matter. Sometimes people are pitching a hustle from the nonprofit sector. You gotta make sure that the people you do business with are aligned to your inclusive line of thinking. This organization [nonprofit] helps me make connections to other people, municipalities, or other nonprofits to get kids connected in meaningful ways.

Strategy 1: Finding Allies

Like James, educators stress the importance of not doing their work in silos. Specifically, they need access to vetted resources (such as lesson plans and materials) informed by best practices centered on fostering student learning, social-emotional wellness, and critical engagement (Darolia, 2020). Educators successful in accessing civics curriculum often strategically partnered with an organization or individual (referred to as a broker). Research within ELA and other instructional programming (i.e., mathematics, STEM) have further highlighted the valuable role of brokers in connecting educators to resources and vetted curriculum (Coburn, 2005; Malin et al., 2018). Brokers come in various forms and may include local community-based organizations, university centers focused on education and outreach, racial justice activist groups and youth organizers, and school district officials, as well as fellow teachers. Such connections are essential to creating a sustainable infrastructure. Brokers are often able to connect educators to an array of resources, professional development support, and a larger community of peers with shared values.

For instance, Katie, a teacher with seventeen years of teaching experience and who is a current doctoral student in education, was inspired to start a coalition in Arizona to support educators in accessing evidence-based resources for teaching civics as well as for garnering relational support:

> I just have a file of facts in my brain. I understand you as a teacher, I understand the community you're serving, here's where I think the best resource is. A lot of our partners, too, will be, "Oh, I have this really great thing." I think that's the beautiful thing about it. It just becomes this big spider web for teachers to say, "We have this really great workshop, or I know so-and-so is doing a workshop." So, it just honestly becomes in the moment, "What is needed? What do I have?" and if I don't know the answer, I know somebody who does. The work is very purposeful. I want to help teachers.

How do I find a broker? Educators in our interviews connected with brokers through a variety of avenues. For some, this included attending national conferences and professional development workshops hosted by universities, state officials, and national organizations. Others met brokers through word-of-mouth from trusted colleagues. Still others looked to individual champions of civics within their local district, region, or at the state level. Lastly, others turned to community groups and youth activists engaged in on-the-ground social justice organizing. Thus, finding a broker involves exploring one's networks both locally and nationally.[1]

Ariana, a teacher with eight years of teaching experience in a suburban school district in Arizona, discussed meeting Katie through the coalition and getting connected to curriculum surrounding participatory schoolwide budgeting:

> When we launched it, [the foundation was] going to all the three different pilot sites learning and helping as well. And so we felt supported that way. When you look at what those kids are learning, the ones who are running the program, they absolutely like to benefit from it. There are so many ways to tie that to our curriculum—it's a no brainer. So, between the principal giving it to me, my colleague who allowed me to do it in his classroom, and the support from the foundation who came in and ran the first launch of the project—they also provided training for the project—it was great.

1. See resource QR code at the end of the essay for identifying potential brokers.

Key Questions for Identifying Brokers

1. Who are the champions (in and outside of school spaces) for social justice and civics education within your network?
2. What meeting spaces (locally and nationally) might allow you to connect with needed resources and supports?
3. What types of resources, connections, or supports might be needed to increase your comfort with engaging in social justice pedagogy?

Strategy 2: Vetting Your Broker

It is important to note that brokers come with varying ideologies, views, and expertise. Thus, another key strategy is that of critical evaluation and disruptive questioning (Vasquez, 2019). The following dimensions are important to research when vetting a broker:

- **Hidden Agendas.** Brokers come with their own beliefs and processes for accessing, vetting, and circulating curricula. Asking, researching, and reflecting on such processes is important to ensure that the information being shared supports student learning and values of social justice.
- **Role of Research.** One way to assess the quality of a curriculum is to ensure that it integrates research-informed best practices in student learning and critical engagement. Determine if the curricula has been evaluated, assessed, or even linked to empirical studies that further highlight its impact on key student learning outcomes. Another key component is assessing if the curricula has been utilized in diverse communities (e.g., novels that have received awards embracing cultural representation, such as Pura Belpré, Corretta Scott King).
- **Equity.** Some civics curricula may be based in research but uphold the status quo (centering in whiteness) and are not reflective of the needs of students and communities from the global majority. It is important to assess if the curriculum uplifts students' voices and lived experiences (i.e., promotes sharing and storytelling), reflects their civic aspirations and struggles (i.e., embraces timely and community relevant topics), and offers a vision of civics that is inclusive (i.e., use of inclusive language and imagery).

Cynthia, a middle school teacher with thirty years of teaching experience in a suburban school district in Vermont who recently relocated to Connecticut, stressed the importance of finding curriculum that upheld best practices on student engagement through project-based learning:

> As I look at the curriculum, I feel like those research elements that talk about how we keep students engaged in meaningful, active learning that's both rigorous and relevant to their lives, I think that's the research that this program is based. It's incredible. So, a lot of the students were focused on the environment, making Connecticut cleaner or more beautiful. They had to do research about the different types of pollution and where the pollution was coming from. They were finding their own voice. We were doing math, science, social studies, ELA, and then sort of the transferable skills with problem solving, critical thinking, and communication. It was amazing.

Key Questions for Vetting Brokers

1. What are the values of the broker? What is their objective in sharing this information?
2. What role does research play in developing and vetting curriculum?
3. Does the curriculum meet the needs of the student body and underrepresented communities? What culturally recognized literary associations might signal support for the curriculum?

Finding curricula and partnering with brokers is no easy feat! However, that is just half of the battle. The next notable hurdle is teaching civics focused on social justice and liberation. We now turn our attention to the strategies educators are using to enact teaching and pedagogy that uphold values of social justice.

Part Two: What Strategies Are Being Used to Teach Civics within Politically Turbulent Environments?

Strategy 3: Building Your Network

Teachers stressed the importance of building a network supporting teaching civics that upholds values of social justice (Lucero & Avelar, 2022; Navarro, 2018). These networks ought to be diverse and encompass relationships with school administrators, community groups, fellow teachers, national organizations, local universities (educational professors), online communities, and, most importantly, youth themselves.

Brenda has been teaching ELA for nineteen years in a middle school located in rural Oregon. With new school board elections, Brenda and her fellow teachers have experienced heightened scrutiny and pressure to remove any books discussing race and LGBTQ issues. One summer, Brenda took a professional development course through the university focused on critical literacy pedagogy. The course provided her the opportunity to explore new pedagogical teaching strategies for discussing race and issues of social justice with aspiring colleagues:

> I think just having the time and the platform just to read and think and talk. As teachers, we just get into the school year, and we just get absolutely buried with all the other stuff. And it was just super-nice to come to a place where you could just sit with other educators who weren't the people that you see every day, who were able to share their thoughts and ideas. And then I was faced with some opposition. And then having it resurfaced in the book, I think, gave me the confidence to do it again. I think those are the baby steps, the introductory things that are somewhat safe in my environment, but also allow students to have a voice.

Another key strategy for cultivating a diverse network includes showing up in one's community. This entails attending local events, supporting school activities and student activists (sports games, festivals, fundraisers), and cultivating one-on-one relationships with students and families, as well as connecting with fellow teachers via informal (reading groups, online forums) and formal (local union chapters) work groups.

Building such deep connections allows educators to feel collectively supported and provides them with the agency and autonomy to teach curriculum centered on principles of equity and justice. Educators stressed that due to these deep connections with the community and school, they were less likely to experience actual

Key Questions for Network Building

1. What spaces (online and in-person) are available for community building among teachers?
2. Do such spaces allow for feelings of safety, vulnerability, and strategizing?
3. What are ways to show up in one's local school and community that can facilitate authentic relationship building?

backlash. This was because parents knew them personally and recognized their investment in their children. Additionally, when they experienced criticism, their colleagues and administrators were active in supporting their work.

Strategy 4: Following Your Students' Lead

Another key strategy educators use to teach social justice-focused civics education is to select a curriculum that incorporates elements of student voice and agency (Darolia, 2020). Such a curriculum encompasses a range of activities such as service-learning projects as well as researching social issues of importance when voting. Central to these projects is that the topic of inquiry is driven by student-led interest. Such inquiry provides an opportunity for students and teachers to co-create a literacy praxis of reflection and action. Here, literacy is used to not only read the world but also as a disciplinary tool to imagine a more just and democratic one (i.e., civic dreaming; see Mirra et al., 2018).

Cynthia, a teacher with twenty-two years of experience in an urban school district in Texas, shared the importance of student engagement and providing a space for students to explore topics that are meaningful to their community.

> It was about teaching students how to have civil discourse, how to come together to solve problems by looking at root causes. We worked with seventh graders, who were reaching out to local city council members. Consistently, what we got back in our feedback was that people could not believe that they were talking to seventh graders. That they were so articulate. That they were organized. Then, these seventh graders, they were astounded by the fact that people were listening to them, and they were having this impact. An issue that they had decided to focus on was domestic violence but particularly in immigrant populations who are afraid to report that, and how we go about getting that support for them. They were trying to advocate for the passage of a bill through the Texas Senate. It felt for the first time, I was really doing what I was supposed to be doing as a teacher. I was creating change-makers.

Educators highlighted the value of engaging students in youth-led participatory action research. As Cynthia notes, her students select and research topics of injustice within their local community. Through this process, they develop skills in sociocultural literacy, research, and critical thinking. Informed by their research, they then develop a plan for social action. This could include presentations to decision-makers, public art pieces, developing a petition to garner community support, or a service-learning project. These hands-on activities provide an interactive framework to understand civics at a local level. It also provides them with experience in advocacy, organizing, and public speaking. While these projects promote best practices in student learning

Key Questions for Promoting Student Voice

1. How might students bring their lived experiences into the classroom?
2. How might students have opportunities to write, read, research, and advocate on social issues of importance to them?
3. What pedagogical shifts and preconceptions need to be challenged in order to create space for student-led civic dreaming within the classroom and in the larger school community?

and engagement (see Kornbluh et al., 2015, for a fuller discussion), they also protect teachers, as the *student-driven nature* of the project made parents and community members less likely to accuse educators of indoctrination.

Strategy 5: Be Transparent

Lastly, educators discussed various strategies for anticipating potential backlash from parents and community members when discussing civics (Ellis & Goering, 2023). Some teachers highlighted the importance of code-switching, in which they used more neutral language. For instance, the term "action civics" was changed to "community service-learning projects."

Lillian is a teacher with twenty-two years of teaching experience in a rural school district in Oregon, where many students come from low-income housing and utilize social services. Drawing from her personal relationships with community members, Lillian has identified which terms are met with resistance from families in her community:

> When [another teacher] and I plan stuff, we have a pretty good idea of some of our kind of hardest families that we kind of in our head keep—I don't say we just cater to them, but we kind of keep in mind some keywords that might push them over the edge. Kids will ask me, usually, not like in full class, but some individual kids will ask me how I vote, and I'm fine to tell them. And like the whole class, I'm pretty kind of, you know, measured and try to be choosing words carefully. Just to not offend, you know, families or get things started up. But I'm still trying to, like, sometimes nudge them toward more critical thinking about an issue in a smiley way. We just try to be smarter than how they're going to react.

They also took efforts to ensure their materials were non-partisan and worked to present "both sides" of a social issue. This strategy is important in the politically tense environment teachers are navigating. However, there have been critiques of such approaches in that presenting both sides of a social injustice can create a platform for false equivalences (see Hlavacik & Krutka, 2021; Kornbluh et al., 2024). Furthermore, such conversations can further traumatize, suppress, and isolate students impacted by such injustices and embolden those who deny such inequities exist. Embracing discussion of socio-political events within the classroom has also been an avenue for fostering critical literacy, in both the unpacking and redesigning of texts (i.e., social media, advertisements, books) with a focus on equity (Darolia, 2020).

Recognizing this complexity, educators in communities with active parent groups pushing for restrictions surrounding social justice education chose the route of *transparency*. These educators welcomed parents to attend the classroom, were explicit in the type of content they were sharing, and encouraged parents to partner with their children in exploring and engaging with assignments. Here, educators really leveraged the role of research to back their work. They highlighted how the curriculum was research-based on promoting high-impact student learning.

Scheana, a union organizer, activist, and veteran ELA teacher of over seventeen years within an urban district in South Carolina, noted her strategy for facilitating civic discussions at home and leveraging research to advocate for the health and wellbeing of her vulnerable students:

> I am incredibly transparent and have a reason for why I am doing this work. The more open you can be, the less they

> can come at you. I do use research to convince parents. I use a mixture of personal stories and statistics. For example, I share with parents around LGBTQ advocacy content the statistics around suicide rates. Humanizing the issues can convince some parents. My students decide the civic issue they are going to focus on. Their first project is interviewing their parents about the project. This creates a bridge between the content of the project and the parents.

Some educators even partnered with researchers themselves (through research-practice partnerships) to develop well-crafted arguments that could highlight the value in the approach and overall content they were using.

Conclusion

The educators in this essay highlighted critical strategies for teaching civics with a focus on social justice. First, they partnered with brokers to access curriculum, resources, and research that facilitated their students' learning and engagement. Second, they vetted these brokers. They ensured the information being shared was grounded in research, reflected values of social justice, and met the needs of their community. Lastly, they were strategic with their teaching. This involved cultivating networks and communities of support, selected curriculum that elevated student-driven learning, and invited parents into the classroom to ease anxiety and fears.

Live Resource Page

Interested in enacting the strategies identified in this essay? Scan this QR code, and it will take you to a resource page for each strategy discussed.

Works Cited

Coburn, C. E. (2005). The role of nonsystem actors in the relationship between policy and practice: The case of reading instruction in California. *Educational Evaluation and Policy Analysis*, *27*(1), 23–52. https://doi.org/10.3102/01623737027001023

Darolia, L. (2020). "He's on fire for justice!": Using critical conversations to explore sociopolitical topics in elementary classrooms. *Journal of Curriculum Studies Research*, *2*(1), 39–54.

Key Questions for Fostering Transparency

1. What are ways to build communication between the classroom and home environment?
2. What training, resources, and support might be needed for you to facilitate critical and racial literacy within the classroom?
3. What are the connections between classroom learning activities and district/state standards? What research might be valuable to have in sharing the importance of a particular pedagogical approach of learning activity?

https://doi.org/10.46303/jcsr.02.01.3

Dover, A. G. (2015). Teaching for social justice and the common core: Justice oriented curriculum for language arts and literacy. *Journal of Adolescent & Adult Literacy, 59*(5), 517–527. https://doi.org/10.1002/jaal.488

Ellis, S. E., & Goering, C. Z. (2023). "I'm really just scared of the White parents": A teacher navigates perceptions of barriers to discussing racial injustice. *English Teaching: Practice & Critique, 22*(4), 531–545. https://doi.org/10.1108/ETPC-05-2022-0067

Gutiérrez, K. D. (2008). Developing a sociocritical literacy in the third space. *Reading Research Quarterly, 43*(2), 148–164. https://doi.org/10.1598/RRQ.43.2.3

Hlavacik, M., & Krutka, D. G. (2021). Deliberation can wait: How civic litigation makes inquiry critical. *Theory & Research in Social Education, 49*(3), 418–448. https://doi.org/10.1080/00933104.2021.1933665

Kornbluh, M., Davis, A., Dunn, A. H., & Brezicha, K. (2024). Exploring the role of evidence-based educational resources and brokering in the wake of political trauma. *Evidence & Policy, 20*(4), 486–503. https://doi.org/10.1332/17442648Y2024D000000026

Kornbluh, M., Ozer, E. J., Allen, C. D., & Kirshner, B. (2015). Youth participatory action research as an approach to sociopolitical development and the new academic standards: Considerations for educators. *The Urban Review, 47*, 868–892. https://doi.org/10.1007/s11256-015-0337-6

Lucero, A., & Avelar, J. D. (2022). Exploring the challenges and possibilities of critical literacy pedagogy: K–8 teacher discussions about race in a virtual professional development course. *English Teaching: Practice & Critique, 21*(4), 483–495. https://doi.org/10.1108/ETPC-05-2022-0065

Malin, J. R., Brown, C., & Trubceac, A. S. (2018). Going for broke: A multiple-case study of brokerage in education. *AERA Open, 4*(2), 1–14. https://doi.org/10.1177/2332858418769297

Mirra, N., Coffey, J., & Englander, A. (2018). Warrior scholars & bridge builders: Civic dreaming in ELA classrooms. *Journal of Literacy Research, 50*(4), 423–445. https://doi.org/10.1177/1086296X18784335

Navarro, O. (2018). We can't do this alone: Validating and inspiring social justice teaching through a community of transformative praxis. *Curriculum Inquiry, 48*(3), 335–358. https://doi.org/10.1080/03626784.2018.1468212

Vasquez, V. M., Janks, H., & Comber, B. (2019). Critical literacy as a way of being and doing. *Language Arts, 96*(5), 300–311. https://doi.org/10.58680/la201930093

Crip Your Civics: A Disability-Informed Approach to More Democratic Learning

ANDREA AVERY

A note on language: I have drawn on my experiences as a disabled woman and my knowledge of disability studies to inform my language choices. Acknowledging that some members of the (large and diverse) disability community prefer person-first language while others prefer identity-first language, I have used both "disabled [people, students]" and "[people, students] with disabilities." I have used the concept of "cripping" throughout this discussion. Like queer, "crip" is at the center of a theory and an aesthetic, having originally been a slur but having been reclaimed by the people against whom it has been used. I have capitalized Black (but not white) to signify shared Black history, culture, and group identity.

Introduction

It is one of the promises of public schooling in the United States in general—and civics education in particular—that students will be provided with the knowledge, skills and dispositions necessary for responsible, engaged citizenship (Hamot, Shokoohi-Yekta, & Sasso, 2005). Indeed, civics education has its antecedents in the original design of public education in America: "preparing people for Democratic citizenship was a major reason for the creation of public schools" (Center on Education Policy, p. 2). Naturally, what it means to be a responsible, engaged citizen has changed over time and is at any moment subjective; the United States is geographically large; racially, religiously, and socioeconomically diverse; and increasingly politically and ideologically divided. What, then, is a "good" citizen, and what knowledge, skills, and dispositions should students be taught?

Indeed, in recent years, alarms have sounded in almost every ideological corner about a "crisis" in civics education; the evidence for such claims usually points to underwhelming, and declining, student proficiency scores in US history and civics as well as surveyed adults' inability to name the branches of government or basics about how the Supreme Court functions (Altschuler & Wippman, 2023; Davenport, 2019). I do not view lackluster test scores or spotty factual recall as the *most* damning evidence of insufficient civics education; instead, I worry most about the state of civics education when I see someone online posting angrily about the injustice of "paying for public schools" when they don't have children who attend them. I agree with those who argue that civic engagement is much more than "knowledge of government structures" but rather the skills and knowledge necessary for "participating as a member of a collective" (Hammer, 2022). Therefore, civic education:

> must teach students to feel empowered to make a difference in their government.... Good civic programs work to teach students that they are valued by the social structures they live in, and that if they aren't being valued then something needs to change. Working outside the structure of government through civil disobedience is still a form of civic engagement. (Hammer, 2022)

It is not my purpose in this discussion to solve the "crisis" in civics education. Instead, with the above definition of civic engagement in hand—participating as a member of a collective, working within and, when necessary, bending structures of government to accommodate, and dignify, all people—my focus will be an aspect of civic education that is particularly underdeveloped and underdiscussed: disability. As a disabled educator and scholar, I will lean on the field of disability studies and the work of disabled scholars to make my argument that high-quality civic education must by definition include, and be informed by, disability. Disabled people exist in all cultures, in all strata of society. A civics education that is not inclusive of disability (in purpose, content, and methods) is no civics education at all.

Perhaps because I am a disabled educator, I am particularly attuned to the ways that pathologizing language is applied to education systems (and, more problematically, to humans inside those systems). As a person with an incurable chronic illness, I have a particular relationship to the very ideas of brokenness and repair, as well as a deep skepticism about "burn it all down" as a viable approach to most problems. In *Against Technoableism: Rethinking Who Needs Improvement,* disabled scholar Ashley Shew (2023) demonstrates via her "transmobile" friend Mallory's flexible, responsive, innovative, context-dependent use of multiple technologies to move about the world as a disabled person that "being disabled gives us more choice," not less (p. 16). I wish to write not in the context of a civics education in crisis but rather within the context of a civics education in flux. I hope to offer some ways that disability wisdom can show us our many choices.

In that spirit, my objectives in this essay are to reinforce those who have argued that disability must be part of civics education because it is a not-insignificant part of the collective with which civics is concerned. Next, I will posit that disability belongs not only in the "what" of civics education (i.e., curriculum) but also in the "how" (i.e., pedagogical approach), and I will share examples of high-quality disability-informed curriculum. Because I intend for my work to have a solid theoretical grounding but still be immediately useful to practitioners, I will offer an example of how a teacher can "crip" an existing civics lesson, both in content and approach, as well as provide some reflective questions teachers can ask of their civics lesson designs to assess how well they include disabled people, voices, history, and perspectives.

Disability Invisibility in School

To be a citizen is to be part of a citizenry. Therefore, meaningful civics education depends on exposure to a diversity of lived experiences and identities and transmission of the idea that "civic society is comprised of and has a responsibility to a wide range of communities" (National Council of Teachers of English, p. 5). One of these communities is the disabled community, more accurately described as a large, multifaceted, loosely affiliated network of disabled communities. Deaf people, for example, have a rich history, culture, and community that may or may not overlap with that of other disabled people—for example, autistic and neurodivergent people, amputees, wheelchair users, or chronically ill people (acknowledging, of course, that many people have multiple disabilities). Still, as members of these communities, disabled people share a vulnerability to erasure, exclusion, marginalization, and abuse in schools and in the community at large. If civic society has "a responsibility to" disabled communities, then it follows that practitioners of civic education have a responsibility to disabled people. Furthermore, a civics education that minimizes or excludes disabled people fails not only disabled students but their nondisabled peers as well, as it depicts for them an incomplete version of the collective society it purports to prepare them for.

Erasing disability from curriculum and avoiding it in discussion with students amounts to what Sapon-Shevin (2017) calls *disability invisibility*, a problem that is "pervasive in K–12 classrooms" (Bialka, Hansen, & Wong, 2021, p. 1). Disability is underrepresented in curricular materials to begin with, and when disability is included in curricular materials and discussions, it can "unintentionally reinforce deficit-laden stereotypes of disability as either pitiable or inspirational" (Bialka, Hansen, & Wong, 2021, p. 1). Teachers have a pivotal role to play in making disability visible and in disrupting deficit-minded approaches to disability, particularly in facilitating disability-related discussions in the classroom (Bialka, Hansen, & Wong, 2021).

However, teachers' "enactment of invisibility is often motivated by their discomfort or their desire to avoid conflict, as they worry that talking about human differences leads to prejudice" (Bialka, Hansen, & Wong, 2021, p. 1). In their study of preservice teachers' engagement with disability in children's texts, Bialka, Hansen, and Wong (2021) found that although most of the teachers "aimed to foster empathy, inclusion, and acceptance, they struggled to disrupt dominant narratives surrounding disability as a deficit and, in many cases, actually perpetuated such narratives" (p. 16). Frequently, disability is framed according to the medical model, whereby disability is produced by bodyminds that are defective or deviant: they fail to do things "normal" bodyminds do. An alternative conceptualization, the social model of disability, posits that disability is produced when bodyminds, which are infinitely variable, interact with a built environment that wasn't designed for them but rather for a narrowly defined "normal." This is not to scapegoat teachers as solely responsible for a systematic phenomenon.

In a study of secondary ELA teachers' engagement with disability-related discussions (DRD) in the classroom, Jacobson and Bialka (2023) found that participants cited internal factors (self-efficacy and theoretical perspectives) as helping or hindering their engagement in DRD. But they also cited important external factors over which teachers have only partial control, including school culture and curriculum. Hansen, Kan, Bialka, and Lundell (2023) found that while internal factors were the most important factors enabling or inhibiting

DRD, teachers also cited curricular flexibility, professional development, administrative/parental support, and curricular relevance as external factors that facilitated their engagement with disability. Teachers perceived external obstacles to DRD in the form of inadequate resources, curricular relevance, time, and parental/administrative support.

It is also important to explore *why* teachers discuss disability in their classrooms when they do. Investigating preK–12 teachers' engagement with disability in the classroom, Hansen, Kan, Bialka, and Lundell (2023) found that most (71.9 percent) of the participating teachers were discussing disability in their classrooms, and that among those, the overwhelming majority (83.1 percent) discussed disability at least occasionally. Some of these conversations occurred in the context of the presence of disability in literature or curricular materials (59.2 percent) and others in the context of health/biology discussions (18.5 percent). However, the context for most of these conversations was students' learning needs (81 percent). It is indeed important for teachers to engage with their students' learning needs, especially given that in the US, 95 percent of students with disabilities are educated in public schools (National Center for Education Statistics).

However, as the aforementioned researchers have posited, approaching disability in an individualized manner, such as by arranging testing accommodations, is not adequate to "dismantle master narratives related to disability," (Hansen et al., 2023, p. 12) nor does it position disability as part of civic life. What I am talking about here is not *only* how to make civic education better for disabled learners (though there is evidence that students with disabilities, deprived of the full promise of high-quality civic education, are not achieving at the level of their nondisabled peers because they are not extended equal opportunities in civic learning [Bueso, 2022; Garwood et al., 2021]). In the context of the current discussion, my argument is broader than improving civics education for disabled learners: I contend that inclusion of disability and disabled people in civics curriculum and use of disability-informed practices are crucial to the civic development of *all* students, irrespective of their disability status, much in the same way that white students need to learn about race and racism.

Cripping the K–12 Classroom

Crip the "What": Disability-Informed Civics Curriculum

As the aforementioned investigations suggest, teachers bring their previous learning and experiences with disability (and the absence of same) to bear on their practice in the classroom. In the context of civics education specifically, and in addition to the internal and external factors already discussed, teachers may struggle to engage with disability because they lack disability content knowledge—it may be that they themselves never learned disabled history, so they may not know, for example, how disabled people have shaped policy and how policy shapes disabled lives (Cairn, 2023). A full civics education would include disabled history: for example, the disability activism of Ed Roberts and the Rolling Quads, who led a push for disability rights at UC Berkeley in the 1970s and whose work has inspired and informed disability activism ever since (Jimenez, 2021). Among the accomplishments of the Rolling Quads, in addition to the creation of the Center for Independent Living and other efforts that increased disabled students' access to higher education, was the implementation of the nation's first "curb cut" (the sloped ramp at curbs that allows wheelchair users to safely use sidewalks) (Jimenez, 2021).

High-quality disability history curricula that center the voices and agency of disabled people and that include disabled history are scant but extant; Emerging America, a program of the Collaborative Educational Services (CES), provides professional development, online resources, and curriculum materials to help "K–12 history educators and students ... develop skills of inquiry, exploration and interpretation of the past through primary sources" (Emerging America, "About Emerging America," 2020). Emerging America has created a full K–12 disability history curriculum called "Reform to Equal Rights." Teachers can use the curriculum in whole or in part, or they can integrate it with existing lessons. Emerging America offers information about how the curriculum aligns with Common Core, some state standards, and the C3 Framework for Social Studies.

In terms of its content focus, "Reform to Equal Rights" was designed to feature "narrative inclusion" and in so doing centers "agency—and voices—of disabled advocates; innovation and tenacity of disabled advocates; identity, community, and citizenship across eras . . . empower[ing] civic action on issues of disability rights; and foster[ing] class responsibility for inclusion" (Emerging America, "Developing a K–12 Disability History Curriculum," 2023). Indeed, the lesson plans available on Emerging America's website demonstrate careful attention to disability history and activism. In lessons for all grade levels, however, Emerging America uses, alongside the ADA definition of disability, this definition from New York Public Schools: "'Disability' is when someone's brain or body works in a way that may require tools or strategies to participate in the community" (Emerging America, "Introduction to Disability History," 2020). Consider the difference between that definition, which identifies the brain or body as requiring adjustment or amendment to participate, and a definition that identifies the community (including the built environment) as requiring adjustment or amendment to include all bodyminds. Even this excellent curriculum invokes mostly a gently medicalized definition of disability, which presents disabled people as people who need and runs the risk of reinforcing "dominant narratives surrounding disability as a deficit" (Bialka, Hansen, & Wong, 2021).

Crip the "How": Disability-Informed Civics Pedagogy

Disability can and should inform not only what is taught in civics but also the "how" of learning and not only for or with students with disabilities. Inclusive pedagogy has the potential to achieve what Angela Glover Blackwell coined "the curb-cut effect," its name derived from that very same instance of disabled activism at UC Berkeley: "the outsize benefits that accrue to everyone from policies and investments designed to achieve equity" (2017), just as wheelchair-friendly curb cuts benefit other, non-wheelchair-using people, disabled and nondisabled alike (people pushing strollers, for example, or lugging suitcases). Similarly, an inclusive pedagogical practice requires

> "a shift in teaching and learning from an approach that works for *most* learners existing alongside something 'additional' or 'different' for those (*some*) who experience difficulties, towards one that involves the development of a rich learning community characterized by learning

> opportunities that are sufficiently made available for *everyone*, so that all learners are able to participate in classroom life" (Florian & Black-Hawkins, 2011, p. 814).

Bones and Evans (2021) extend Mezirow's (2009) framework for transformative learning, which "transforms problematic frames of reference to make them more inclusive, discriminating, reflective, open, and emotionally able to change" (p. 22) to a specific form of inclusive pedagogy, what they call "disability-informed instruction" (Bones & Evans, 2021, p. 2). This includes use of universal design for learning (UDL) and multimodal learning; autonomy and centering the student; own voices; plain language; and (a)synchronicity and flexibility (Bones & Evans, 2021). McKinney (2014) positions disability "not merely as a concept or an object of study, but as an approach to producing knowledge" (McKinney, 2014, p. 125). In its design of "Reform to Equal Rights" curriculum, Emerging America prioritizes not only narrative inclusion, as discussed in the previous section, but physical and pedagogical inclusion as well. This means that all students have unfettered access to learning materials, spaces, resources, and educators as well as accommodations when needed; that students' choices and questions drive investigations; and that principles of UDL are applied throughout planning and instruction to address representation, engagement, action and expression, and cultural considerations ("Developing a K–12 Disability History Curriculum," 2020).

Competency-Based Education as Disability-Informed Practice

One approach that holds great potential for educators interested in inclusive pedagogy is competency-based education (CBE). CBE is a "systems-change approach intended to reshape traditional understandings of what, when, where, and how students learn and demonstrate academic content knowledge and skills" (Evans, Landl, & Thompson, 2021, p. 1). Central to CBE is a prioritization of students' authentic demonstrations of mastery as evidence of learning rather than accrual of seat time, credit hours, or time on task (Evans, Landl, & Thompson, 2021, p. 13). The Aurora Institute, in its 2019 updated definition, describes seven features of competency-based education. These are shown in Table 1.

Table 1: Seven features of competency-based education (CBE) (Aurora Institute, "What is Competency-Based Education?", 2019)

Students are empowered daily to make important decisions about their learning experiences, how they will create and apply knowledge, and how they will demonstrate their learning.
Assessment is a meaningful, positive, and empowering learning experience for students that yields timely, relevant, and actionable evidence.
Students receive timely, differentiated support based on their individual learning needs.
Students progress based on evidence of mastery, not seat time.
Students learn actively, using different pathways and varied pacing.
Strategies to ensure equity for all students are embedded in the culture, structure, and pedagogy of schools and education systems.
Rigorous, common expectations for learning (knowledge, skills, and dispositions) are explicit, transparent, measurable, and transferable.

Naturally, CBE depends on an articulation of competencies. These are the "rigorous, common expectations for learning (knowledge, skills, and dispositions)" (Aurora Institute, 2019) that students are learning, practicing, and demonstrating. This is most often done through a competency framework or competency set, which identifies a set of transferable skills; operationalizes them as observable, measurable actions or behaviors; and describes them in stable, explicit, transparent terms. Some communities (states, districts, or schools) create their own competency frameworks; others adopt or adapt existing frameworks. One such framework is the Future9 Competencies, a free, open-source competency framework created by reDesign, LLC.

Some of the features of CBE with the potential to "crip" K–12 education are as follows:

- A competency framework takes as its premise that all people, irrespective of (dis)ability, can do things, and all people can grow and develop. The language used to describe skills is affirmative and asset based. It describes what learners can do, not what they lack or can't do.
- CBE is predicated on the idea that human development is variable, both between individuals and within individuals. Progress is not tied to age or grade level, because there is fixed "normal" at any age or grade level. Individuals' development of competency skill may also be "jagged," with students spending a long time developing a skill at one level and speeding through others.
- CBE can be a powerful equity move by articulating and stabilizing expectations for learning and the language used to describe it. Without this transparency and stability, expectations and evaluations (e.g., of engagement, creativity, collaboration, communication) are subject to implicit and explicit bias.
- Shifting control of learning from teachers to students "pivots the center" (Collins, 1990).

Even so, CBE is not a simple "fix" for disability invisibility (or any other education problem). Competency frameworks are created by people and therefore vulnerable to ableist biases pervading the language of skill development (e.g., requiring eye contact or verbalization as the primary or sole ways to express understanding or engagement). Additionally, a competency set, like a curriculum or a reading list, is a selective list. Choices reveal what matters (and what might not), and no competency framework (or lesson or curriculum, for that matter) is above critique. For example, the Future9 competencies, though described by reDesign as "nine essential skill sets for preparing young people to navigate and shape our future world . . . a whole-learner, trans-disciplinary, outcomes-driven framework for learning design, assessment, growth measurement and reporting" (reDesign, LLC), do not include competencies related to environmental stewardship or sustainability. A disability-informed critique of this framework might object to the omission of environmental skills from a supposedly comprehensive set of "essential" skills, given that "people with disabilities around the world bear more of the burdens of climate change" and are more vulnerable to climate catastrophes ("Disability in a Time of Climate Disaster," 2020).

Additionally, CBE cannot fulfill its potential if it is implemented by educators who hold ableist beliefs about disability or disabled learners. This is true whether that teacher's students are disabled or not. A small study of CBE in Zimbabwe with students with learning disabilities found that teacher-reported barriers to effective implementation included not only poor teacher preparation, inadequate resources, and a lack of stakeholder collaboration but also negative attitudes toward learners with learning disabilities (Mpofu & Sefotho, 2024). According to the National Center for Education Statistics, as of fall 2022, approximately 15 percent of US public school students have disabilities, about a third of whom have specific learning disabilities. The overwhelming majority of students with disabilities (95 percent) attend public schools, and the majority (67 percent) spend 80 percent or more of their time in general classes. So, it is vital that teachers learn to disrupt harmful narratives of disability. Even if a teacher defied odds and never taught a disabled student, ableist, normative, deficit-oriented beliefs about disability would also impede their ability to see, affirm, and support the full range of human variability that exists even in nondisabled learners.

As with any significant systems-level educational change, full implementation of CBE is challenging and slow, and it depends on the engagement and support of multiple stakeholders: teachers, administrators, parents, and students. Additionally, a move to CBE often requires educators learn new pedagogical skills and strategies. Perhaps more challenging than CBE-supportive skill development are the necessary mindset shifts (KnowledgeWorks). CBE entails a redistribution of power from traditional learning models (e.g., between students and teachers and between teachers and administrators) and a focus not only on designs and practices but on sustainable learning culture.

Moving from a traditional learning model to CBE means learning a new way to move about a community as a teacher, leader, or learner, with the opportunity/excitement and fear/loss that this entails: it can mean suddenly not knowing what you're doing, or it can mean figuring out new ways to get a job done and a deep reconsideration of purpose and identity. In this way, for individuals and for communities, adopting CBE (or learning other methods for inclusive pedagogy) can be a little like becoming disabled.

Crip This Lesson

To "crip" something is "to bend, compress, twist, subvert, and imbue disabled wisdom into systems, institutions, and cultures" ("Crip"). It is quite in keeping with disability aesthetics to "hack" an existing resource to make it work better (Shew, 2023). Having been a classroom teacher, I know that we often need to adapt existing curriculum, lessons, and activities to suit our learners, our community, our moment. To that end, I will demonstrate how existing civics materials can be "cripped." I will make all my choices and moves clear in the hope that other teachers will find some ideas for making their own civics teaching more disability informed. I have used free, publicly available materials for my "cripped" lesson.

The example I chose to adapt comes from iCivics, created in 2009 by Justice Sandra Day O'Connor. iCivics describes itself as "the nation's premier nonprofit civic education provider of high-quality, non-partisan, engaging, and free resources to more than 9 million students annually, in all 50 states. That equates to the majority of our nation's middle and high school students" (iCivics, "Who We Are," 2009; MacArthur Foundation, 2008). As evidence of its stature and regard, iCivics was the recipient of a 2015 MacArthur Foundation Award.

iCivics is among the groups heralding a crisis in civic education, but it could be argued that it is also among the first responders. iCivics has founded a cross-partisan coalition to improve civic education, and the iCivics digital library includes educational video games, digital literacy resources, professional learning material—and, of course, lesson plans (iCivics, "Who We Are," 2009). It is these classroom-ready lesson plans that I will use to model a process by which teachers can

The Scenario

Imagine you are a judge. You have been asked to hear a case brought by Alicia Mims, who has accused a Texas cheerleading organization of discriminating against her Deaf nine-year-old daughter by preventing her access to a sign-language interpreter. As a judge, you must come to a decision that is based on the evidence presented in the case. And you must also be able to explain the legal rationale for the decision—the laws, previous cases, or examples that you used to reach their decision. You will explore the Americans with Disabilities Act as well as the case of *PGA Tour, Inc. v. Martin* (2001) to help you make your decision.

What You Will Make/Do

You will deliver your opinion on Mims's case in a form of your choosing (writing, video, audio).

What Does Success Look Like?

Table 2 is a rubric you can use to self-reflect as you develop your opinion and prepare to share it.

Table 2. Single-point rubric for revised lesson

Glows	Target: Read the World: Engage and Critique Perspectives, Level 5	Grows
	• I can describe and characterize the **main arguments put forth in Mims's case**, and draw connections to **the Americans with Disabilities Act and *PGA Tour, Inc. v. Martin* (2001).** • I can ask and answer questions about the supporting evidence, purpose, and/or context of **Mims's case** to evaluate its quality, integrity, relevance, and/or significance **as I make my decision**. • I can reflect on my own biases, and discuss the limitations of my perspectives, evidence base, or analysis of the **case**.	

examine and adapt whatever civics curriculum they are using to make it more disability informed.

There are only two lesson plans in the iCivics digital library that explicitly name disability. The first, designed for grades 6–8, is called "Getting Involved." In this lesson, "[s]tudents learn the basic steps of civic engagement and what it takes to make change. Along the way, they explore the change-making examples of four key movements: women's rights, disability rights, Native American rights, and migrant farm worker rights" (iCivics). The second lesson plan, for grades 9–12, is called "*PGA Tour, Inc. v. Martin* (2001)." In this "mini-lesson," students learn about the Americans with Disabilities Act (ADA) through the lens of the Supreme Court's ruling that the PGA had to accommodate golfers with disabilities.

As written, the PGA Tour lesson plan includes the activation of students' prior knowledge about accessibility and the role of government in enabling access, an explanation of the ADA and the PGA case, a reading about the case, a class discussion of the case and the Court's decision, a written matching exercise to explore accessibility measures in public places (e.g., guide dogs, closed captioning), and an opportunity for students to recapitulate and evaluate, in writing, the court's decision.

Table 3 (see next page) shows how I "cripped" the lesson in ways consistent with the forgoing discussion of disability. On the left, you'll find some questions for reflection and self-assessment that you can use for your own adaptations. On the right, I've provided some discussion of how that reflection question prompted my revision choice and how I would teach this lesson.

The Future Is Disabled

I have argued throughout this discussion that disability belongs in civic education, not only for the benefit of disabled learners, but also for currently abled learners. Disability will affect the lives of every student who passes through a classroom, at some point in their lives. To teachers, I would say that your students will acquire disabilities or will age into disability. They will fall in love and partner with disabled people, and the abled people they love will acquire disabilities or age into disability. They will have disabled children, and they will have "healthy" children who acquire disabilities or age into disability. Alongside conversations of "college, career, and civic readiness," we should be talking about "disability readiness." We should be endowing students with knowledge of disabled culture, history, and activism so they can draw on it as a source of empowerment and community in their disabled futures. We should be cultivating meaningful, transferable skills that they can use to navigate their disabled futures.

We should be teaching them in ways that disrupt narrow, normative ideas of success and that honor the great diversity of the human experience, so that they can do the same in their disabled futures. The future, Leah Lakshmi Piepzna-Samarasinha has told us, is disabled (2022). If we do not include disability in civic education—in what we teach and how we teach it—we are defaulting on our responsibility to prepare students for the future.

Table 3. Reflection questions and revision choices

<table>
<tr><th>Reflection Question: How and to what extent does the lesson as written:</th><th>My revision</th></tr>
<tr><td>disrupt negative, deficit-based models and definitions of disability, including the medical model of disability?</td><td>As students brainstorm ideas about the challenges people with disabilities face in gaining access to public events and spaces, I would direct their focus to the built environment and the decisions that were made in constructing that built environment that cause the inaccessibility. I would invite students to consider who made these decisions, and why? Who was involved in these design decisions? Doing so reinforces that disability results when environments are designed for a narrow set of bodyminds (i.e., the social model of disability).</td></tr>
<tr><td>center the voices and experiences of disabled people, not only as objects but as experts and knowledge-makers?</td><td>I would include, for example, video of Casey Martin talking about his own career, experience, and legal case in his own words, as well as available video of Ari Mims discussing her experiences as a cheerleader in her own voice.</td></tr>
<tr><td>disrupt monolithic depictions of disability and provide access to varied, diverse, intersectional narratives of disability that illustrate many ways of being disabled as there are ways to be nondisabled?</td><td>Including a secondary case for students to consider doubles the number of disabled people they encounter in the lesson, reinforces that disability does not preclude athleticism, and expands students' exposure to the diversity of disabled experience (Mims and her daughter are Black) as a counterpoint to the white disabled people in the PGA case.</td></tr>
<tr><td>refuse us/them framing (e.g., "What can we do to help disabled people?") Remember that disabled people are likely in the room with you, or in the homes of your students.</td><td>As we discuss the lesson's matching exercise, I would invite students to explore the ways that they benefit from accessibility measures, irrespective of their disability status. Who uses closed captions and why? Automatic doors? Voice-to-text? Doing so reinforces students' understanding that they are beneficiaries of disabled activism (curb-cut effect).</td></tr>
<tr><td>leverage UDL and multimodal learning to include all learners?</td><td>I would offer students the opportunity to explore the ADA, and the PGA Tour, Inc. v. Martin (2021) in a variety of modes and formats, not only via teacher explanation and reading. Similarly, I would curate a variety of modes and formats for students to explore Mims's case.</td></tr>
<tr><td>"pivot the center" so students experience agency and choice in what they learn and how they demonstrate their learning?</td><td>I reconsidered the demonstration of learning that students would be invited to produce at the end of the lesson. Instead of asking them to simply restate and evaluate the Supreme Court's decision in writing as the original lesson does, I invited them to transfer their learning to a novel, but related, real-world scenario (much in the way that judges rely on precedent and case law to inform their opinions).</td></tr>
<tr><td>include, in addition to content knowledge, the opportunity to practice and apply meaningful, durable, transferable skills?</td><td rowspan="2">I created a single-point rubric to make clear to students what skills they are developing and to encourage self-reflection on their development of those skills. The first-person language on the rubric ("I can") is affirmative and asset-oriented, and a single-point rubric design allows for a range of performance levels to be recognized and supported with targeted feedback. My rubric is adapted from language used in Future9, a free, open-source competency framework (reDesign, LLC). I organized the task around the skill "engage and critique perspectives," part of the "Read the World" competency.</td></tr>
<tr><td>make expectations of learning transparent and explicit to learners?</td></tr>
</table>

Works Cited

Altschuler, G. C., & Wippman, D. (2023, May 31). We have a civics education crisis—and deep divisions on how to solve it. *The Washington Post*. https://www.washington-post.com/made-by-history/2023/05/31/civics-education-history/

Bialka, C. S., Hansen, N., & Wong, S. J. (2021). Erasure or empowerment?: How pre-service teachers address disability when using children's literature. *International Journal of Qualitative Studies In Education*, *36*(2), 102–120. https://doi.org/10.1080/09518398.2021.1956629

Blackwell, A. G. (2017). The curb-cut effect. *Stanford Social Innovation Review*, *15*(1), 28–33.

Bones, P. D. C., & Evans, A. (2021). Cripping the COVID classroom: Centering students through transformative disability-informed instruction. *Journal of Transformative Learning*, *8*(1), 1–9.

Boren, R. (2022). Crip. In Stimpunks, *Glossary Terms*. Retrieved June 1, 2024 from https://stimpunks.org/glossary/crip/

Bueso, L. (2022). Civic equity for students with disabilities. *Teachers College Record*, *124*(1), 62–86. https://doi.org/10.1177/01614681221086092

Cairn, R. (2023, August 1). Developing a K–12 disability history curriculum. *Emerging America*. https://www.emergingamerica.org/blog/developing-k-12-disability-history-curriculum

Cairn, R. (2023, September 5). Disability history is essential history—2023 report on the teaching of disability history. *Emerging America*. https://www.emergingamerica.org/blog/disability-history-essential-history-2023-report-teaching-disability-history

Collins, P. H. (1990). *Black feminist thought: Knowledge, consciousness, and the politics of empowerment*. Routledge.

Connor, D., & Bejoian, L. (2007). Cripping school curricula: 20 ways to re-teach disability. *Review of Disability Studies: An International Journal*, *3*(3).

Davenport, D. (2019, April 5). The civic education crisis. *Hoover Institution*. https://www.hoover.org/research/civic-education-crisis

Emerging America. (n.d.). *About Emerging America*. Retrieved August 14, 2024 from https://emergingamerica.org/about-emerging-america

Evans, C. M., Landl, E., & Thompson, J. (2020). Making sense of K–12 competency-based education: A systematic literature review of implementation and outcomes research from 2000 to 2019. *The Journal of Competency-Based Education*, *5*(4), Article e01228. https://doi.org/10.1002/cbe2.1228

Florian, L., & Black-Hawkins, K. (2011). Exploring inclusive pedagogy. *British Educational Research Journal*, *37*(5), 813–828. https://doi.org/10.1080/01411926.2010.501096

Garwood J.D., Ciullo, S., Wissinger, D.R., & McKenna, J. W. (2021). Civics education for students with learning disabilities and emotional and behavioral disorders. *Intervention in School and Clinic*, *56*(4), 250–254. https://doi.org/10.1177/1053451220944143

Hammer, B. (2022, April 8). What is civics education and why is it important? Carsey School of Public Policy. https://carsey.unh.edu/blog/2022/04/what-civic-education-why-it-important

Hamot, G. E., Shokoohi-Yekta, M., & Sasso, G. M. (2005). Civic competencies and students with disabilities. *Journal of Social Studies Research*, *29*(2), 34–45.

Hansen, N., Kan, I. P., Bialka, C. S., & Lundell, A. (2024). Are teachers talking about disability?: An investigation of factors associated with discussion in PK–12 classrooms. *International Journal of Disability, Development and Education, 71*(6), 849–865. https://doi.org/10.1080/1034912X.2023.2211017

Harvard University Center for the Environment. (2023, January 19). *Disability in a time of climate disaster.* https://environment.harvard.edu/news/disability-time-climate-disaster

iCivics (n.d.). *Getting involved.* Retrieved June 1, 2024, from https://www.icivics.org/teachers/lesson-plans/getting-involved

iCivics (n.d.). *PGA Tour, Inc. v. Martin (2001).* Retrieved June 1, 2024, from https://www.icivics.org/teachers/lesson-plans/pga-tour-inc-v-martin-2001

iCivics (n.d.). *Who we are.* Retrieved from https://web.archive.org/web/20240618075614/https://www.icivics.org/who-we-are

Jacobson, R., & Bialka, C. S. (2023). Identifying factors that promote or inhibit disability-related discussion in secondary English language arts classrooms. *English in Education, 57*(3), 219–236. https://doi.org/10.1080/04250494.2023.2218879

Jimenez, D. V. (2021). *Disability rights movement highlights.* UC Berkeley Life. Retrieved June 1, 2024, from https://life.berkeley.edu/disability-rights-movement-highlights/

Kober, N., & Rentner, D. S. (2020). *History and evolution of public education in the US.* Center on Education Policy. https://files.eric.ed.gov/fulltext/ED606970.pdf

Kuhlmann, J. (2024, January 9). For leaders, from leaders: Mindset shifts for sustainable change. *KnowledgeWorks.* https://knowledgeworks.org/resources/education-leaders-growth-mindset-systems-change/

Levine, E., & Patrick, S. (2019). *What is competency-based education? An updated definition.* Aurora Institute. https://aurora-institute.org/wp-content/uploads/what-is-competency-based-education-an-updated-definition-web.pdf

MacArthur Foundation (n.d.). *iCivics.* Retrieved June 1, 2024, from https://www.macfound.org/grantee/icivics-43099/

McKinney, C. (2014). Cripping the classroom: Disability as a teaching method in the humanities. *Transformations: The Journal of Inclusive Scholarship and Pedagogy, 25*(2), 114–127. https://doi.org/10.1353/tnf.2014.0024

Mezirow, J. (2009). Transformative learning theory. In J. Mezirow & E. W. Taylor (Eds.), *Transformative learning in practice: Insights from community, workplace, and higher education* (pp. 18–31). Jossey-Bass.

Mpofu, J., & Sefotho, M. M. (2024). Challenges of competency-based curriculum in teaching learners with learning disabilities. *African Journal of Disability, 13*(0), Article a1268. https://doi.org/10.4102/ajod.v13i0.1268

National Center for Education Statistics. (2024). Students with Disabilities. *Condition of Education.* U.S. Department of Education. Retrieved June 1, 2024, from https://nces.ed.gov/programs/coe/indicator/cgg

National Council of Teachers of English. (n.d.). *Civics guide: Reading, writing, & raising voices: The centrality of literacy to civic education.* Retrieved May 14, 2024, from https://ncte.org/civics-guide-for-ela-educators/

Piepzna-Samarasinha, L. L. (2022). *The future is disabled: Prophecies, love notes and mourning songs.* Arsenal Pulp Press.

reDesign. (n.d.). *Future9 Competencies.* Retrieved

May 31, 2024, from https://www.redesignu.org/future9/

Reform to Equal Rights. (n.d.). *Introduction to disability history: Grades 6–12 history units introductory lesson* [Google Slides]. Emerging America. Retrieved August 15, 2024, from https://emergingamerica.org/curriculum/disability-history-curriculum/grades-6-8-disability-civic-engagement-and-government

Sapon-Shevin, M. (2017). On the impossibility of learning "not to see": Colorblindness, invisibility, and anti-bias education. *International Critical Childhood Policy Studies Journal*, *6*(1), 38–51.

Shew, A. (2023). *Against technoableism: Rethinking who needs improvement.* W. W. Norton & Company.

White, J. (2017). Towards a relational aesthetic in disability art: Interdependence and crip futurity. *Knots: An Undergraduate Journal of Disability Studies*, *3*(1), 133–143.

"It's on a Banned Book List": Moving through a Landscape of Book Censorship in Literacy Classrooms

JESSICA MURDTER-ATKINSON,
RACHEL RANSCHAERT &
ERIN ASHCRAFT

As our nation continues to contend with increasingly hostile rhetoric, educators must consider their role in ensuring the interruption of such discourse (Rembert et al., 2019). Teaching in today's context in the United States means navigating many sociopolitical tensions, including, but not limited to, a global pandemic, racial violence, the narrowing of many curricular standards and materials by state legislatures (De Lissovoy, 2014), and increased censorship in literacy classrooms (Burmester & Howard, 2022). As of the 2022–2023 school year, 3,362 texts had been banned from schools nationwide, which is a 33 percent increase from the previous school year (Meehan et al., n.d.). Additionally, the topic of book banning has received increased attention in the media and across state legislatures.

As Texas teacher educators, we've noticed a trend whereby the preservice teachers we work alongside self-censor the texts they select in their work with students. We've observed that policy and media impacted their instructional decision making, perhaps even more so than their teacher preparation program. We took note of these influences and considered potential responses. In this essay, we share information about the current sociopolitical context and anecdotal stories to illustrate what we see in our respective spaces. Lastly, we offer suggestions for how educators may navigate classroom censorship issues and engage in civic futurity.

Situating the Work within the Broader Context

Legislative Context

The historical sociopolitical context of book bans and seemingly controversial texts in the United States is part of a complex, longstanding, and broader intersection of differing cultural values, beliefs, political agendas, and educational policies (Meehan et al., n.d.). At the heart of the current contestation surrounding book banning is a systemic collusion of extreme ideologies, legislation, and policymakers that impacts librarians, educators, students, and preservice teachers entering the field (Schwartz, 2023). While not a new phenomenon, book banning has reached a fever pitch recently and focused on topics such as sexuality, gender, and race (Gilbard, 2023). The terms *sexually explicit*, *age-appropriate*, and *divisive* are often used to justify the removal of texts (Schwartz, 2023). These specific words appear to stoke fear and uncertainty, which can lead to self-censorship.

Protocol regarding what book banning looks like across individual states and school districts varies. At the federal level, significant precedents function to shape state policies. For instance, *Pico v. Board of Education*, a 1982 landmark Supreme Court case, has been used to justify further book censorship legislation in the forty years since it was passed. The ruling placed the onus of responsibility to uphold the First Amendment regarding censored books to school boards. Gilbard (2023) remarked that such cases allow school boards to "make decisions that prioritize community values first and access to information second" (Gilbard, 2023, para. 9). While the decision stated that banning books is unconstitutional, it has not stopped further efforts by some communities that continue to challenge specific texts on moral and racial grounds despite the unconstitutional nature of their claims.

In our Texas context, legislative policy and rhetoric have attacked books containing LGBTQ+ themes, claiming they are pornography (Pen America, 2023). For instance, House Bill 900, which is also known as The READER Act (Restricting Explicit and Adult Designated Educational Resources), was passed in 2023 and uses the language "'sexually explicit material' to mean any communication, language, or material, including a written description, illustration, photographic image, video image, or audio file, other than library material directly related to the curriculum" (HB900, 2023). This broad definition has been implemented to remove texts that feature LGBTQ+ characters and storylines. This bill requires book vendors to rate the content of books on a scale of sexual explicitness. An "explicit" book cannot be sold to a school or at a school book fair and must also be removed from school library shelves once rated (Schwartz, 2023). The bill has been challenged in lower circuit courts, causing confusion about who is responsible for rating and prohibiting texts (Texas Library Association, 2024). Further, books by Black authors and texts that feature topics such as the history of slavery, racial violence, and police brutality are also being removed from libraries, claiming that these topics are intended to imbue guilt over racial identity, pointing to an alarming trend that impacts communities and classrooms (Gilbard, 2023).

In 2024, *Book People Incorporated v. Wong*, which was petitioned by a coalition of Austin-based booksellers, authors, bookstores, and publishers, found HB900 to violate the First and Fourteenth Amendments. This ruling put the legislation under further scrutiny and claimed, "the Law is vague, overbroad, and operates as a prior restraint on speech" (American Booksellers Association, 2023). Even with small wins, book banning shows no signs of slowing in the national and local context, and we have seen the effects of book bans and restrictions firsthand.

Book Banning in the Media

For many, knowledge of moves to ban texts available in schools may be filtered through various forms of media, including traditional news media, online media sources, and social media, to name a few. Below, we discuss a few noteworthy phenomena that appear more broadly in media coverage of book banning across Texas and the United States.

US Media Coverage of Book Bans Amplifies Partisan Discourse

Frequently, national media coverage of book bans is framed through ideological lenses that lead to the reification of binary partisan discourse. For example, publications that tend to be categorized as more right-leaning on scales, such as the Ad Fontes media bias chart, tend to promote the censorship of texts in schools by emphasizing parents' rights and the need to protect what they forward as "traditional family values" (e.g., Joseph, 2024). Contrastingly, more liberal-leaning media sources tend to emphasize the importance of representing diverse voices and perspectives in schools. Further, traditionally left-leaning publications often highlight the dangers of banning books on educational equity and freedom of thought (e.g., Alter, 2024).

Divisions in media discourse are particularly meaningful given the ways that contemporary media dissemination creates an echo-chamber effect (Rhodes, 2022), meaning that in increasingly algorithm-driven media consumption landscapes, individuals are more likely to continually be exposed to only one of the ideological poles around book banning and censorship. This ideological bifurcation of media coverage can result in an environment in which powerful individuals, such as legislators and school board members, may feel the need to align with a partisan stance on book banning rather than the needs of children and adolescents in schools.

Texas Media Coverage Highlights Consequences for Teachers

In our Texas context, media coverage of book banning also tends to focus on the severe consequences teachers can face for including books in their schools or classrooms deemed too controversial or dangerous. For instance, significant media coverage focused on the reprimanding of a fourth-grade schoolteacher who included Tiffany Jewell's *This Book Is Anti-Racist* on her classroom library shelves after a parent expressed concern (Hixenbaugh, 2021). Another teacher was fired from her eighth-grade teaching position for including a graphic novel adaptation of *The Diary of Anne Frank,* which was alleged to include sexual content (Madani & Sheeley, 2023). These stories highlighted the dire consequences teachers faced for including challenged books in their classrooms.

As teacher educators, we see this trend in media coverage as perhaps the most consequential. It can perpetuate a chilling effect, with teachers becoming increasingly hesitant to include books in their curricula that could be deemed controversial for fear of retribution (Schwartz, 2023). In what follows, we present our own accounts of how preservice teachers in Texas are experiencing and responding to the current legislative and media landscape of book banning and challenges.

Who We Are and the Work We Do

Our Positionality

We are former and forever K–8 teachers, mothers, and literacy learners. We are also teacher educators who have adopted critical perspectives and applied critical lenses in our teaching and research work. As white, cisgender women, we are aware of the limitations of our perspectives. As part of our teaching and research, we engage in critical reflexivity, considering how our individual identities influence our teaching and research.

As teacher educators, we work alongside preservice teachers (PTs) enrolled in their professional development sequence at a large Southwestern public university. In this capacity, we have taught literacy methods courses and coached PTs in their respective field placements. Through these different roles, we noticed that media, policy, and critically oriented teacher preparation influenced PTs' instructional decisions with their mentor students and in their field placement(s). We share some anecdotal stories below, illustrating the ways the context of book banning appears in our interactions with PTs.

Our Observations

In our instructional contexts, we gathered data that pointed to concerns about book bans, which repeatedly surfaced in class discussions. This intrigued us because conversations around book bans had yet to surface in local school governance. For example, censorship surfaced during an interactive read-aloud of *Milo Imagines the World* by Matt de la Peña. After the text was read aloud, space was opened for the whole class to discuss. A PT, Kate (all names are pseudonyms), immediately raised her hand and said, "This is a great book, and I would like to read it with my class, but I can't because it's on a banned book list."

A collaborative conversation ensued, and several PTs joined in to confirm whether it was indeed on a banned book list (they also believed it was). Another course instructor, Dr. Fuller, asked the PTs to say more and point to the evidence that it was banned. Another PT, Victoria, cited the recent state legislation (e.g., HB 900) regarding Texas library purchasing requirements. The class conversation led to an inquiry whereby the course instructors and PTs researched the guidelines for choosing and sharing instructional materials. After studying district protocol, the conclusion was reached that none of the three campuses where PTs were placed for student teaching had formally removed any books from the shelves or received parent complaints about specific texts. This interaction demonstrates that although the PTs had some knowledge of state policy, they also did not fully understand the legislation. Yet it was influential nonetheless.

While concern for potential pushback against selected texts influenced safe choices among PTs, this was not always the case. In a different example, in their formal observation, Victoria chose to include a text that highlighted identity in her lesson and fostered student discussions. In the pre-conference and post-conference, the student expressed that she knew the text she chose for the read-aloud could be considered controversial or on a banned book list. Still, Victoria resisted and refused to let that concern her, instead centering her students in the lesson.

At the time of these examples, the PTs we worked with were not directly affected by oppressive policies restricting the texts and contents they read with their students. Yet we acknowledge that many educators face different realities (Alter, 2024). We hope that the ideas we share in the next section can be helpful tools for any educator navigating threats to intellectual freedom.

Where Do We Go From Here?

In the face of growing and restrictive moves toward book bans and censorship across the United States, we seek to equip teachers with strategies to make sense of the present moment and continue to do the vital work of educating and supporting students' growth and learning. First and perhaps most importantly, we suggest educators turn inward and participate in critical reflection to better understand how their storied identities and beliefs shape instructional practice. We contend that the essential work of self-reflection comes before any other critically oriented civic action.

Delve into Critical Reflection

Engage in Self-Reflection

To create more equitable schooling spaces for all children, educators must critically examine how their perspectives, beliefs, and actions influence the texts they select and the instructional practices they use in their teaching and learning. We recommend that educators begin this reflective process by first interrogating their beliefs and values and then moving into shared reflection with others.

We draw on Dr. Yolanda Sealey-Ruiz's Archeology of the Self (Sealey-Ruiz, 2021), or the process of digging deeply and examining the layers of one's lived experiences. Sealey-Ruiz argues that, as educators, we have been conditioned in our work with preservice and inservice teachers to focus on standards (i.e., what is taught) and the curriculum (i.e., how it's taught). Such an approach to teaching literacy is reductive in nature and doesn't account for students' cultural and linguistic assets. To counter such a subtractive approach, we encourage all educators to explore their familial, cultural, and linguistic histories as well as their own schooling experiences, as our lived experiences undoubtedly influence how we, as teachers, show up in classroom spaces. We suggest that PTs, teacher educators, and inservice professionals take up this cyclical, reflective work.

Sealey-Ruiz (2021) offers questions for educators to begin this process, which largely focuses on messages we've received from our families and communities. We have expanded them below, hoping they will serve as useful tools for critical reflection.

- What are the norms of the place I teach in now?
    - What are those norms rooted in?
    - Do those norms center the children that I work with? If not, whose voice is left out?
- How might I question, reframe, or disrupt inequities that I see?
    - What happens to people like me who break the rules? Follow them?

These questions are not meant to be exhaustive but rather a starting point for educators to examine their own histories and beliefs.

Building Allyship by Engaging in Shared Reflection

After initiating the ongoing process of self-reflection, examining their own storied identities and lived experiences, educators can participate in reflective conversations with others. We encourage educators to share their individual critical reflections with their students, colleagues, and the larger community (i.e., families, community members, etc.).

Educators in K–12 and higher education alike should invite their students into moments of critical reflection. These reflective opportunities should be presented as ongoing and recurring and not just reserved for the end of the time together. These reflections may look differently in response to individual teachers' contexts and students. In the same way, we suggest teachers examine their own identities, beliefs, and schooling experiences, and they may invite their students to do the same. As educators learn more about their students' backgrounds, needs, and interests, they can build on their assets to create a learning environment that is culturally responsive and sustaining (Ladson-Billings, 1995; Paris & Alim, 2017).

In addition to opening up space for identity study, we recommend educators ask their students to share their experiences, successes, and challenges working with the teacher, other members of the class, and the greater school community. In this way, they are prioritizing and valuing the voices of the students they work with and for each day. We lovingly caution that teachers may hear feedback that is challenging to sit with, and we invite educators to reflect on this discomfort before responding. We offer below a few question stems that may assist you in this process:

- What are some of the ways you've appreciated working with your peers?

What has been challenging?

- Do you feel like your voice is heard in our community?
- How can we work together to make our classroom community a more inclusive learning space?

By engaging in deep self- and shared reflection, educators can discover who they are in a safe, nonjudgmental way and become more aware of how they approach their teaching practice. Hopefully, this shared reflection might lead to broader coalition building and civic engagement.

Familiarize Yourself with the Relevant Policy

While the constant onslaught of the discourse surrounding book bans and censorship can be confusing and constraining, having a firm grasp on the laws, policies, and legislation can be an area to address with PTs to discuss which books are banned and how to move forward with social justice frameworks integrated within their coursework. This is especially important for PTs entering the field since it is a place of tension and confusion, and open and candid discussion in their university coursework can be a location where students can gather and share resources and navigate the technical and confusing policies and practices.

Teacher educators can facilitate activities and opportunities to help PTs investigate, research, and deconstruct the legislation federally, statewide, and in districts where students are interested in teaching. Familiarity with the language of the laws and how individual school districts have interpreted them is also essential to combating unfair and unjust practices and policies. Additionally, encouraging PTs to become knowledgeable about local school board races and government may empower early career teachers to shape their local communities. The looming fear of repercussion can be combated by a thorough understanding of policy and identifying where to resist in an era of compliance.

By familiarizing themselves with legislation, teachers can take agency over their classroom libraries and resist policies aimed at restriction and dehumanization. Knowing the history of book censorship and current policy can equip educators with a firm grasp of the legalities and wording, which can be protective and build confidence for all educators.

Taking Civic Action in the Classroom and Beyond

After deconstructing legislation and engaging in reflection, teachers must next consider how they will respond to the specter of book bans and community backlash in their curriculum. While there are no clear-cut or simple solutions, we suggest three strategies for teachers to consider: managing literature selections, asking layered questions with mandated texts, and connecting to larger teacher networks.

Manage Literature Selections

It is crucial that teachers recognize that it is both possible and vital to include texts that represent the cultural, linguistic, gender, racial, and social identities of the students in the classroom and of the communities beyond the classroom. Even if teachers encounter banned book(s) lists or divisive concepts legislation impacting their school or classroom, there are likely additional texts that represent identities relevant to the students learning in their classrooms. Teachers may consult a broad range of resources to encounter these texts. However, one beneficial place to start might be book award lists for prizes such as the Coretta Scott King Award, the Batchelder Award, the Pura Belpré Award, or the Rainbow Book List, to name a few. Importantly, when selecting these texts, it is imperative that teachers prepare a clear rationale for the curricular needs that each text meets for their students.

Ask Layered Questions with Mandated Texts

It is possible that teachers may find themselves in a district or school that has a strictly mandated curriculum accompanied by restricted book lists. Even in these settings, there are generative possibilities for critical analysis and anti-oppressive teaching. Responding to previous iterations of book-banning frenzies, Kumashiro (2015) asserted that the classics can be used in anti-oppressive lessons and that what has been framed as "multicultural literature is not inherently anti-oppressive: they can reinforce stereotypes if teachers fail to ask questions about how students are reading them" (pp. 80–81). In other words, while reading only "classic" texts as part of a constrained curriculum does limit what might be represented in the literature in our classrooms, it does not constrain the possibility for critical questioning of those texts. Thus, Kumashiro suggests that teachers approach the literature they read in their classrooms with four layers of questioning: questions about factual issues/comprehension, questions about literary analysis, questions that connect to self, and questions that connect to and critique society. In this final category, Kumashiro offers sample questions such as "Who has the most power in this story? How does that power affect other characters?" or "How do the characters respond to differences" (pp. 80–81). By engaging these questions, teachers can continue to do critical work with whatever texts are made available in their classroom.

Connect to Larger Networks

Given the breadth of proposed book-banning legislation, teachers do not have to look far to find others undergoing similar experiences. Engaging with organizations like the National Council of Teachers of English (NCTE) and the American Library Association (ALA) can provide invaluable guidance, resources, and solidarity. Joining these networks offers access to a wealth of information and research on book bans and connects teachers with a community of like-minded professionals who share their commitment to intellectual freedom and the promotion of diverse voices in literature. Through active participation in conferences, webinars, and online forums, educators can stay informed about current challenges and strategies in combating book banning, ultimately empowering them to advocate effectively for the freedom to read in their schools and communities. Additionally, we encourage all educators to connect with local civic groups advocating for change in the community.

Conclusion

In this essay, we sought to trace the legis-lative and media environment surrounding book bans and challenges in the United States, connect that environment to our observations as teacher educators, and present steps teachers can take to maintain agency in the face of book bans. Educators might move toward more equitable civic futures by engaging in critical reflection, deconstructing legislation, exercising creativity in curricular design, and connecting to more extensive networks.

Works Cited

Alter, A. (2024, April 16). Book bans continue to surge in public schools. *The New York Times*. https://www.nytimes.com/2024/04/16/books/book-bans-public-schools.html

American Booksellers Association (2023, July 5). ABA files suit challenging Texas censorship law. https://bookweb.org/news/aba-files-suit-challenging-texas-censorship-law-1629754

Burmester, S., & Howard, L. C. (2022). Confronting book banning and assumed curricular neutrality: A critical inquiry framework. *Theory into Practice*, *61*(4), 373–383. https://doi.org/10.1080/00405841.2022.2107343

De Lissovoy, N. (2015). *Education and emancipation in the neoliberal era: Being, teaching, and power.* Palgrave Macmillan.

Gilbard, M. (2023, September 6). *What you need to know about the book bans sweeping the U.S.* Teachers College Press. https://www.tc.columbia.edu/articles/2023/september/what-you-need-to-know-about-the-book-bans-sweeping-the-us/

Hixenbaugh, M. (2021, October 8). *Southlake, Texas, schools restrict classroom libraries after backlash over anti-racist book.* NBC News. https://www.nbcnews.com/news/us-news/southlake-texas-anti-racist-book-school-library-rcna2734

Joseph, J. (2024, April 9). *American Library Association claims 'censoring' sexually explicit books targets LGBTQ+ community.* Fox News. https://www.foxnews.com/politics/american-library-association-claims-censoring-sexually-explicit-books-targets-lgbtq-community

Kumashiro, K. K. (2015). *Against common sense: Teaching and learning toward social justice* (3rd ed.). Routledge.

Ladson-Billings, G. (1995). Toward a theory of culturally relevant pedagogy. *American Educational Research Journal*, *32*(3), 465–491. https://doi.org/10.2307/1163320

Madani, D., & Sheeley, C. (2023, September 20). *Texas teacher removed after using Anne Frank graphic novel with sexual content.* NBC News. https://www.nbcnews.com/news/education/texas-teacher-removed-using-anne-frank-graphic-novel-sexual-content-rcna108039

Meehan, K., Friedman, J., Baêta, S., & Magnusson, T. (2023, September 1). *Banned in the USA: The mounting pressure to censor.* PEN America. https://pen.org/report/book-bans-pressure-to-censor/

Paris, D., & Alim, H. S. (Eds.). (2017). *Culturally sustaining pedagogies: Teaching and learning for justice in a changing world.* Teachers College Press.

PEN America (2023, April 10). *Banned in the USA: State laws supercharge book suppression in schools.* https://pen.org/report/banned-in-the-usa-state-laws-supercharge-book-suppression-in-schools/

READER Act, Tex. Stat. § 33.021 (2023). https://capitol.texas.gov/tlodocs/88R/billtext/pdf/HB00900F.pdf#navpanes=0

Rembert, K., Harris, P., & Hamilton, F. (2019, November 6). Being an antiracist educator is a verb. *National Council of Teachers of English.* Retrieved March 12, 2020, from https://ncte.org/blog/2019/11/being-an-anti-racist-educator-is-a-verb/

Rhodes, S. C. (2022). Filter bubbles, echo chambers, and fake news: How social media conditions individuals to be less critical of political misinformation. *Political Communication*, *39*(1), 1–22. https://doi.org/10.1080/10584609.2021.1910887

Schwartz, J. (2023, October 11). *Book bans in Texas spread as new state law takes effect.* The Texas Tribune. https://www.texastribune.org/2023/10/11/texas-library-book-bans/

Sealey-Ruiz, Y. (2021). The critical literacy of race: Toward racial literacy in urban teacher education. In H. R. Milner & K. Lomotey (Eds.), *Handbook of Urban Education* (2nd ed., pp. 281–295). Routledge. https://doi.org/10.4324/9780429331435

Texas Library Association. (n.d.) *HB 900 implementation.* https://txla.org/advocacy/hb-900-vendor-ratings-for-school-library-materials/hb-900-implementation/

High School English Teachers Advancing Civic Possibilities through Assessment

DANIEL P. MOORE & KEVIN HO

Introduction

For those who want to construct a different social reality that is grounded in justice and joy, we can't only critique the world as it is. We have to build the world as it should be to make justice irresistible.
—Ruha Benjamin (2022, p. 11, as cited in Howard, 2023)

In education, the past few years have featured conversations about portals to new futures (Roy, 2020), hard resets (Ladson-Billings, 2021), the building of new worlds (Mirra & Garcia, 2023), and the imagining of otherwises (Levine et al., 2023). These calls to action have inspired civically minded scholarship and pedagogy grounded in the idea that it is not enough to critique the status quo; we must actually "build the world as it should be." This essayfocuses on one group of English teachers who have both dreamed of and built toward a different educational reality—all through the lens of assessment.

Research has shown that high-stakes standardized tests exert detrimental effects on the school experience of students, particularly students of color from marginalized backgrounds (Au, 2022; Woodard et al., 2017). For example, high-stakes testing narrows English curriculum (Crocco & Costigan, 2007), prioritizing exam-driven skill work and Eurocentric content and epistemologies over multicultural, anti-racist, justice-oriented learning (Au, 2022; Picower & Mayorga, 2015). High-stakes tests have also been criticized for being punitive, for discouraging culturally sustaining practices, and for reinforcing a status quo characterized by white supremacy and inequality (Au, 2022; Moore, 2024; Woodard et al., 2017). And yet these exams are so entrenched in our schooling system that many struggle to imagine another way.

Thus, a necessary frontier in education is that which explores alternative forms of assessment, ones that are more humanizing and equitable (Moore & Penuel, 2023; Moore & Bawany, 2025; Taylor, 2022). Two such alternatives include culturally sustaining assessment (Paris, 2012; Taylor, 2022) and liberatory assessment (Au, 2022). This essay aims to establish a clearer picture of what culturally sustaining and liberatory assessments look like in action. It aims to do so by centering the voices of teachers who are using their classrooms as laboratories for this work and by drawing from the wisdom of their practice (Shulman, 2004).

This study followed an online professional learning community (PLC) of secondary English teachers; it investigated what happens when teachers apply the principles of culturally sustaining and liberatory assessment to their work by designing and enacting alternatives to traditional assessments. Over one school year, this group explored possibilities for an "otherwise" in literacy assessment (Levine et al., 2023). They designed, implemented, and received feedback on new assessments. They named themselves the Alternative Assessment Collective (AAC). The AAC functioned as a civic project, building toward a better, more equitable future.

Some context about us: Dan is a teacher educator who taught secondary English for ten years, mostly in New York City. Kevin, who also goes by Kei, is in their fifth year as a high school English teacher in Chicago. Dan identifies as a white man who uses he/him pronouns, and Kei identifies as a genderqueer Vietnamese American who uses he/they pronouns. Both of us participated in the AAC, Dan as an organizer and facilitator and Kei as one of the teacher participants. We met through a professional development fellowship program, a two-year learning experience focused on pedagogy and social justice. Initially, Dan was assigned to be Kei's instructional coach, but together—along with five other program teachers—we formed the AAC based on a shared interest in developing more culturally sustaining and liberatory assessment alternatives.

This study explored what happens when teachers are invited to design more humanizing assessments for their classrooms. While the concepts of liberatory pedagogy and culturally sustaining pedagogy have been well theorized and researched, this study builds on that work by examining how English teachers operationalize those principles when designing assessments. We've taken a practical focus, showcasing the work of teachers in the AAC in hopes that these examples may be useful models for other educators who are building toward justice.

Literature Review

Teachers as Civic World-Builders

This work draws on ideas regarding civic literacy and the practicing of civic futures by English teachers. Specifically, it draws on Mirra and Garcia's (2023) framework for world-building civic education. This framework views schools as portals to the future and is grounded in three non-neutral principles: "1) All teaching is political and all teachers are civics teachers; 2) Our teaching must demand just futures, not just submit to the world as it is; and 3) We can interrogate and innovate our teaching by embracing world-building commitments in the classroom" (p. 4). Inspired by lessons from speculative fiction, Mirra and Garcia argue that teachers must be "world-builders" who interrogate the status quo and innovate toward new possibilities. In other words, we must think not only about the schools we have but the schools we need (González, 2024; Williamson & Moore, 2021). We view the AAC's work of imagining an "otherwise" in literacy assessment as a civic project accomplished by a community of world-building teachers. This project moved from the essential step of imagining a different assessment future to actually advocating for it and experimenting with it in real classrooms.

Reclaiming Assessment

In light of the detrimental effects of traditional, retributive assessment and the testing enterprise, scholars and teachers have made calls to "reclaim assessment" (Au, 2022; Gallagher, 2007). Several have proposed more culturally sustaining and liberatory approaches to assessment.

Culturally Sustaining Assessment

Culturally sustaining assessment prioritizes the tenets of culturally sustaining pedagogy: criticality, student-centeredness, and linguistic and cultural pluralism (Paris, 2012). Teachers who utilize culturally sustaining assessment embrace high expectations and collaboration while rejecting deficit thinking and long-standing assessment practices grounded in dominant culture (Taylor, 2022). In place of high-stakes tests, teachers routinize ongoing, localized formative assessment practices rooted in growth and learning.

Performance-based assessments represent one form of culturally sustaining assessment (Taylor, 2022). Unlike a single, sit-down exam, performance-based assessments provide an extended opportunity to draw upon funds of knowledge, to address community-based needs, and to work collaboratively with peers or other community members (Lee, 1998). Project-based learning—or "assessment as learning" (Dann, 2014)—also has culturally sustaining potential. Students learn and practice while doing projects rather than striving for a certain proficiency score.

Such assessments are more likely to connect to students' communities and feature a political dimension (Taylor, 2022). Other assessments with culturally sustaining potential might include student self-assessments, running records, interviews, or portfolios (Meier & Knoester, 2017). They center growth over retribution; involve children, teachers, and families; promote reflection on learning; and offer accountability to oneself and the community rather than to test makers.

Liberatory Assessment

Liberatory assessment (Au, 2022; Miller, 2008) draws from the principles of liberatory pedagogy, which views education as a pathway to freedom (Freire, 1970). It exists in opposition to carceral or punitive logics (Annamma, 2017), such as assessment practices that aim to surveil, label, and "fix" students. Instead, liberatory assessment empowers students to understand and act upon the world around them (Miller, 2008). By definition, liberatory assessment is culturally sustaining in that it is rooted in students' cultural schema, is democratically constructed, and centers the language and experiences of students (Miller, 2008).

Au (2022) has advocated for two types of liberatory assessment. First, "restorative assessment" centers healing, identity development, self-knowledge, cultural knowledge, and the processing of internalized oppression (Au, 2022). For example, antiracist writing tasks (Inoue, 2015) may invite students to consider the roles of race, class, and language in their lives or to write through pain they may have experienced (Christensen, 2009). "Transformative assessment," meanwhile, engages an activist lens to confront injustice, systemic racism, white supremacy, and settler colonialism (Au, 2022). For example, teachers and students might codevelop assessments (Moore, 2025) that demonstrate students' knowledge of strategies for confronting systemic problems at a local or national level. Such assessments can check for understanding of the skills and knowledge required to be an effective activist.

Together, these ideas around civic world-building and reclaiming assessment inspired the AAC's work: experimenting to see what culturally sustaining and liberatory assessment can look like in action.

Who Is the Alternative Assessment Collective (AAC)?

Six high school English teachers from around the country formed the AAC. All met through the same professional development fellowship program, and all teach at schools primarily serving minoritized students from marginalized groups. The collective formed based on a shared interest in experimenting with more humanizing approaches to traditional assessment. The teachers self-identify as female (four teachers), male (one), and genderqueer (one); and as White (two), Latinx (two), Black (one), and Asian (one). Though the meetings were teacher-led, Dan helped with scheduling and facilitation, drawing on his background as an ELA teacher, teacher educator, instructional coach, and professional developer.

The AAC's Journey

Over one school year, the AAC met monthly. Most gatherings occurred on Zoom, with one in-person session. Meeting activities included:

- Setting collective goals and individual goals
- Sharing school contexts, assessment norms, and requirements
- Exploring theories of alternative approaches to assessment (e.g., culturally sustaining, liberatory, transformative, restorative assessment)
- Codeveloping a list of principles of culturally sustaining and liberatory assessment
- Perusing examples of liberatory and culturally sustaining assessments
- Critiquing examples of "status quo" assessments and discussing ways to modify them to be more liberatory or culturally sustaining
- Brainstorming and co-planning assessments
- Getting feedback on assessment drafts
- Sharing artifacts and student work
- Reflecting through activities like ranking the assessment principles teachers viewed as most important to them
- Reflecting on how the AAC had developed their thinking

Teachers also participated in individual planning sessions. Both group and individual meetings were recorded. All data was transcribed using otter.ai before uploading to Dedoose for qualitative analysis. Analysis was inductive with iterative development of codes and themes (Charmaz & Belgrave, 2012). Triangulating findings through analysis of several data sources fostered a stronger understanding of how teachers conceptualized this work. Member checks helped ensure teachers felt they were being represented accurately and with integrity.

Findings and Takeaways

Three Assessment Stories

Given this book's audience of practitioners and community-engaged teacher educators and researchers, we have chosen to spotlight three "assessment stories" to showcase how some teachers in the AAC put principles of culturally sustaining and liberatory assessment into action. For the sake of space, these examples represent only a slice of the impactful work achieved by all six members of the AAC, which we plan to detail more comprehensively in future publications.

Briana's Assessment Story:
"Assessing the Ability to Care and Heal"

In years past, Briana's twelfth-grade English class had concluded the year with a traditional senior research essay. This time, Briana set out to develop an assessment that was more transformative and civically minded. With input from her students and the AAC, Briana designed a "Civic Engagement Capstone" assessment. As a capstone, it was not just the final assessment of the year but the final assessment of students' high school careers. The purpose was to assess students' understanding of a chosen social issue impacting the community, as well as to assess their development of a feasible action plan. Students were also invited to enact that action plan and share their work at a "Civic Engagement Fair" that was open to the school and the community.

First, students reflected on their values and the issues they cared about—"anything that is of personal importance, no matter the scale," Briana explained. They explored the idea of civic engagement through questions like "What inequities in your local community or in our larger society would you like to fix?" They considered "intellectual challenges," "research queries," and "ethical dilemmas." Student-selected topics included cleaning up public parks, reducing pollution in Lake Michigan, substance abuse, mental health for Latino youth, safer driving conditions, and reducing gun violence.

Students researched the missions, values, and track records of three local organizations connected to their topic. They emailed experts to learn how they might meaningfully contribute. Students then developed a civic action plan with concrete steps, accompanied by a "feasibility assessment" to ensure that the plan was doable during the home stretch of the school year. Students also conducted research and gathered community data. For example, many administered surveys with community members, asking questions like "To what extent are you concerned about (this topic/ civic issue)?" This assessment concluded with a "Civic Engagement Fair" in which students shared posterboards outlining their research and a summary of their civic engagement. The whole school was invited, as was the wider community, in hopes of encouraging community members, teachers, and students in younger grades to engage civically as well.

Briana said, "This project highlighted the importance of empowering students to think about their values and act on them." Students found the work "healing" because it provided "an opportunity to reflect" on themselves and to process challenges in their lives. Students also cited personal growth that came with the "opportunity to lead and solve problems," including possibilities for civic action and world-building beyond the school. To Briana, this project "embodied liberatory and culturally sustaining assessment because it centered . . . self-reflection . . . healing . . . and critical consciousness." She added, "It made me realize our communities and what we leave behind is in good hands. And because our students care about the world, we just need to give them the tools to show us." She also noted, "It's like assessing the ability to care and heal. And of course they do."

Eve's Assessment Story: "A Glimpse into My Life"

In previous years, Eve's sophomore English students wrote a traditional literary analysis essay after finishing the play *A Raisin in the Sun* by Lorraine Hansberry. As an alternative, this year Eve designed a map-based autoethnography assessment titled "A Glimpse into My Life: A Chicago Story Map." The goal was to assess not only students' understanding of how the setting of Chicago was important to the play but also to demonstrate students' own sense of place in the Chicagoland area (and beyond).

Eve's class first explored the genre of autoethnography and ideas like participant observation, self-study, interviewing, and humanizing research. They considered how autoethnography empowers folks to comment on places about which they themselves are experts. In addition to identifying places that were essential to the development of *A Raisin in the Sun*, students selected eight to ten personally important locations, reflecting on how these places and their experiences there have shaped them. Students had access to a web-based program from Northwestern University called knight lab StoryMap (storymap.knightlab.com). Students could drop pins and then click through those locations for a "tour" of Chicago. Many students also included locations outside of Chicago, especially students who had grown up elsewhere, internationally or within the US.

In writing about the stops on their autoethnographic journey, students considered:

- "How did this location (or things that have occurred at this location) shape your life?"
- "What does this stop on your journey mean to the larger community?"
- "How does this pin make you think about place, space, or culture?"
- "Are there differences in how this place is perceived by others versus how you see it?"

Students were also encouraged to "think intertextually" and to "make a connection(s) to a character, setting, or theme within *A Raisin in the Sun* or other texts."

Students pinned places like their homes, schools, places of work, grandparents' homes, corner stores, bus stops, places where their families went through challenges like a divorce or periods of unemployment, places that brought them peace and joy, and neighborhoods relevant to or different from their own cultures. Students reflected on family experiences, like moving to different neighborhoods, making connections to the Younger family's move in *Raisin*. Students wrote about intersections of race and geography, discussing experiences with different diverse and monoracial spaces in Chicago as well as racial and geographic aspects of the setting in the play. The class interrogated the idea of the American Dream, drawing on the text and their own lives.

Eve said her goal was to develop an authentic assessment that was "more community centered, more student centered." She described the autoethnography as a form of world-building because of how it invited students to demonstrate learning in more personal, culturally sustaining ways than status quo assessments do. She said this map-based assessment was "very self-reflective . . . thinking about places and locations as important in their life." She added, "I've had better luck at getting students to engage creatively or critically" and "my thinking in general has kind of just expanded about assessments." Regarding the AAC, she said, "To have thought partners was incredibly helpful . . . to see other people's work and how they were reimagining their assessments . . . it definitely was very beneficial for me and my practice."

Kei's Assessment Story: "Humanizing Global Issues"

During preceding school years, most of Kei's assessments were traditional writing assignments. With goals of fostering community and assessing students' civic mindedness, they developed a new assessment called "Global Solutions: Speech and Service." Students first selected a global issue, researched its history, and explored current activist efforts. "Global issues," defined expansively, could include those affecting a country outside the US or the Chicagoland community. Kei encouraged students to make this work personal by choosing topics or places they felt connected to in terms of identity, culture, or experiences. Kei said a major inspiration for this assessment was the remarkable diversity in their classroom—over half of students were born outside of the United States—and the fact that students knew little about their classmates.

Ultimately, students gave a speech to inform classmates about the global issue, outline potential solutions, and persuade them to engage civically as activists or advocates. Rather than a unidirectional speech, students facilitated dialogue with classmates so everyone could share responses, connections, and questions. These conversations made space for collaborative dreaming about potential solutions. Kei said this emphasis on dialogue and personal responses helped with "humanizing global issues" and experiences rather than merely considering them academically. Instead of focusing strictly on social issues, students also shared aspects of their culture or homeland that they were proud of or that brought them joy.

Some students shared topics relevant to Chicago or the US, such as the gender pay gap, gun violence, antisemitism, and accessible and affordable healthcare. Others focused on international issues like air pollution in Kyrgyzstan, conflict in the Tigray region of Ethiopia, ethnic division in Bosnia, and xenophobia toward Chechen and Ingush in Russia. Students considered solutions both at the system and individual level. For example, after a peer's presentation about the Syrian Civil War, the class discussed legal and policy change, electoral change, and the rebuilding of homes, neighborhoods, and infrastructure. However, students also considered ways they as individuals could be activists and advocates even from afar, such as sending food, water, or clothes; supporting and donating to relevant organizations; and raising awareness online.

Kei said this assessment was culturally sustaining because "students have different opportunities to talk about their own lives and culture." They added that "this is an opportunity for windows and mirrors" and "a moment for students to show and tell from their own identity and experiences." This assessment fostered classroom community as students learned about their peers' lives and home countries, often for the first time, and made "connections based on some shared experiences." They reflected that "this has been healing for students," especially for "folks who have come to America and maybe felt they lost some of their culture; this assessment helped students preserve their identities." Kei viewed this assessment as a form of civic world-building because it asked students to interrogate the status quo while being innovative about ways to respond.

Reflections and Conclusion

This essay has explored what happens when teachers are invited to "build the world as it should be" and design more liberatory, culturally sustaining assessments for their classrooms. An ongoing goal of the AAC has been to leverage these principles to see what they look like in action. We hope the overview of the AAC's work and the three assessment story examples provide a glimpse into how teachers can dream of and build toward a different reality in literacy assessment. Hopefully, these examples are useful models for other educators to learn from and to iterate on.

This work has been exciting, in large part due to the collaborative power of the collective. Teachers used the time together not just to "beg, borrow, and steal" but also to codesign, workshop, and serve as thought partners. One teacher said, "These are new ideas to me, so it helps to bounce things off the group." Another said, "Even if it's not for my classroom, I can help my teammates design assessments that are more liberatory."

This work has also been a meaningful civic project, driven by a community of world-building teachers. The AAC created assessments rooted in activism, advocacy, and transformativity. By design, the AAC served to interrogate "the way things are" in literacy assessment. Most importantly, the group moved beyond the essential step of imagining an alternative to actually experimenting with assessment alternatives in real classrooms. As one teacher said, "I've never done assessments like this. It feels more real than another analysis essay."

The AAC emerged in response to growing evidence that high-stakes tests and other traditional forms of assessment cause harm and perpetuate inequality. We acknowledge that standardized tests remain deeply entrenched in schools and that students and teachers remain accountable to them (Hutt & Schneider, 2018), with real implications for teaching and learning. However, it is our hope that this study contributes to informing a better future, one where teachers not only disrupt traditional modes of assessment but where they co-construct alternatives that advance equity and justice. We hope it can aid in answering the question of what it means to assess students in liberatory, culturally sustaining ways.

Works Cited

Annamma, S. A. (2018). *The pedagogy of pathologization: Dis/abled girls of color in the school-prison nexus*. Routledge. https://doi.org/10.4324/9781315523057

Au, W. (2023). *Unequal by design: High-stakes testing and the standardization of inequality* (2nd ed.). Routledge. https://doi.org/10.4324/9781003005179

Benjamin, R. (2022). *Viral justice: How we grow the world we want*. Princeton University Press. https://doi.org/10.2307/j.ctv2h439xx

Charmaz, K., & Belgrave, L. L. (2012). Qualitative interviewing and grounded theory analysis. In J. F. Gubrium, J. A. Holstein, A. B. Marvasti, & K. D. McKinney (Eds.), *The SAGE handbook of interview research: The complexity of the craft* (2nd ed., pp. 347–365). SAGE Publications. https://doi.org/10.4135/9781452218403

Christensen, L. (2009). *Teaching for joy and justice: Re-imagining the language arts classroom*. Rethinking Schools.

Crocco, M. S., & Costigan, A. T. (2007). The narrowing of curriculum and pedagogy in the age of accountability: Urban educators speak out. *Urban Education*, *42*(6), 512–535. https://doi.org/10.1177/0042085907304964

Dann, R. (2014). Assessment *as* learning: Blurring the boundaries of assessment and learning for theory, policy and practice. *Assessment in Education: Principles, Policy & Practice*, *21*(2), 149–166. http://doi.org/10.1080/0969594X.2014.898128

Freire, P. (1970). *Pedagogy of the oppressed* (M. B. Ramos, Trans.). Continuum.

Gallagher, C. W. (2007). *Reclaiming assessment:*

A better alternative to the accountability agenda. Heinemann.

González, R. A. (2024). "I've always had the abolitionist spirit in me": Preservice teachers of color and pedagogies of abolitionist praxis. *English Education*, *56*(3), 143–169.

Howard, T. (2023). *Dismantling racial injustice and constructing educational possibilities: A call to action* [Meeting theme]. 2024 AERA Annual Meeting. https://www.aera.net/Events-Meetings/Annual-Meeting/2024-Annual-Meeting-Presidential-Program-Theme

Ladson-Billings, G. (2021). I'm here for the hard re-set: Post pandemic pedagogy to preserve our culture. *Equity & Excellence in Education*, *54*(1), 68–78. https://doi.org/10.1080/10665684.2020.1863883

Lee, C. D. (1998). Culturally responsive pedagogy and performance-based assessment. *Journal of Negro Education*, *67*(3), 268–279. https://doi.org/10.2307/2668195

Levine, S., Moore, D. P., Bene, E., & Smith, M. W. (2023). What if it were otherwise? Teachers use exams from the past to imagine possible futures in the teaching of literature. *Reading Research Quarterly*, *58*(1), 5–24. https://doi.org/10.1002/rrq.488

Meier, D., & Knoester, M. (2017). *Beyond testing: Seven assessments of students and schools more effective than standardized tests*. Teachers College Press.

Miller, s. (2008). Liberating grades/liberatory assessment. *International Journal of Critical Pedagogy*, *1*(2), 160–171.

Mirra, N., & Garcia, A. (2023). *Civics for the world to come: Committing to democracy in every classroom*. Norton Professional Books.

Moore, D. P. (2024). Culturally sustaining catch-up? How English language arts teachers "compensate" with culturally sustaining pedagogy after the state exam. *Urban Education*. Advance online publication. https://doi.org/10.1177/00420859241266605

Moore, D. P. (2025). Students as assessment advocates in the ELA classroom: The case for "little a" advocacy, and what it looks like in action. *Voices from the Middle*.

Moore, D. P., & Bawany, M. (2025). Try, translate, relate: A student voice tool for remixing ELA assessment prompts. *International Journal of Student Voice*.

Moore, D. P., & Penuel, W. R. (2023). *Making the most of teacher team time to support equitable assessment* [Policy brief]. Stanford Public Scholarship Collaborative. https://publicscholarship.stanford.edu/sites/default/files/uploads/scholarships/making_the_most_of_teacher_team_time.pdf

Paris, D. (2012). Culturally sustaining pedagogy: A needed change in stance, terminology, and practice. *Educational Researcher*, *41*(3), 93–97. https://doi.org/10.3102/0013189X12441244

Picower, B., & Mayorga, E. (Eds.). (2015). *What's race got to do with it? How current school reform policy maintains racial and economic inequality: Vol. 2. Critical multicultural perspectives on whiteness*. Peter Lang.

Roy, A. (2020, April 3). The pandemic is a portal. *Financial Times*. https://www.ft.com/content/10d8f5e8-74eb-11ea-95fe-fcd274e920ca

Shulman, L. S. (2004). *The wisdom of practice: Essays on teaching, learning, and learning to teach* (S. M. Wilson, Ed.). Jossey-Bass.

Taylor, C. S. (With Nolen, S. B). (2022). *Culturally and socially responsible assessment: Theory, research, and practice* (J. A. Banks, Ed.). Teachers College Press.

Williamson, P., & Moore, D. (2021). Preparing teachers for the schools we have and the schools we need. In S. S. Serger, A. Malmberg, & M. Benner (Eds., with Goksör, M., Hättestrand, C., Kettis, Å., & Rindefjäll, T.), *Renewing higher education: Academic leadership in times of transformation*, (pp. 167–190).

Woodard, R., Vaughan, A., & Machado, E. (2017). Exploring culturally sustaining writing pedagogy in urban classrooms. *Literacy Research: Theory, Method, and Practice*, *66*(1), 215–231. https://doi.org/10.1177/2381336917719440

Teachers of Writing and Their Experiences: *Cuentos* from a Community Writing Workshop

MÓNICA BALDONADO-RUIZ, CELINA RODRÍGUEZ & ALEXIA ENRIQUEZ

Introduction

When one thinks about teacher professional development and teacher preparation programs, one does not often think about art supplies, handwritten notebooks, or unscripted community building. When one thinks about writing instruction, there is also a disconnect between task and community. In the workshop we are going to describe for you here, we did the unexpected. We came together as preservice, novice, and inservice experienced teachers to write in and about the communities we serve. We gathered together with art supplies and composition notebooks to learn and write together. We wrote, discussed, and unpacked what it means to be a writing teacher in the borderlands. What follows highlights the experiences of two participant collaborators. This essay will examine how the workshops were designed and will reflect upon the ways in which the workshops shaped how teachers thought about writing instruction.

Purpose and Background

The purpose of the week-long workshop was to provide professional development for teachers with a range of experience levels to learn about providing curricular writing opportunities for youth from historically marginalized groups to reflect on, write about, and make public their lived experiences and family histories within the formal language arts curriculum. An additional goal of creating a professional development community of teacher writers and learners was to situate the learning space in its own historical, cultural, and political background (Kinloch, 2016; Paris & Alim, 2017). To that end, teachers who taught or were about to enter student teaching in a border region of the US were invited via email to participate because of their connection to their location. Further, in the context of writing and teaching writing in the borderlands, this workshop invited a perspective on teaching writing that is situated in drawing on the strengths of the community (Baldonado Ruiz et al., 2022; Gonzalez Ibarra & Marroquin, 2024; Yosso, 2005).

Community Cultural Wealth

Teachers who consider their students' homes and communities and view them as assets to the classroom are better able to build classroom communities that are student centered. Further, this writing workshop focused on highlighting Yosso's (2005) community cultural wealth model. The community cultural wealth model posits that students of color and the communities from which they come hold intrinsic value. Additionally, these communities provide a foundation on which educators can build a curriculum that is reflective and inclusive of their students, their languages, their cultures, and their communities. The model includes a discussion of six types of cultural capital: 1) aspirational capital; 2) familial capital; 3) social capital; 4) navigational capital; 5) resistant capital; and 6) linguistic capital.

Aspirational capital refers to the ways in which minoritized communities and families have hopes for success for their students within the dominant society. Familial capital discusses the ways in which families provide support for their students. Social capital is a concept that highlights the ways in which interfamilial connection and support help students obtain positions and scholarships and provides support toward success. Navigational capital refers to the need for students of color to learn to draw on their community's support to navigate often hostile spaces. This is tied to resistant capital, which holds that communities of color are well versed in resistance and the need to resist oppression. Finally, linguistic capital is the ways in which students can draw on a rich linguistic history that allows them to draw on multiple linguistic skills.

When creating this professional development opportunity, the cultural capital of the communities in which the workshops took place was of the utmost importance. The workshop curricular decisions and activities were grounded in the idea that the assets of the community, in which all of the teachers taught, were paramount to the work in which we were engaged. Each activity was designed to ask participants to examine writing instruction from the perspective of the assets students and their communities could bring into the secondary classroom space.

Identity-Driven Writing Instruction and Teacher Professional Development

Teacher professional development opportunities that "encourage identity-driven instruction are powerful ways to begin to learn how to approach the teaching of writing from a different perspective" (Baldonado-Ruiz et al., 2022, p. 13). Thinking about writing instruction from the perspective of the community, ties to the community, and ways students can engage their community can empower teachers to create writing spaces in which students are engaged and have true ownership of their own writing development.

We explored identity-driven writing instruction through the lens of testimonio writing. The Latina Feminist Group (2001) writes about the importance of testimonio "as a crucial means of bearing witness and inscribing into history those lived realities that would otherwise succumb to the alchemy of erasure" (p. 2). Further power can be found in the purpose of testimonio described by Baldonado (2023) as going "beyond simply telling our individual stories. It is in telling a story of us, a story that involves an individual connection with our community" (p. 89). Inviting teachers to write in this way invites change to the future landscape of what counts as writing in schools.

Participant Collaborators

The two participant collaborators and coauthors of this piece were workshop attendees, teach at the same school, and have been invited to lead future iterations of the workshops.

Celina is a former community organizer who was drawn to teaching in a project-based learning high school where she has a great deal of autonomy in curriculum design. She attended the workshops because she was interested in finding community and in exploring ways to come to writing and writing instruction that appeared reminiscent of her Chicana/o studies background. Having grown up in two border communities and being of mixed Latiné and white background gives her a perspective on writing instruction that is tied to culture. She wrote in her closing reflection that "the big takeaway for me in this work was that it was affirming that much of what I already do when it comes to writing instruction in my classroom was validated by what we did this week." In her own humanities classroom, Celina centered writing activities and assignments around students' lived experiences in the San Diego-Tijuana borderland, community, and local culture. Empathy interviews with classmates, sharing circles, peer feedback, personal reflection, and class presentations are a regular part of the curriculum. Within humanities, Celina's comfort is in teaching history and less in the English language and writing instruction. For her, the workshop confirmed her instincts of centering students' lived experiences, community, and culture to engage them in writing instruction.

A practice that Celina integrated into her classroom post-workshop is getting students outside of the classroom and into their local community to write. While writing *about* the experiences of the local community was a regular practice in her writing instruction, Celina had never considered having students write *in* a community setting. Inspired by the "Writing Marathon" activity of the workshop, Celina equipped her students with notebooks and now incorporates walking her students through local neighborhoods, parks, and various spots around campus to journal and reflect. Moving students outside of the classroom, away from laptops, and into local spaces will continue to be a regular part of her writing instruction.

Alexia grew up with a strong sense of wanting to become a teacher. She was excited to officially begin her journey as an educator in her own community. (In fact, she attended the middle school that hosted our workshops.) She decided to attend the workshops because of a book club and a writing group she did with the workshop leader, Mónica, earlier in the year. She said, "That group made me really interested in exploring more about writing and doing writing in the community." Though she is a humanities teacher in her context, she always felt stronger in the history aspect of the course rather than the writing instruction. Reflecting on her own insecurities around writing about her personal experiences, she wanted to push herself to find a stronger sense of her writing voice and hoped this experience would put her in the shoes of the students. The biggest takeaway for her from the workshop series was that "she found that writing instruction didn't always have to be formulaic and formal" but much of the value could be gained through more low-stakes and informal approaches.

The workshops grounded the idea that writing instruction can prioritize student choice rather than beginning with the formal expectations of writing style. She felt the most comfort in being able to choose how much of herself she wrote about during those workshops. "I'm not really comfortable writing and sharing about myself, but the ways that we did it here, I could write about my car and feeling uncomfortable . . . and feel okay with that." Recreating this feeling about writing for her students became a goal for Alexia going into the upcoming school year. A practice she added to her class projects was to provide more chances for free responses and quickwrites as essential steps to the project process. She also modeled a stronger comfortability with messy first drafts and showed value toward students getting their initial thoughts onto paper without the premature concern for the end results.

Mónica is an assistant professor of literacy, and she held a dual role in the workshops: She was both researcher and the workshop leader. She organized and led the workshops. Her view is that in order to create writing instructional practices that are moving students toward ownership, writing teachers must move away from insular and formulaic writing that limits the audience and purpose of writing to school. Her goal for the workshops she teaches is to center the teacher voices in the writing communities that the workshops produce.

Workshop Design

This workshop took place for five days and was modeled on the National Writing Project (NWP) summer institute (Gray, 2000) in which teachers participated in the writing instructional practices they are learning. In addition, this particular workshop was thematic in nature and focused on writing instructional strategies that highlighted the testimonio genre of writing (Baldonado-Ruiz, 2023; Latina Feminist Group, 2001), which is a personal genre of writing that is written in solidarity with one's community for the purpose of making change. Each day consisted of four-hour sessions.

Day-one activities included introductions and definitions of the testimonio genre. This included creating self-portraits and writing artist statements. Self-portraits are a genre of writing that include visual representations of self, so in the context of our workshop we used a collage approach for this (see Figure 1). Participants wrote artist statements (Early, 2023) based upon these portraits.

Day-two activities focused on writing about our own communities and identities. Day three was dedicated to a community mapping event in which participants traveled through the borderland region to write, reflect upon, and map the community. This activity is based upon the writing marathon, outlined by Sassi (2022) and described in detail below.

During the final two days, participants engaged in a testimonio writing workshop of their own on their own lived experiences in connection to their communities. Below, we describe one of the activities that Mónica called Humans of New York. The final goal of the workshop was to do the work of making public their own testimonios and to complete a reflection upon how they might create a unit plan of their own to take into their work as student teachers and teachers. We achieved making public teachers' testimonios through a celebratory storytelling event on the last day of the workshops that was video recorded for future sharing. Figure 2 illustrates the invitation to write and workshop curriculum.

Borderlands Writing Marathon and Trauma-Informed Writing Instruction

The writing marathon has been a staple of The National Writing Project (NWP) and can be transformative for both teachers and student participants in the way they see the communities they explore (Sassi, 2022). A writing marathon is an activity in which groups of participants move through a space to reflect upon and explore that space through writing in any genre they choose. Participants can freewrite, write poetry, draw, or even make lists to expand later. The writing marathon that was the centerpiece of this writing workshop was created with community cultural wealth and funds of knowledge in mind. I asked teacher participants to engage in the writing marathon with two questions in mind: 1) What do you notice? and 2) What do you wonder?

When reflecting upon the writing marathon, participants overwhelmingly agreed that it changed the ways they viewed the community, even a community in which they themselves grew up. The following exchange between Alexia and Celina helps us see how intentionality in exploring community spaces can be both important to do and should be approached with mindfulness.

> ***Alexia:*** *I have spent so much time crossing the border, like as a child, but I have never sat and written there. It's a space that you rush through, you know? Like, get in and get out.*
>
> ***Celina:*** *I thought of it as you are taking a moment to reflect, but it's not always comfortable to do that.*
>
> ***Alexia:*** *Yes, I think if I were to do this with students, I would need to remember that not everyone has the same relationship with the border. It could be triggering for some.*
>
> ***Celina:*** *Oh, yes, we have to be mindful and intentional about the ways we ask students to engage in this kind of identity exploration. This is good to think about.*

In listening to these exchanges and reading reflections about how each of the teachers who attended our workshop responded, we realized the transformative power of writing in community. Through these exchanges and reading reflections, we were able to see the deep thinking and considerations for how we approach difficult topics and the stories that are difficult. Dutro (2011) discusses the ways in which "exposed wounds and the exposing of wounds" (p. 194) work in writing classrooms. Thinking clearly about how the writing assignments, especially those that are personal in nature, will affect our students is at the heart of being intentional, mindful, and with an eye toward care. If students do not feel brave (Arao & Clemens, 2013) in the activities that we are implementing, then we are only perpetuating a sense of mining of trauma for our own benefits. Thinking about these stories that expose wounds can be better understood in conjunction with the care that bell hooks (1994) notes: "To teach in a manner that respects and cares for the souls of our students is essential if we are to provide the necessary conditions where learning can most deeply and intimately begin" (p. 13). Approaching the stories of our students' communities with this level of respect is at the core of creating a culture in our classrooms that nurtures and builds brave writing communities.

Inspired by this writing marathon activity and the "Remember" poetry activity, Alexia developed an entire project entitled "Words That Burn." During this project, Alexia's students picked a memory, read and analyzed a mentor text by a Chicano author, and then mirrored the mentor text in their writing to tell the story of their chosen memory. The students also created a watercolor and wood-burned art piece to go with their writing piece, both of which were exhibited to the community.

Humans of New York and Other Teacher Takeaways

The Humans of New York (HONY) activity is based upon work Mónica did when she was a high school English teacher in central Arizona. The activity combines the journalistic attributes of the Humans of New York Instagram account with the idea that the stories of humans in each community are pivotal to understanding the community dynamics. Additionally, this activity asks teachers to contemplate the purpose of writing as well as ownership of one's story. Baldonado-Ruiz (2023) explores the concept of ownership of one's story as being a way to give voice and take agency in telling your own story in the way you want to tell it.

This activity asks writers to study the stories of Humans of New York and decide how those stories are told. Writers quickly realize that HONY stories are told in the exact words of the people who are interviewed. That is to say, this genre of writing is personal and quoted verbatim rather than interpreted by the interviewer. Writers are then asked to take the lessons learned about this genre and interview those people who are important to them and their communities. The final step of this process is to create an Instagram account for their own community space. This can be done as a class or school community. Both Celina and Alexia described this project as one that they will take into their classrooms.

> ***Celina:*** *Alexia and I have been talking about how we can use the Humans of New York activity to build a cross-grade connection.*
>
> ***Alexia:*** *Because I teach ninth grade and Celina teaches eleventh grade, we thought, what a great way to build school community across grades and to build this, like, feeling of care for who tells our stories.*

This exchange and the plans to use this lesson from the workshops makes clear that when exposed to different ways of incorporating students' stories into writing instruction, teachers begin to find ways to build community in classrooms that begin with the stories of students' communities.

Making Public and Bearing Witness

One of the tenets of testimonio as described by Baldonado (2023) is that the story be made public for the community to witness. In our workshop, the last day was reserved for this bearing witness to the cuentos of our colleagues. We had spent time writing together and sharing bits of our writing during the week. Teacher participants were given time to write and revise and to choose which stories they wanted to share aloud with the group in a celebratory space where we shared lunch. Our community for this week was one another, the storytelling celebration was, in the words of Alexia, "hard, and also, what I needed to do. I don't write about myself, but telling a story that changed me also changed the way I think about personal writing." This public sharing of stories solidified the purpose of testimonio, which is to share cuentos of struggle and triumph with community in order to call for change.

What Does This Mean for Writing Instruction?

One of the criticisms of personal identity writing in the secondary classroom is that it can often devolve into teachers becoming voyeurs to the traumas of their students. Something we learned in the context of this workshop is that when teachers are asked to participate in professional development programs that ask them to take on the role of writer while simultaneously thinking about pedagogy, something transformative happens. Teachers

Figure 1: Alexia's self-portrait and artist statement

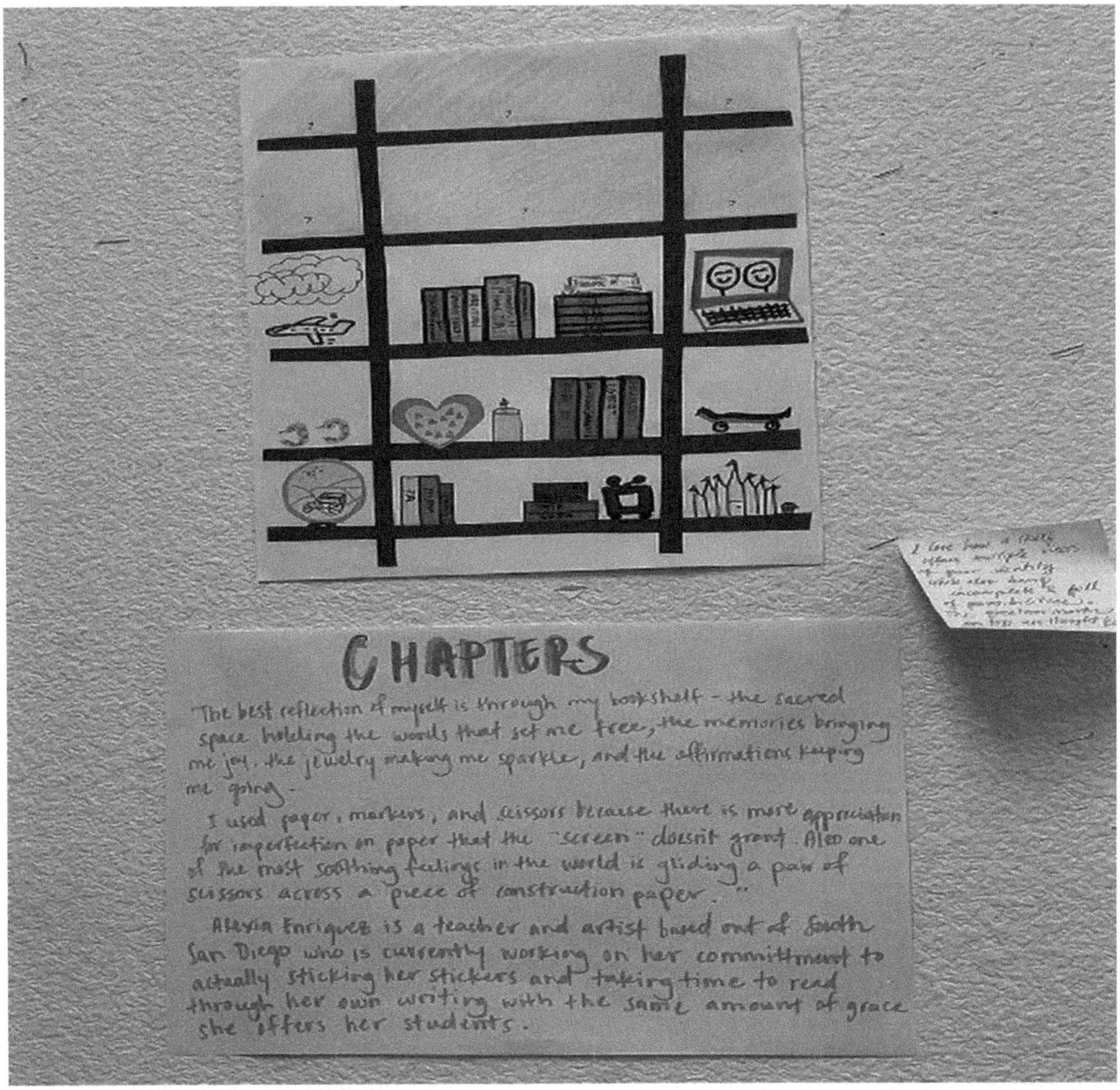

begin to think about personal writing as a way to connect with the communities of their students. In teacher professional development programs we often believe that it is enough to teach teachers strategies or incorporate the newest educational buzzword. What we forget is that in the real world of teaching, community-centered teaching is not about a teacher toolbox; instead, it is about those lasting relationships with students, their families, and the communities that have entrusted us with their education. It's not enough to teach the standards of writing; in a world that is fast becoming simultaneously more technologically connected and more isolating, the futurity of writing classrooms must be brave spaces that center, honor, and show care to the histories, cultures, and cuentos of their students' communities. In honoring the histories of communities, we can also create a future literacy learning landscape where more of our students feel they belong.

Figure 2. Invitation to write and learning schedule

Cuentos Invitation to Write

Welcome to our Cuentos Writing Workshop!

We are inviting you to write a testimonio this week to share with our community of writers. Your testimonio, as you will learn this week, can take many different forms. It could be a personal memoir, a family story/oral history that shares an aspect of your family, an op-ed or editorial about your community, a series of journal entries, or a letter to yourself, your students, your community, or it could be a corrido or a poem. What matters is that it is a story that is unique to you, your community, and the purpose for which you write.

You choose your genre: This week, we'll explore a few genres of writing and from those, you'll choose what to write about. At the end of the week, we'll share our final stories in a celebration with lunch on Friday!

Learning Schedule

AGENDA	Monday: 6/10	Tuesday: 6/11	Wednesday: 6/12	Thursday 6/13	Friday 6/14
8:30–10:30	Intros Logistics Self-Portraits	Community Cultural Wealth Community Maps	Community Writing Marathon	Who Owns Our Stories? Humans of New York	Polishing Writing Sharing Celebration!
10:30–10:45	Break	Break	WM	Break	Break
10:45–12:15	Remember Poetry Writing Time	Gallery Walk Self-Portraits Accents and Remembering Lobo Writing Time	WM	Writing Time	Sharing Celebration!

Works Cited

Arao, B., & Clemens, K. (2013). From safe spaces to brave spaces: A new way to frame dialogue around diversity and social justice. In L. M. Landreman (Ed.), *The art of effective facilitation: Reflections from social justice educators* (pp. 135–150). Routledge. https://doi.org/10.4324/9781003447580-11

Baldonado-Ruiz, M. (2023). Stories of self, stories of us: Bearing witness and writing testimonios. *English Journal, 113*(2), 81–89. https://doi.org/10.58680/ej202332739

Baldonado-Ruiz, M., Yap, A., & Arenas, S. (2022). Twilight professional development: Implications for teacher leadership and identity driven writing instruction. *English Leadership Quarterly, 45*(1), 9–14. https://doi.org/10.58680/elq202231975

del Alba Acevedo, L., Alarcón, N., Alvarez, C., Behar, R., Benmayor, R., Cantú, N. E., Cocco De Filippis, D., Cuádraz, G. H., Fiol-Matta, L., Flores-Ortiz, Y. G., Hernández-Avila, I., Morales, A. L., Lomas, C., López, I. O., Quintanales, M. N., Rivero, E., Souza, C., & Zavella, P. (2001). *Telling to live: Latina feminist* testimonios. Duke University Press. https://doi.org/10.2307/j.ctv116891w

Dutro, E. (2011). Writing wounded: Trauma, testimony, and critical witness in literacy classrooms. *English Education, 43*(2), 193–211. https://doi.org/10.58680/ee201113426

Early, J. S. (2023). *Next generation genres: Teaching writing for civic and academic engagement.* Norton Professional Books.

González Ybarra, M., & Marroquin, E. (2024). Rethinking and redrawing teaching and learning: Latinx preservice teachers documenting their pedagogies of the home through comic strips. *Journal of Adolescent & Adult Literacy, 67*(6), 389–402. https://doi.org/10.1002/jaal.1348

Gray, J. (2000). *Teachers at the center: A memoir of the early years of the national writing project.* National Writing Project.

hooks, b. (1994). *Teaching to transgress: Education as the practice of freedom.* Routledge. https://doi.org/10.4324/9780203700280

Paris, D., & Alim, H. S. (Eds.). (2017). *Culturally sustaining pedagogies: Teaching and learning for justice in a changing world.* Teachers College Press.

Sassi, K., Martens, S., & Dawkins, J. (2022). A thousand teens writing across America: A virtual marathon. *English Journal, 112*(1), 24–32. https://doi.org/10.58680/ej202232064

"You're Letting the Kids Really Go There": Practices of Novice Teachers Mentored by Experienced and Innovative Educators

SARAH BONNER
& ROBYN SEGLEM

When you do an inquiry framework, and you're letting the kids really go there with their questions, and you're not telling a kid that their question is right or wrong or that it doesn't fit on the test, or it's not on the quiz or we're not going to talk about it or it's not the reading guide—you let them wrestle with whatever questions they're talking about or whatever topic they're talking about . . . with inquiry, you just see such a higher level of engagement and critical thinking, and that's where I'm more willing to let go and try new things.

—Caila

The Tale of Two Teachers

As James Baldwin states, "Nothing can be changed until it's faced." While many new teachers *want* to engage in meaningful, student-centered, civically engaged work with their students, there are factors that can potentially inhibit novice educators from stepping into these spaces: lack of administration support, community backlash, and district-mandated curriculum, to name a few. In an effort to keep new teachers thriving—not just surviving—in our profession, it becomes essential to rethink how mentoring can play an ongoing role in this fragile space.

What happens when developing teachers have the opportunity to bear witness to adaptability, civic mindfulness, and real-world connectedness within the classroom? And what happens to the professional decision making from that new teacher's experience when stepping into their own classroom for the first time? For Sarah—an experienced eighth-grade language arts teacher—she saw the need to infuse civics into her classroom early on in her career. She implemented inquiry frameworks and community-based work into her classroom culture because she saw the need for her students to be engaged with more than just superficial packets and worksheets. However, not only was there a need to do this work with students, but it became equally vital to do this work alongside novice teachers as a way to reimagine teaching and learning in the ELA classroom.

This is the tale of two teachers: Caila and Kyle. Both of these teachers student-taught with Sarah throughout separate school years and moved forward into their own classrooms. Many benefits came from these interactions between the three of them, but the heart of this story focuses primarily on the instructional practices and professional decision making of new teachers. Ultimately, this work urges us to rethink the ways in which new teachers can be supported in their formative stages as we seek to transform and reimagine new possibilities for teaching and learning and dream of a stronger, civically engaged future.

Making the Case to Let Go

Education research points to the positive outcomes that student-centered approaches to teaching and learning can have for all students. Studies have highlighted this approach not only as effective for learners but also as a means to reduce learning inequities (Dole et al. 2016; Gray et al., 2018; Wegner, 2000; Wingfield, 2017). Additionally, there is strong literature support for engaging students in learning relative to their lives, interests, curiosities, and their need to have a say in the learning process. To expand further, a student-centered approach to learning creates an important difference for students—especially for those who may not respond to teacher-centered practices (Jacobs et al., 2010; Kuh, 2008). In our ever-changing world, we know that skills continue to expand and evolve. As educators, we have a responsibility to our learners to expose and incorporate these skills on a regular basis. Integrating inquiry-based practices that create student-centered learning environments can be key in this process. Students construct new knowledge by formulating connections between new information and their existing knowledge, experiences, and ideas. While these practices support student learning, they also ask teachers to explore various ways students learn and connect to their prior experiences (Aguilar, 2012). To add to this, we know that teaching and learning occurs within a wider social and political context. Bridging student-centered practices rooted in inquiry and agency welcomes the integration of social justice practices in the classroom as well. Students who are in the driver's seat of their own learning not only lean into their own personal curiosities through inquiry but also become invested and motivated when learning becomes tangible and actionable in ways that matter to them.

Transforming Teacher Practices

Rejecting Initial Conceptualizations of Teaching

When it comes to being a justice-oriented and student-centered educator, rejecting traditional forms of teaching, boxed curriculum, and tools such as pacing guides is not surprising. Letting go of these former practices leaves space for teachers to reimagine teaching and learning in new, innovative ways in an effort to connect learners with the world around them. Very often, teachers connect their own learning experiences to the ones they create for their students. Traditional patterns and practices continue to be recycled because it's comfortable, safe, and easy. However, as Caila and Kyle reflected on their own teaching identities, it became clear that tension existed between what was happening and what was best for student learning. As Kyle expressed:

> My clinical experiences were very teacher centered: me telling students the answers, students memorizing the answers and spitting them back to me. The difficulty of their work was determined by the Lexile or levels of the books they were reading, not by levels of thinking, analysis, or any actual "doing."

Caila and Kyle also identified moments of implementing critical thinking strategies and how that appears differently throughout other classrooms. Most frequently discussed were examples when these teachers observed mentoring teachers implement low-level comprehension strategies or standardized assessment practices with students related to studied texts in the language arts classroom. For example, Caila spoke about how her students frequently engaged in higher-order thinking questions around text connected to their own personal experiences and interests. Both Caila and Kyle demonstrated fence testing to their work with learners while they participated and observed in standardized, traditional learning spaces; they also believed that their students were capable of doing more and wanted to engage in practices that extrapolated these thoughts.

Power and control not only pushed the boundaries of their own power as educators and what they could do with their students, but the pressure and control of being the only "expert" in the classroom shifted as well. Caila had the opportunity to integrate young adult literature into a unit related to her students' interests and questions at the time. As her students read, her classroom culture provided a safe space for asking questions and discussing pointed topics. Throughout this experience, Caila found herself at a crossroads: continue to control the class narratives by presuming to be the only expert in the room or invite outside experts into her learning space and give up the teacher-centered control that she had observed for so long. She noted:

> When reading *The Hate U Give* (Thomas, 2017), it's irresponsible for me to stand up and say what it's like to be part of a Black Lives Matter space—that's irresponsible, and so bringing in those outside expert sources is necessary.

While this shift in power and control within the classroom demonstrated a sense of logic, it also highlighted a sense of hesitation and fear among these new teachers. Kyle began to reflect on the crossroads teachers face when approaching change—moving in a safe direction that emulates what he saw as a young learner or moving in a direction that features many unknown variables like student responses, parent reactions, and the messages of outside experts, to name a few. As Caila noted that she had a responsibility to her students to give up pieces of her classroom control, Kyle initially struggled to think about what this could look like in practice. Throughout his student teaching experience, Kyle alongside Sarah had the opportunity to work with author Samira Ahmed and her book *Internment*. Not only did they have the chance to connect with this author to discuss the book, but they also had the unique opportunity to host a panel discussion between Ahmed and their students. Prior to starting this novel study with students, Kyle explained his initial reactions:

> I immediately loved the book. But I was really nervous as soon as I read it because, like, not having done something like this before, I knew that it could be, there are topics, although they shouldn't be controversial, are. And so, knowing the dynamics of a small town and understanding how politics can play a role in understanding where we are today, um, that was something really nerve-wracking for me.

Caila and Kyle emphasized the importance of how hard their work can be with students and how that can be translated to the stakeholders connected to their classrooms. The choice to integrate meaningful inquiry experiences by infusing contemporary texts as well as affording students space to investigate the issues that matter the most to them were easy decisions to make. However, they also described the hesitation and fear they must work against when attempting to move forward in their critical work with students as they continue to reject familiar teacher-centered practices. Even though both Caila and Kyle experienced teacher-centered learning as students and observed these practices throughout their university programs, their student teaching work with students pushed against traditional models of teaching. They both saw what teaching could be like in a student-centered learning environment.

Empowering Students as Catalysts for Learning

While formulated in different ways, both Caila and Kyle emphasized a high importance on centering students in the design of their classrooms. Both teachers highlighted the importance of regularly integrating inquiry, student interests, and contemporary social issues. Authentic inquiry was an embedded practice within their classrooms. The nature of inquiry invites students to not only shape the ongoing work through questions and topics, but it also creates a community of shared decision making. Centering student questioning was foundational to Caila's work with learners. To her, questions served as an entry point into critical thinking and sparked a new level of engagement among her students. Similar observations were made in connection to combining contemporary social issues with inquiry and student decision making as Caila connected to her work with Genius Hour (Juliani, 2022). She noted that students were at the center of not only the design of her curriculum but also were the conductors of meaningful learning. When relying on students to determine the questions and the direction of classroom learning, it is fair to acknowledge that this "unknown" might be intimidating to many teachers. However, Caila depended on her students to guide the direction of her classroom.

Kyle asked his students to think about the world around them when he decided to integrate inquiry into his classroom practices using a literature-based inquiry framework (Seglem & Bonner, 2022). The framework asks ELA teachers to use contemporary literature as an entry point into researching and taking action on social issues. Kyle saw what this framework did in his classroom and how this work empowered his students. As contemporary issues, inquiry, and student interest continued to embed in the work of these teachers, it also emphasized the importance of strengthening student voices. While Caila implemented frameworks like Genius Hour (Juliani, 2022), she took inquiry further by encouraging students to speak up and speak out about the social issues that mattered the most to them in the moment. For Kyle, his students participated in a unit entitled "What Does It Mean to Be a Teen in Today's World?" This unit title and essential question took his students on a journey to develop a collaborative student podcast series that involved a collection of various social issues relative to his students' lives. As Kyle stated on his unit for his students:

> If literature can be seen as a mirror into modern society, then it's essential that we use literature to grapple with conflicts that teens face in our current world. In the safe environment of the classroom, we can read, question, explore, discuss topics that teens interact with, and unpack such topics through the comforts of characters and fictional stories. In connection with these fictional texts, we'll be using the NPR podcast *This American Life* to explore true-to-life stories in connecting themes.

Young adult literature served as a launching pad into these questions and investigations by students, but the end resulted in students being empowered to authentically construct something that represents not only who they are but how they view the world.

For many teachers, empowering student voices could be seen as a triggering experience for both the classroom teacher and the stakeholders connected to the learning space (parents, administrators, and community members, to name a few), as it could potentially invite negative attention. As teachers today face the scrutiny and criticism of infusing personal agendas within the classroom—especially when focusing on controversial topics—centering students' questions and partnering that with their own research discoveries creates a community of learners. Caila witnessed these social topics integrate into her classroom because she empowered her students to think, question, and research the issues that mattered to them the most. Providing this power to students established an entry point to meaningful, critical work that learners need when shaping their own personal beliefs and civic identities.

As educators, we experience change on a daily basis. From constructing meaningful lessons to integrating the latest research findings, we reflect in order to do what is best for all of our learners. But how often do we ask our students to both design and experience change? How often do we ask our students to get uncomfortable with learning? We may be familiar with the notion of change, but is it the type of change that completely uproots our comfort in an effort to stretch the boundaries of what we can do with students? Repeating the same practices in our classrooms—especially when it comes to the text choices we provide our students—can bring comfort to teachers. Caila spoke about her inner struggle with getting comfortable and why she aspired to make changes despite how those changes might take her to uncomfortable spaces:

> I had talked about new texts. I kinda got comfortable with the same book because this is a lot to take on. It is. And when you're the only teacher doing it in your school, you get a lot of crap for it, for lack of a better word. So, it's like this part of me that wants it to be comfortable and the whole point of it is that I'm not and we're not. School isn't a place that we're all supposed to be comfortable all of the time . . . I'm trying to push myself next year in going there a little bit more difficult with content, asking some tougher questions, bringing in some more social justice, bringing in some more diversity, really kind of pushing my kids a little bit more.

Through this reflection, Caila began to reflect upon the importance of being uncomfortable due to her work with inquiry and student-centered practices. As she situated her definition of school being a place where learners go to stretch and grow their thinking, she acknowledged that what she asked of her students, she must ask of herself. Teacher participants view change as an endless cycle of aspiration and discovery. For Caila, she aspired to integrate more depth into her beginning practice but—as many new teachers do—took small steps to develop her learning culture over time.

Texts can also represent those entry points that students and teachers need when contemplating change. In thinking about the nature of many language arts classrooms, there's a reason why canon exists. Texts that continue to be mantled and repeated in the classroom year after year become a staple to many language arts educators. Many teachers justify their text choices through their state's learning standards, limited access and availability of texts, or even the simple reason "because it has always been done in this class." Discourse around canonical texts and contemporary texts continue to grow. And while Caila and Kyle were both required to incorporate more traditional texts into their teaching practices, they also implemented and valued contemporary texts. Taking time to observe how students think, write, speak, act, and process the world around them invites a conversation about the way we as 'teachers interject texts among our learners. Kyle extended these thoughts as he reflected on the decision to integrate Samira Ahmed's *Internment* (2018) with his work with students:

> We started out talking about internment camps, and somehow we've got kids who are doing entire [awareness] campaigns on mental health. And so, the critical thinking that they were able to do as far as, like, what's happening in our text and seeing that there are these deeper issues—even if they're not 100 percent highlighted—was really cool to see. They could make real-world connections with the text and pull things out that maybe aren't... that go beyond the surface level.

Just as Caila experienced with her students and Genius Hour, Kyle demonstrated a similar line of thought when he infused young adult texts with inquiry principles. For both of these teachers, change continued to be an ongoing theme because of how the decisions they implemented as teachers ignited students to think differently about themselves as well as their communities.

Reimagining a New Future to Support New Teachers

This essay began with a quote from Caila as she reflected on her student teaching experiences and how that carried forward into her own classroom infrastructure. Her comment speaks to the need new teachers have when it comes to seeing inquiry and student-centered teaching in action. It became clear that both teachers were able to think divergently about their craft and understand fully how their mentorship and early experiences as educators impacted their own teaching. Figure 1 illustrates a continuum that reflects the major themes Caila and Kyle experienced throughout their journey as they entered the profession on their own beyond student teaching.

In this tale of two teachers, Caila and Kyle both began their journeys by rejecting past concepts of what they believed teaching should look like. Kyle noted that much of his learning experience was rooted in teacher-centered learning practices—lectures, rote memorization activities, desks in rows, to name just a few practices. It was when he discovered new ways of teaching and learning that he was able to conceptualize a new inner framework for teaching. This discovery allowed him to integrate more risk taking, like bringing in community members and empowering his students to design and publish a class podcast.

For Caila, this continuum holds true for her as well as she reflected on her beginning days as a student teacher. As she worked with Sarah during her student teaching semester, she became more comfortable with trying new strategies and conferencing with student groups during regular reading and writing workshop

Figure 1: Instructional practices continuum of novice teachers

Rejecting initial conceptualization of teaching			Empowering students as catalysts for learning
Rejecting	**Discovering**	**Integrating**	**Empowering**
Rejecting teacher-centered approaches to learning Ex: Classroom lectures, passive receiving of information, complete control of content, little to no collaboration among students	Discovering new teaching practices beyond what has been modeled in the past Ex: Exploring student identities, getting uncomfortable and shrinking hesitation and fear, rethinking the role of a teacher, playing with new strategies to engage students	Integrating contemporary social issues and community to support learning Ex: Using inquiry methods with contemporary social issues, inviting community voices into the classroom, using student interests to teach skills, utilizing more contemporary novels with students	Empowering students as catalysts for learning Ex: Mantling student voices to take action around social issues, using students' questions and interests to co-design learning, encouraging text freedom and reader autonomy, placing students in the driver's seat of the learning environment

sessions. The semester continued by them working together to connect students with various community members relative to the class novel and eventually empowering the students to develop public service campaigns to create awareness around social issues that mattered to them. When she gained her own classroom, she furthered this work by implementing Genius Hour.

As these teachers shaped their craft in new ways under these themes, the outcome can also be considered a new—possibly threatening—means of teaching for others. The global pandemic challenged teachers to think of new avenues of teaching, and the struggle to continue this important work became real. Kyle, for instance, knew that his work was important to students but felt deflated when he couldn't connect with his students' interests in real time. Being able to see the work in action and having the support to infuse student-centered practices still mattered to Kyle's development as an educator. Having weathered that storm and since reconnected with students, he remains committed to student-centered learning principles. For Caila, however, professional bullying took its toll on her confidence. Rather than establishing an ongoing mentorship in her school district, teachers in Caila's department vehemently worked against her and her classroom practices with students. And while Caila had the positive support of her students, their families, and administrators, she ultimately left the classroom permanently due to these negative interactions.

While this study did not directly address teacher education programs, several implications can still be drawn from this work. The teachers who entered this study willingly wanted to explore literature in new ways with their students. As teachers opened up to the idea of inquiry and what the inquiry-based framework

(Seglem & Bonner, 2022) was asking them to do in their classroom, it also felt foreign to these teachers to engage in these practices. The framework highlighted a variety of skills that students needed in order to participate in this work–formulating research-based questions, deciphering between fiction and nonfiction, and constructing authentic writing aligned to student interest, for examples. While students were challenged to implement these new skills, teachers were equally challenged to teach those skills to their students in ways that met the students' needs as learners. Ultimately, this framework pushed both teachers and students to think, act, write, and speak differently.

For new teachers to be able to step into spaces like this, teacher education programs can promote studying the nature and needs of learners (Dole et al., 2016; Grudnoff, 2011). Teacher education programs must consider this reevaluation and play a part in modeling this change by not only rejecting teacher-centered practices that are still being implemented but also by maintaining strong connections to primary and secondary educators who continue to implement innovative practices with students. By rejecting the use of lecture-based, teacher-centered practices in teacher education programs, there is an opportunity to model these pedagogical practices for all teachers entering the field (Barrett et al, 2009; Caughlan et al., 2017; Kahl et al., 2010; Stoetzel & Shedrow, 2021;). Prior to student teaching, Caila and Kyle reminded us that they had observed a limited number of teaching strategies throughout their time as learners as well as preservice teachers in their preparation programs. The student-centered learning practices they experienced during student teaching were only discussions and very rarely modeled for them as developing teachers within their university programming.

As we see in many novice teachers, there is a growing disconnect between what learners in the classroom need and how these needs are modeled in teacher education spaces (Jenset et al., 2018; König et al., 2017). By modeling and practicing inquiry, teachers have an opportunity to witness firsthand how these strategies can look and feel in a classroom (Lammert, 2020). And as we saw by Sarah's impact on Caila and Kyle as their mentor teacher, programs can also reconsider how preservice teaching placements are assigned. As we saw in both Kyle and Caila, placing novice teachers with experienced, innovative educators has the power and influence to ripple into future classrooms (Goldhaber et al., 2017; Kretchmar & Zeichner, 2016). These intentional mentorship placements provide new teachers with experience in this work in both safe and meaningful ways. When entering Sarah's classroom, Caila and Kyle knew they wanted to do this work, but they did not feel confident or comfortable doing it on their own. Over the course of their semester-long student teaching experience, Sarah worked alongside these new teachers to codesign as well as co-teach within a student-centered and inquiry-based framework. Rather than leaving new teachers by themselves, intentional placements and an emphasis on collaboration and co-teaching can promote more confidence and therefore create more meaningful teaching experiences that set a precedent for how new teachers continue to develop their own identities as educators (Pasternak et al., 2018).

While Caila and Kyle's stories ended differently from each other, their early teaching experiences proved that change in teaching practices is possible. This offers a sense of hope as we look to the future to rethink and evolve our current classrooms. Nevertheless, as education seeks to find and retain strong, civic-centered teachers for our classrooms, where our teacher candidates are placed, what they observe in the classroom setting, and how they absorb pedagogical knowledge can all serve as a new path to letting go of old practices and ushering in a new way of teaching all students.

Works Cited

Aguilar, E. (2012, March 27). Beyond student engagement: Achieving a state of flow. *Edutopia*. https://www.edutopia.org/blog/student-engagement-elena-aguilar

Ahmed, S. (2019) *Internment*. Little, Brown and Company.

Baldwin, J. (1962, January 14). As much truth as one can bear; to speak out about the world as it is, says James Baldwin, is the writer's job as much of the truth as one can bear. *The New York Times*. https://www.nytimes.com/1962/01/14/archives/as-much-truth-as-one-can-bear-to-speak-out-about-the-world-as-it-is.html

Barrett, S. E., Solomon, R. P., Singer, J., Portelli, J. P., & Mujuwamariya, D. (2009). The hidden curriculum of a teacher induction program: Ontario teacher educators' perspectives. *Canadian Journal of Education, 32*(4), 677–702.

Caughlan, S., Pasternak, D., Hallman, H. L., Renzi, L., Rush, L. S., & Frisby, M. (2017). How English language arts teachers are prepared for twenty-first-century classrooms: Results of a national study. *English Education, 49*(3), 265–297. https://doi.org/10.58680/ee201729043

Dole, S., Bloom, L., & Kowalske, K. (2016). Transforming pedagogy: Changing perspectives from teacher-centered to learner-centered. *Interdisciplinary Journal of Problem-Based Learning, 10*(1), 45–58. https://doi.org/10.7771/1541-5015.1538

Goldhaber, D., Krieg, J. M., & Theobald, R. (2017). Does the match matter? Exploring whether student teaching experiences affect teacher effectiveness. *American Educational Research Journal, 54*(2), 325–359. https://doi.org/10.3102/0002831217690516

Gray, J. A. (2018). Leadership coaching and mentoring: A research-based model for stronger partnerships. *International Journal of Education Policy & Leadership, 13*(12). https://doi.org/10.22230/ijepl.2018v13n12a844

Grudnoff, L. (2011). Rethinking the practicum: Limitations and possibilities. *Asia-Pacific Journal of Teacher Education, 39*(3), 223–234. https://doi.org/10.1080/1359866X.2011.588308

Jacobs, H. H. (Ed.). (2010). *Curriculum 21: Essential education for a changing world*. ASCD.

Jenset, I. S., Klette, K., & Hammerness, K. (2018). Grounding teacher education in practice around the world: An examination of teacher education coursework in teacher education programs in Finland, Norway, and the United States. *Journal of Teacher Education, 69*(2), 184–197. https://doi.org/10.1177/0022487117728248

Juliani, A. J. (2022, October 3). *How to use design sprints, PBL, and genius hour to get kids making*. Retrieved from https://web.archive.org/web/20221003143647/https://www.ajjuliani.com/blog/how-to-use-design-sprints-pbl-and-genius-hour-to-get-kids-making

Kahl, D. H., & Venette, S. (2010). To lecture or let go: A comparative analysis of student speech outlines from teacher-centered and learner-centered classrooms. *Communication Teacher, 24*(3), 178–186. https://doi.org/10.1080/17404622.2010.490232

König, J., Ligtvoet, R., Klemenz, S., & Rothland, M. (2017). Effects of opportunities to learn in teacher preparation on future teachers' general pedagogical knowledge: Analyzing program characteristics and outcomes. *Studies in Educational Evaluation, 53*, 122–133. https://doi.org/10.1016/j.stueduc.2017.03.001.

Kretchmar, K., & Zeichner, K. (2016). Teacher prep 3.0: A vision for teacher education to impact social transformation. *Journal of Education for Teaching, 42*(4), 417–433. https://doi.org/10.1080/02607476.2016.1215550

Kuh, G. D. (2008). *High-impact educational practices: What they are, who has access to them, and why they matter.* American Association of Colleges and Universities.

Pasternak, D. L., Caughlan, S., Hallman, H. L., Renzi, L., & Rush, L. S. (2018). *Secondary English teacher education in the United States.* Bloomsbury Academic. https://doi.org/10.5040/9781350032040

Seglem, R., & Bonner, S. (2022). *Igniting social action in the ELA classroom: Inquiry as disruption.* Teachers College Press.

Stoetzel, L., & Shedrow, S. (2021). Keeping it collaborative: Differentiating coaching practices for beginning teachers. *Kappa Delta Pi Record, 57*(2), 80–85. https://doi.org/10.1080/00228958.2021.1890444

Thomas, A. (2017). *The hate u give.* Balzer + Bray.

Wenger, E. (1998). *Communities of practice: Learning, meaning, and identity.* Cambridge University Press. https://doi.org/10.1017/CBO9780511803932

Wingfield, A. H. (2020). Where work has been, where it is going: Considering race, gender, and class in the neoliberal economy. *Sociology of Race and Ethnicity, 6*(2), 137–145. https://doi.org/10.1177/2332649220903715

Equipping Educators to Nurture Student Civic Advocates through Social Justice Pedagogy

MARÍA LUISA GARCÍA UNDERWOOD
& RESHMA RAMKELLAWAN-ARTEAGA

Introduction

In the realm of civics education, educators face a daunting challenge: how to effectively convey the complexities of history and contemporary social issues without succumbing to the temptation of presenting a single narrative (Adichie, 2009). Too often, the teaching of civics relies on sanitized versions of historical events and sole biographies of celebrated figures, which can inadvertently perpetuate the myth that racism and social injustices are relics of the past. Historical figures, such as Dr. Martin Luther King Jr., are often portrayed in isolation, stripped of the contexts and contradictions that shaped their actions and beliefs (Busey & Walker, 2017; Tschida et al., 2014). This approach not only oversimplifies the realities of systemic inequities but also fails to equip students with the criticality necessary to navigate and challenge the complexities of their world. Moreover, it overlooks the voices and experiences of marginalized groups, whose stories are essential for a comprehensive understanding of civic engagement and social change.

To combat this, there is a growing recognition of the importance of social justice pedagogy. Educators, therefore, face the crucial task of moving beyond traditional narratives in their mandated curriculum to embrace a more inclusive and nuanced approach that acknowledges the ongoing impact of institutional racism. This transformative or antiracist curriculum can facilitate the teaching of social justice pedagogy (Haddix & Price-Dennis, 2013; Thomas, 2016; Xie, 2000).

In this essay, we will address the role of teachers in making informed decisions about curriculum content, particularly in the context of literacy instruction. Recognizing the inherently political nature of narratives, we will explore how educators can navigate sensitive topics such as race and racism in the classroom. Our aim is to equip teachers with the strategies needed to facilitate meaningful discussions and to promote antiracist classroom practices.

At the core of our essay is a research-based framework designed to help educators guide students in analyzing and questioning racism and social injustices. This framework emphasizes identifying social justice and racial themes in texts, integrating project-based learning, and culminating performance tasks with a social purpose. By engaging students in critical inquiry and civic-oriented assignments, we aim to empower them to actively participate in creating positive change within their school and community. Our essay will provide practical guidance for teachers seeking to transform their curriculum, fostering a more inclusive and socially just learning environment.

Defining Social Justice Pedagogy

The need for social justice pedagogy (SJP) in civics education becomes increasingly evident in fostering students' critical consciousness and preparing them for active involvement. Inherent in the pillars of SJP is their alignment with civics curricula, which allows educators to offer students opportunities for exploring complex issues from multiple perspectives. The definition of social justice pedagogy that frames the practices we discuss in this essay is derived from Ayers, Quinn, and Stovall (2009). They posit that social justice pedagogy exists through three pillars: equity, activism, and social literacy.

Figure 1 represents the iterative nature of this theory. Social justice work intentionally disrupts previously held beliefs and acquires new information, resulting in our continual growth, which is represented by Figure 1 and its iterative nature. Table 1 (next page) offers a breakdown of each pillar's definition.

This approach encourages empathy and understanding and empowers students to identify and challenge inequities (Kumashiro, 2001, 2009). As English educators, we advocate for the use of SJP, as it can be applied universally to many texts, classrooms, and contexts. Such an inclusion promotes civic-based practices. By engaging students in projects based on themes in literacy units, teachers can empower students to advocate for social justice issues in their communities. Projects such as examining historical documents through diverse lenses or researching contemporary social issues such as food insecurities, gentrification, standards of beauty, or school discipline can be powerful tools for bridging the gap between theory and practice in civics education (Banks, 2014).

Despite the benefits, teachers may encounter obstacles in implementing social justice pedagogy due to inadequate support, legislative restrictions, and limited professional development opportunities. Agarwal et al. (2009) highlighted the challenges teachers face when teaching for social justice and stress the importance of proper preparation and support from

Figure 1. A diagram representing the definition of social justice pedagogy

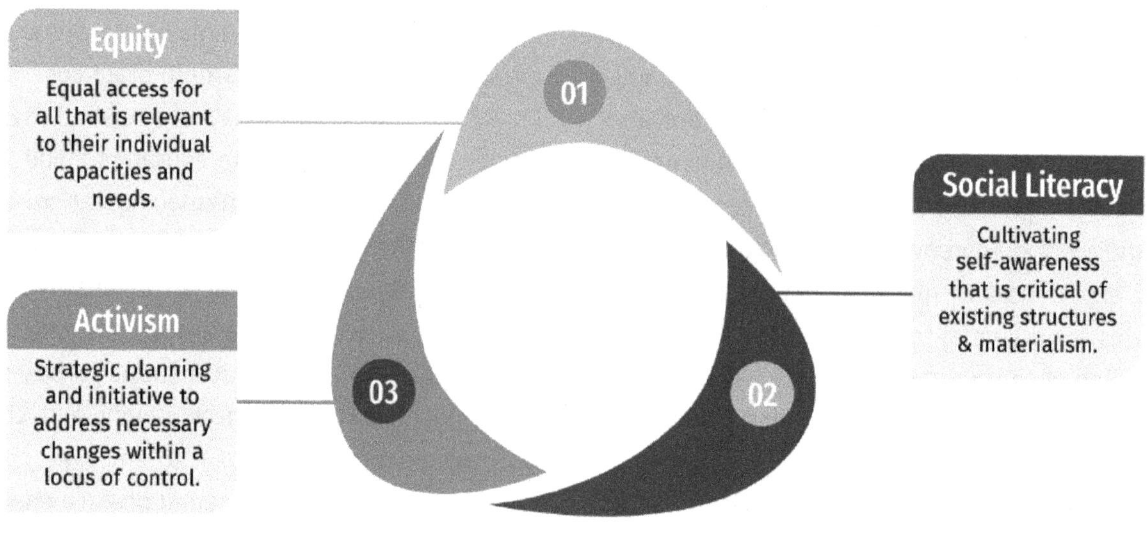

Table 1. Definition for each pillar of SJP

Equity	Equity asserts that the high standards provided to the most privileged should be available to all students. Additionally, equity involves ensuring fair outcomes and addressing historical and systemic injustices. Example: Allowing students to self-select advanced courses based on self-perceptions of readiness.
Social Literacy	Fostering an awareness of our identities and connections with others, highlighting the dedication, perseverance, bravery, and achievements of those who have historically sought justice. It also emphasizes the link between ideas and the broader economic, historical, and cultural contexts in which we live. Example: Questioning end-stage capitalism and the implications for global and national human rights violations.
Activism	Preparing young people to understand, engage with, and, when necessary, transform their surroundings. It encourages moving away from passivity, cynicism, and despair. Example: Using research and traditional assignments to investigate topics of importance to the community and developing a strategic plan to solve noted issues.

teacher educators. Gruenewald (2003) emphasized educators' need to consider local context and community dynamics when addressing educational, social justice issues. Such practices reinforced social literacy, allowing students and teachers to intentionally advocate for immediately relevant courses.

Integrating SJP requires the teacher to take risks by diverging from a preestablished curriculum and exploring issues and information that may question the ideas espoused in the traditional curriculum (Flores et al., 2019). The traditional literacy programs in the United States do not have a foundation in cultural relevance, critical thinking, or social justice. The educational resources utilized for teaching literacy are positioned to be race-evasive and do not address racism and social justice issues. Perceptive teachers and teacher educators begin with the premise that all equity-oriented narratives innately include a cultural and racial aspect.

Embracing social justice pedagogy offers a pathway to engage students in meaningful dialogue about the complexities of civic life and empowers them to become agents of change. By integrating diverse perspectives and themes of equity into literacy-based projects, educators can foster a deeper understanding of social issues and cultivate students' commitment to justice and equality.

Teacher Role in Promoting Civic Activism and Social Justice Pedagogy

Civic activism in education refers to the process of equipping students with the skills and dedication required for the successful functioning of a democratic society (Westheimer & Kahne, 2004). Teachers are vital in promoting critical literacy and social awareness among students. They do this by facilitating deliberative classroom activities and promoting democratic peer norms, which in turn contribute to civic involvement among young people (Lee et al., 2012). The challenges teachers encounter in fostering student participation encompass the requirement for proficient teaching methods, curriculum development, a ssessment, and educational policies that correspond with various interpretations of citizenship and democracy (Westheimer & Kahne, 2004).

Teachers have challenges finding the right balance between active learning tactics and traditional civic education approaches to cultivate a call of action among students (Feitosa, 2020). Teachers who promote critical literacy and social consciousness are ultimately responsible for civic activism in education. Classroom teachers play a crucial role in social justice teaching by advocating for students and supporting efforts for social change within a democratic society. Teaching for social justice, or "good and just teaching," is essential to promoting equity and fairness in education (Cochran-Smith et al., 2009). Teachers can incorporate social justice education by utilizing social reconstructionist approaches and by enacting related teaching practices in their classrooms (Agarwal et al., 2009). Even in mathematics classrooms, social justice pedagogy can contribute to promoting a more just society (Gutstein, 2003).

In the context of classroom justice, teachers can enact fairness through distributive justice, procedural justice, and interactional justice, influencing students' perceptions of justice within the classroom (Estaji & Zhaleh, 2022). Teaching for social justice requires teachers to reimagine their classrooms, represent diverse identities, problematize social and political conditions, and become allies and advocates with as well as for their students (Wild, 2023). It is crucial for teacher education programs to emphasize the significance of social justice and assess teacher candidates' dispositions related to social justice (Villegas, 2007). Classroom teachers play a pivotal role in social justice teaching by advocating for equity, promoting fairness, empowering students to challenge societal inequities, and providing opportunities for students to take on social justice projects.

Social Justice Teaching: Teacher Learning Needs

In the realm of social justice teaching, supporting educators in their professional development is crucial to effectively integrating social justice issues into the curriculum and empowering students to become agents of change in society. The literature has identified several key strategies to enhance teacher learning needs in this area.

Collaborative inquiry and critical reflection are essential to teacher professional development (Eshchar-Netz & Vedder-Weiss, 2020). Engaging teachers in communities of practice that foster collaborative, reflective inquiry can support their professional and situated learning (Eshchar-Netz & Vedder-Weiss, 2020). This approach allows teachers to actively engage in reflective practices within a supportive community, leading to enhanced teaching practices that incorporate social justice principles.

Experiential learning opportunities play a significant role in helping teachers engage with social justice issues (Coffey et al., 2015). Educators can develop a critical, social justice-oriented perspective in their teaching practices by providing authentic learning experiences, such as using museums as pedagogical tools (Coffey et al., 2015). These opportunities encourage teachers to reflect on their teaching methods and inspire them to enact courage in addressing social justice topics in the classroom.

Incorporating culturally responsive pedagogy is another vital aspect of social justice teaching development (Hofmann et al., 2021). Professional development programs that promote cultural literacy learning through dialogic teaching can equip teachers with the necessary tools to create inclusive and equitable learning environments (Hofmann et al., 2021). This can often be the greatest obstacle to fully enacting SJP within the classroom: Layers of lived experience can influence how one sees the importance of equity and activism in any curriculum. Social literacy, an essential element of SJP, requires a keen sense of self-awareness and external observation of gaps that exist within society that one might benefit from. By enhancing teachers' cultural competence and awareness, educational institutions can better prepare educators to address social inequities and to advocate for social justice in their classrooms.

Educational institutions can effectively support social justice educators by embracing collaborative inquiry, experiential learning opportunities, and culturally responsive pedagogy in teacher professional development. Professional development, as we have alluded to, would benefit all educators. School leaders can also integrate structures for professional learning communities and intervisitation that explicitly align with the three pillars of SJP that we have previously discussed. These approaches address the challenges and limitations of educational leadership for social justice and empower teachers to integrate social justice principles into their teaching practices, ultimately fostering a more equitable and inclusive educational experience for all students (Capper & Young, 2014).

Social Justice Pedagogy Curricular Framework

To effectively implement social justice pedagogy, we strongly recommend beginning with a thematic unit plan centered around a specific topic that speaks to the values of SJP and ultimately civics. This approach fosters deep exploration and engagement through interconnected educational activities and project-based learning opportunities. In the next section, we will provide an example of how to integrate SJP through a curricular framework. Our curated curricular framework provides comprehensive guidance for educators as they embark on this design process based on foundational principles from Dr. Gholdy Muhammad's seminal work *Cultivating Genius* (2020) and Gloria Ladson-Billings's pillars of culturally responsive pedagogy (2009). It empowers teachers to create enriching learning experiences. McAnuff Gumbs (2020) posited that educators often benefit from structured curricular support to delve deeply into topics, facilitate discussions, and encourage students to confront and navigate biases.

The four-part framework contains guiding questions that teachers can use to develop thematic unit plans. These prompts are crafted to provoke thoughtful exploration and critical analysis among students, promoting resilience and openness in confronting challenging societal issues. Structuring lessons using this framework ensures that teachers can effectively scaffold learning experiences that foster deep understanding and meaningful engagement with social justice and racial themes. Integrating these strategies, educators can create cohesive and purposeful thematic units that deepen students' knowledge and that empower them to actively address and challenge inequities within their communities.

This framework equips teachers with the tools needed to facilitate transformative learning experiences that promote critical consciousness and civic engagement among students. To effectively

Figure 2: SJP framework for instructional planning

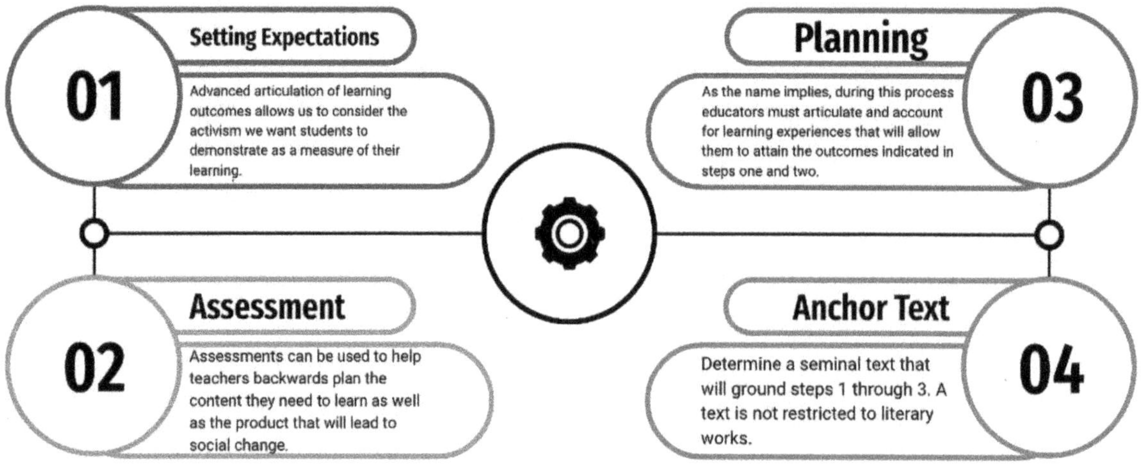

guide students through their learning journey with the chosen text, teachers must start by identifying clear learning goals and desired outcomes. This process helps frame the educational experience and align instructional strategies with the intended results. Figure 2 offers an overview of the framework as well as its connections to SJP.

The framework follows a process similar to that of Understanding by Design. Notably different from this approach, however, is the layering of SJP with the intentional outcome of students articulating civics-oriented outcomes that can be used to promote advocacy.

The next step in the framework guides teachers in assessing student mastery effectively. How will students demonstrate mastery? Assessing student mastery of content is crucial for gauging their understanding and application of the themes and implications derived from the texts they engage with. Teachers ensure that assessments are comprehensive and meaningful by setting clear criteria for success aligned with understanding, application, reflection, and communication. Moreover, incorporating student choice and nontraditional (or multimodal) assessment methods promotes creativity, critical thinking, and a deeper connection to the texts studied. Ultimately, this approach measures academic achievement and cultivates skills essential for lifelong learning and civic engagement—the core pillars of SJP.

The next step in the framework involves effectively planning the teaching and learning process. By aligning teaching and learning processes with clear objectives and engaging strategies, educators can create dynamic and purposeful learning experiences. Emphasizing thematic exploration through instructional design fosters deeper connections with the text and promotes meaningful learning outcomes. Moreover, integrating diverse assessment methods expands opportunities for students to demonstrate their understanding beyond conventional measures, thus nurturing holistic development and academic growth. This approach enriches the educational experience and equips students with the skills and insights necessary for success in both academic and real-world contexts.

Table 2: Setting expectations

***Setting expectations and learning targets*—What are the takeaways for students? Consider the plot and characters' experiences in the chosen text.**

Step 1	Actions
Identify Goals	Articulate the desired learning outcomes and goals for students. Ensure that the goals are grounded in equity and based on individual readiness.
Communicate Expectations	Communicate these goals to students, ensuring understanding.
Monitor Progress	Assess and adjust teaching strategies based on student progress.
Reflect and Adjust	Reflect on outcomes and make necessary adjustments to improve learning experiences.

Questions

- **What should students have learned about themselves and their community at the end of the text?**
    - We want to encourage students to reflect on personal growth and insights gained through their engagement with the text. This focuses on self-discovery and understanding of how literature can illuminate aspects of one's own identity and experiences. Internalized reflections or growth can support the development of social literacy.

- **What connections can students make between the characters and their lives, lived experiences, and identities?**
    - By prompting students to draw parallels between the characters' experiences and their own, we encourage empathy and deeper connections with the text. This question encourages students to explore universal themes and relate them to their own individual circumstances. Making connections can create a sense of urgency related to activism.

- **How do we extend the desired results beyond academic or literary standards?**
    - We are challenged to consider broader impacts on students' personal growth and development as a whole. This encourages us to foster skills such as critical thinking, empathy, and self-awareness that are transferable to multiple aspects of students' lives.

Table 3: Assessment/criteria to demonstrate understanding

***Determine assessment or mastery*—What are your criteria for success or mastery by students? Students should demonstrate a connection to the texts they have read, grounded in a call to action.**

Step 2	Evidence
Understanding of Themes	Students demonstrate a nuanced understanding of the themes and implications explored in the text.
Application to Real-World Context	Students make connections between the text and real-life scenarios, proposing actionable ideas or solutions and encouraging activism.
Depth of Reflection	Students engage in reflective practices. Reflective practices foster a greater understanding of social literacy.
Effective Communication	Students engage in reflective practices that reveal they considered the themes in the text.

Questions

- **How will I know that students have considered the implications and themes of the text provided? How might this spur them to action?**
  - This prompts teachers to assess students' depth of engagement with the text's themes and implications. It encourages us to look for evidence of critical thinking and the application of concepts beyond surface-level comprehension.

- **How might I use nontraditional modes of assessment to allow students to explain what they have learned?**
  - By exploring nontraditional assessment methods such as presentations, multimedia projects, or debates, educators can provide opportunities for students to demonstrate their understanding in creative ways and in a manner that showcases multiple intelligences. Nonbinary assessment products can serve as the foundation for activist causes. This approach fosters student autonomy and encourages deeper exploration of the text's themes. Empowerment yields grounding in one's community and aspirations for change.

- **How might I include student choice and voice in the learning outcomes?**
  - By allowing students to choose topics for analysis, select presentation formats, or propose action plans based on their interpretations of the text, teachers can empower students to take ownership of their learning.

Table 4: Plan learning and teaching processes

***Plan learning experiences and teaching processes*—What is the trajectory of learning for students to engage with? Performance tasks and daily objectives should center on the novel's themes rather than only academic skills.**

Step 3	Actions
Learning Objectives	Define specific objectives that emphasize understanding and application of thematic content in the text.
Instructional Strategies	Select strategies that promote active learning, critical thinking, and exploration of themes through discussion, analysis, and reflection.
Student Engagement	Incorporate activities and tasks that encourage student involvement, collaboration, and personal connection to the text.
Assessment Integration	Integrate ongoing assessment methods that align with learning objectives and that measure comprehension beyond traditional assessments.

Questions

- **How do we design performance tasks that extend beyond traditional modes of measuring student comprehension?**
  - This question challenges us to think creatively about assessment methods that require students to apply their understanding of the text in practical and innovative ways. Performance tasks such as simulations, roleplays, or project-based assessments can effectively gauge comprehension while encouraging deeper engagement and alignment with an SJP framework.

- **How do learning objectives emphasize themes from the text as opposed to standards/skills? Where is the happy medium?**
  - Balancing thematic emphasis with skill development is crucial. Learning objectives should articulate both the exploration of themes and the acquisition of essential skills (e.g., critical analysis and communication). The happy medium lies in crafting objectives that integrate thematic exploration with skill development, ensuring that students not only grasp the content but also acquire transferable skills for lifelong learning.

Table 5: Social justice-oriented texts

***Social justice-oriented texts*—What are the themes that are pertinent to your students' lives? The themes in the texts should have contemporary connections. Students should note evidence and real-world scenarios that speak to the ideas being explored in the text.**

Step 4	Thematic Contemporary Connections
Identity and Representation	Representation in media; stereotypes versus authentic portrayal; single story, generalization. The layering of supplemental texts for canonical pieces in order to shift into a contemporary narrative.
Equity and Access	Educational opportunities addressing socioeconomic, racial, cultural, and linguistic disparities in social justice texts.
Community and Activism	Local and global social movements through youth activism as spurred through larger textual connections.
Cultural Heritage and Diversity	Cultural identity, traditions, and celebrations in a multicultural society that move toward joy and healing.

Questions

- **What resources or supplemental pieces of literature reinforce the themes of the text?**
    - Educators can enrich students' understanding by integrating supplementary resources such as articles, videos, poems, or novels that further explore the themes of social justice and culturally responsive pedagogy (CRP). These materials provide diverse perspectives and deepen students' engagement with the issues discussed in the primary text.

- **How can students connect what they read with their daily lives?**
    - Facilitating connections between text and daily life involves guiding students to identify parallels between the themes, characters' experiences, and real-world situations they encounter. This approach encourages critical thinking and empowers students to apply their learning to personal experiences and community contexts.

- **How can the unit support teachers' aspirations around social justice and culturally responsive sustaining education (CR-SE)?**
    - The unit can support teachers' aspirations by fostering a learning environment that values and respects diverse cultural backgrounds, promotes critical consciousness about social injustices, and encourages students to become agents of change. Incorporating CR-SE principles ensures that educational experiences affirm and celebrate students' identities while challenging inequities and promoting inclusivity.

In the last step of this framework, teachers are to carefully identify the relevant themes, incorporate diverse resources, and facilitate personal connections to create a robust learning experience that aligns with social justice and culturally responsive pedagogical principles. Naming themes of social justice and culturally responsive pedagogy requires educators to select texts that resonate with students' lives and contemporary issues. Having a core or foundational text will allow teachers to maneuver other layers of this framework to enact SJP in their classroom. These themes encourage students to explore evidence and real-world scenarios that reflect the ideas explored in the text, fostering deeper understanding and relevance. This approach enhances students' academic engagement and equips them with the skills and perspectives needed to navigate and contribute to a diverse and equitable society. By nurturing empathy, critical thinking, and activism, educators play a pivotal role in preparing students to confront societal challenges and to advocate for positive change.

We recently applied this framework to a unit plan associated with the novel, *Monday's Not Coming*. While Figure 2 offers a linear approach, the reality is that the novel itself served as the grounding force for the curricular framework. Based on the plot and themes, one of the performance tasks called for students to investigate problematic tendencies in their communities' social service infrastructure as well as present a potential solution. The solution would not simply live in the domain of the school; instead, teachers would encourage students to reach out to local officials and heads of agencies to discuss potential application of their ideas.

Enacting SJP can often feel overwhelming, especially in light of larger mandates and expectations. The framework we present allows educators to "plug and play" practices that they might typically use to cultivate intentionally disruptive learning spaces.

Conclusion

In this essay, we have emphasized the critical role of educators in fostering social justice education. By embracing social justice pedagogy, teachers can empower students to navigate complex societal issues and to challenge inequities. We highlighted the importance of equipping educators with the necessary tools and strategies to foster social justice pedagogy. However, challenges such as inadequate support, limited instructional frameworks, and professional development opportunities hinder the effective implementation of social justice pedagogy. Therefore, a call to action is proposed for teacher educators and policymakers to prioritize ongoing support, targeted professional development, and cohesive instructional frameworks that prioritize social justice education.

Future research and practice in promoting civic activism through teacher education should address these challenges and gaps in support. Research should aim to explore innovative strategies for integrating social justice principles into teacher professional development programs and develop additional instructional frameworks that facilitate meaningful dialogue and critical inquiry on issues of race, identity, and social justice. By fostering a continuous learning and growth culture among educators, we can strive toward a more equitable and democratic society in which students are empowered to advocate for justice and equity broadly.

Works Cited

Adichie, C. N. (2009, July). *The danger of a single story* [Video]. TED Conferences. https://www.ted.com/talks/chimamanda_adichie_the_danger_of_a_single_story/transcript?language=en

Agarwal, R., Epstein, S., Oppenheim, R., Oyler, C., & Sonu, D. (2010). From ideal to practice and back again: Beginning teachers teaching for social justice. *Journal of Teacher Education, 61*(3), 237–247. https://doi.org/10.1177/0022487109354521

Ayers,W.,Quinn,T.,& Stovall,D.(Eds.).(2009).*Handbook of social justice education.* Routledge. https://doi.org/10.4324/9780203887745

Banks, J. A., & Banks, C. A. M. (2004). *Multicultural education: Issues and perspectives* (5th ed.). Jossey-Bass.

Busey, C. L., & Walker, I. (2017). A dream and a bus: Black critical patriotism in elementary social studies standards. *Theory & Research in Social Education, 45*(4), 456–488. https://doi.org/10.1080/00933104.2017.1320251

Capper, C. A., & Young, M. D. (2014). Ironies and limitations of educational leadership for social justice: A call to social justice educators. *Theory Into Practice, 53*(2), 158–164. https://doi.org/10.1080/00405841.2014.885814

Cochran-Smith, M., Shakman, K., Jong, C., Terrell, D. G., Barnatt, J., & McQuillan, P. (2009). Good and just teaching: The case for social justice in teacher education. *American Journal of Education, 115*(3), 347–377. https://doi.org/10.1086/597493

Coffey, H. M., Fitchett, P. G., & Farinde, A. A. (2015). It takes courage: Fostering the development of critical, social justice-oriented teachers using museum and project-based instruction. *Action in Teacher Education, 37*(1), 9–22. https://doi.org/10.1080/01626620.2014.971136

Eshchar-Netz, L,. & Vedder Weiss, D. (2020). Teacher learning in communities of practice: The affordances of co planning for novice and veteran teachers' learning. *Journal of Research in Science Teaching, 58*(3), 366–391. https://doi.org/10.1002/tea.21663

Estaji, M., & Zhaleh, K. (2022). The enactment of classroom justice through explicit instruction: Deciphering the changes in English as a foreign language teachers' perceptions and practices. *Frontiers in Psychology, 13,* Article 821763. https://doi.org/10.3389/fpsyg.2022.821763

Feitosa, F. (2020). Does civic education foster civic duty? A systematic cross-country analysis of the effect of three forms of civic education on the sense of civic duty to vote. *Canadian Journal of Political Science, 53*(4), 887–901. https://doi.org/10.1017/s0008423920000669

Flores, T. T., Vlach, S. K., & Lammert, C. (2019). The role of children's literature in cultivating preservice teachers as transformative intellectuals: A literature review. *Journal of Literacy Research, 51*(2), 214–232. https://doi.org/10.1177/1086296X19839181

Gruenewald, D. A. (2003). The best of both worlds: A critical pedagogy of place. *Educational Researcher, 32*(4), 3–12. https://doi.org/10.3102/0013189x032004003

Gutstein, E. (2003). Teaching and learning mathematics for social justice in an urban, Latino school. *Journal for Research in Mathematics Education, 34*(1), 37–73. https://doi.org/10.2307/30034699

Haddix, M., & Price-Dennis, D. (2013). Urban fiction and multicultural literature as transformative tools for preparing English teachers for diverse classrooms. *English Education, 45*(3), 247–283. https://doi.org/10.58680/ee201323559

Hofmann, R., Vrikki, M., & Evagorou, M. (2021). Engaging teachers in dialogic teaching as a way to promote cultural literacy learning: A reflection on teacher professional development. In F. Maine & M. Vrikki (Eds.), *Dialogue for intercultural understanding: Placing cultural literacy at the heart of learning* (pp. 135–148). Springer. https://doi.org/10.1007/978-3-030-71778-0_10

Kumashiro, K. K. (2001). "Posts" perspectives on anti-oppressive education in social studies, English, mathematics, and science classrooms. *Educational Researcher*, *30*(3), 3–12. https://doi.org/10.3102/0013189X030003003

Kumashiro, K. K. (2009). *Against common sense: Teaching and learning toward social justice* (Rev. ed.). Routledge.

Ladson-Billings, G. (2009). *The dreamkeepers: Successful teachers of African American children* (2nd ed.). Jossey-Bass.

Lee, N., Shah, D. V., & McLeod, J. M. (2012). Processes of political socialization: A communication meditation approach to youth civic engagement. *Communication Research*, *40*(5), 669–697. https://doi.org/10.1177/0093650212436712

McAnuff Gumbs, M. (2020). A multiple case study of the diversity richness of seven early literacy classrooms in upstate New York. *The Journal of Negro Education*, *89*(2), 97–121.

Muhammad, G. (2020). *Cultivating genius: An equity framework for culturally and historically responsive literacy*. Scholastic.

Thomas, E. E. (2016). Stories *still* matter: Rethinking the role of diverse children's literature today. *Language Arts*, *94*(2), 112–119. https://doi.org/10.58680/la201628803

Tschida, C. M., Ryan, C. L., & Ticknor, A. S. (2014). Building on windows and mirrors: Encouraging the disruption of "single stories" through children's literature. *Journal of Children's Literature*, *40*(1), 28–39. https://scenicregional.org/wp-content/uploads/2017/08/Building-on-Windows-Mirrors.pdf

Villegas, A. M. (2007). Dispositions in teacher education: A look at social justice. *Journal of Teacher Education*, *58*(5), 370–380. https://doi.org/10.1177/0022487107308419

Westheimer, J., & Kahne, J. (2004). What kind of citizen? The politics of educating for democracy. *American Educational Research Journal*, *41*(2), 237–269. https://doi.org/10.3102/00028312041002237

Wild, N. R. (2023). Teaching for social justice: A teacher researcher's journey and evolution. *The Reading Teacher*, *77*(3), 360–370. https://doi.org/10.1002/trtr.2252

Xie, S. (2000). Rethinking the identity of cultural otherness: The discourse of difference as an unfinished project. In R. McGillis (Ed.), *Voices of the other: Children's literature and the postcolonial context: Vol. 10. Children's literature and culture* (pp. 1–17). Routledge. https://doi.org/10.4324/9780203357682

ELA Teacher Educators and Activism: Concepts, Curricula, Barriers, and Possibilities

MIKE P. COOK & BRANDON L. SAMS

Introduction

As teacher educators and former secondary English language arts (ELA) teachers, we find ourselves thinking often about the current sociopolitical context and feel compelled to use our teacher preparation classrooms to advance equity and justice. Given the ongoing attacks on teachers and teaching and the ways education is being co-opted by conservatives who whitewash history and maintain existing systems of white supremacy in education, it is vital that we continue to prepare future teachers to help students interrogate systems of power and develop the tools necessary to fight for change.

This, we acknowledge, is not a new idea. In fact, many others continue to argue that teaching is inherently a political act (e.g., Nieto, 2006) and that teachers and teacher educators have an obligation to act in and on the world in their professional lives (e.g., Schneider, 2013). Butler (2016), for example, asks educators to grapple with what activism can and should look like in educational contexts. Within the field of ELA, Morrell (2005) and others have argued for almost two decades for a critical English education that promotes an activist view of literacy and its relationship to the world. Others (e.g., Blackburn et al., 2018; Cook, 2021, 2022; Cook & Yeilding, 2022; Haddix, 2015; Haddix & Price-Dennis, 2013) have specifically looked at implementing activism into work with ELA preservice teachers (PSTs) and inservice teachers. What the field and those invested in activist approaches to teaching may benefit from, however, is a broader view of the ways activism is variously conceptualized and enacted by ELA teacher educators across the US, including how activism may be context-specific and/or tied to particular values and interests of educators and communities.

In this essay, we provide this broader view by drawing on our own research to highlight ways ELA teacher educators discuss activism as part of their efforts to prepare classroom teachers to construct liberatory spaces and prepare students to question and dismantle the systems that harm and oppress communities. We were interested in better understanding how ELA teacher educators (1) engage in activism in their own lives and (2) make activism part of their preparation of future ELA teachers by exploring questions such as: How do

ELA teacher educators conceptualize activism? How do they integrate activist themes into their preparation of ELA teachers? What tensions arise when ELA teacher educators promote activism and activist teaching, and how do they navigate those tensions? How do teacher educators prepare future teachers in ways that move beyond passivity to actively fight for and with communities? We hope that writing through our experiences with these questions highlights the commitments these teacher educators hold for civic action and offers readers new or additional ideas for their own classrooms.

A Bit about Our Project

We spent approximately three years surveying, interviewing, and observing ELA teacher educators across the United States who expressed commitments to advancing justice in and through their teaching, particularly via activist connections to the ways they prepare future ELA teachers. To better understand these connections, we talked with them about activism in their personal lives, about how they engage in activism through their teaching, about their activist inspirations, and about the support they experience from their students, institutions, etc. Building on the responses we received, we engaged in more focused conversations with nineteen ELA teacher educators from across the US (Great Lakes Region, Mid-Atlantic, Midwest, Northeast, Pacific Northwest, South, Southeast, West). Although we knew several of them previously, we met others for the first time during the project. Together, they represent a range of university positions, from high school teachers who serve as adjunct instructors to graduate students to full professors, and contexts, from teaching-focused universities to research-intensive institutions across urban, suburban, and rural spaces. The teacher educators who shared their activist teaching with us also identified across a diverse range of self-reported social identities. Their racial/ethnic identities included white, Thai, and People of Color. They identified their gender as male, female, and gender queer. And they represented diverse queer, pansexual, and cis-het sexual identities.

Contextually, they work with undergraduate preservice teachers (PSTs), those seeking alternative teacher licensure, and classroom teachers pursuing graduate degrees. They each position themselves, albeit in humble ways, as critical teachers and scholars who are invested in using their teaching to construct a more equitable and just world. They each also believe in the power of education to challenge the status quo and of the necessity to prepare teachers who work with students to address the oppressions they see and experience. The ways they talked about their teaching made these commitments clear to us, and we focus this essay on highlighting their voices and they ways they conceptualize and engage activism in their teacher preparation classrooms and communities.

We found that drawing on the tenets of critical literacy helped us to better understand the ways these teacher educators talked about activism in their lives. Because critical literacy offers a helpful lens for considering power dynamics in the world and for positioning both teachers and students as active participants in remaking the world, it offered us a pathway to better understanding their perspectives and the ways they make activism part of their teaching. In fact, the teacher educators we talked with used critical literacy themselves to read, understand, and act upon their world as a form of activism. Throughout their talk about activism as it relates to their teaching, they—similar to Freire (1970) and Luke (2000)—made connections between critical literacy and their work with future ELA teachers to challenge dominant discourses and institutions that compose the world, including ELA curricular histories and legacies. Throughout our conversations, it became clear that critical literacy helped these teacher educators conceptualize activism, and it helped us develop a better understanding of the activist goals they hold and the tensions they experience.

In what follows, we describe four broad themes we recognized across our conversations. First, we share some of the ways they conceptualized activism. Then, we offer snapshots of how they engage in activist teaching. Third, we provide examples of the barriers to activism these teacher educators noted, including ways they navigate those barriers. We close by describing how their students, in turn, engage in activism themselves.

During our talks with these ELA teacher educators, we noticed a range of ways they described activism, themselves as activists, and the relationships they saw between the two. Their discussions included insight into how they thought about activism, which helped us to better understand not only how they positioned activism as part of (or not) their teaching and lives but also provided us examples of the myriad ways activism and activist teaching are currently happening more broadly.

Here we share four of these themes, along with examples and discussions of each. We see genuine possibility in the work these teacher educators do and in the ways they prepare teachers to go into classrooms and do the same, and we see relevance for other classrooms and school communities. They are each dedicated to the notion of teaching as political, and they frame their teaching as socially engaged and as part of and responsible to the communities they serve. Within that shared commitment, however, we noticed different ways they talked about activism, and we seek to highlight those below.

Conceptualizing Activism in ELA Education

In their conceptualizations of activism, one thread that stood out to us included a handful of teachers who maintained that their teaching is political and should be socially engaged but who did not describe their teaching as "activist." Their hesitancy was in part tied to compelling student action or intervention in the world as a course requirement, which they felt varying degrees of tension around. These teacher educators expressed more comfort creating awareness than compelling action. They viewed compelling action as inauthentic and a version of "telling students what to think." These educators viewed ELA curriculum as an opening of possible doors. It was the students' choice, not the teachers' mandate, to walk through those doors.

In contrast to this position, many of those we spoke with described activism as integral to justice and equity, and they viewed teaching as a means to reproduce this position and to help students act on the world. These teacher educators used keywords to describe activism such as "power relations," "injustice," and "change" and often viewed their English methods classrooms, and/or other ELA teacher preparation courses, as scenes of learning about these concepts and intervening in the world to address oppression, often in open-ended ways.

Several of these educators made clear connections between activism and values, specifically, as Henry shared, in "putting my values into practice." The relationship between values and action emerged across many of our conversations and appear to be at the heart of how they think about activism. Others framed an activist education as obvious and clear—that is, transparent and explicit—as focused and intentional and as actively seeking to move the needle toward equity and justice.

Being more specific with the language she used, Ivy defined activism related to education as "standing up and stepping up and speaking out . . . and also associating that with actions." She went on to note that, for her, activism must be both well-informed and involve a measure of risk taking. Adding to Ivy's notion, Henry shared a view of activism that included "building and participating in transformative communities that redistribute the way people share power" and "creating, sustaining, and participating in communities or groups of people with a focus on sharing . . . rather than imposing power." Ivy's and Henry's conceptions of activism are useful when imagining how to create English teacher preparation programs that foreground distributive power, community building, and transformative action.

Further complicating these stances, others viewed teaching as advocacy rather than activism—feeling the former described strategic coalition and relationship building while the latter connoted "lone wolf" efforts to make change. Regardless of the labels or language they use, we are encouraged by the ways these teacher educators think and talk about activism as connected to values, as explicit and outward facing, as requiring research and risk, and as collaborative. For us, this nuanced understanding of activism provides a truly helpful lens for reflecting on our own teacher preparation and for making necessary revisions to ensure we are preparing teachers who use their positions to create change in classrooms, schools, and society.

ELA teacher educators looking for practical connections to these conceptualizations of activism or ways to bring this into their classrooms may consider asking students early in courses to brainstorm working definitions of activism, advocacy, and justice. At the same time, we believe it's important for students to think about teaching values and goals and how those connect to activism, advocacy, and justice. Evolving views and perceptions related to values, activism, advocacy, and other driving concepts can also be documented after key readings, activities, and/or discussions. There are also numerous course texts that can serve as touchstones for this work in classrooms, including Sonja Cherry-Paul's (2024) *Antiracist Reading Revolution* and Lorena Escoto Germán's (2021) *Textured Teaching*.

Engaging in Activism in ELA Teacher Education

In addition to helping us understand how they conceptualize activism, the educators we spoke with also talked about how and when they bring activist ideas into their teacher preparation courses. In this section, we share some of the unique ways they engaged in activist teaching in their classrooms.

While some participants asked PSTs to grapple with important social issues in theoretical terms, others tasked them with addressing issues that matter to them through activist projects. Others still pushed PSTs to design instruction to prepare their future students to address meaningful issues in their communities. Discussing activism in his teaching, Elijah talked about his internship classes, where he works to help PSTs "consider why ungrading is a way that we should head [and] that they should [take] into their classrooms." Here, Elijah frames his activist teaching as theoretically driven—that is, to help future teachers think about possibilities—but grounded in one classroom practice (i.e., removing or decentering grades) he feels teachers can use to positively impact equity and agency.

Others view activist teaching as rooted in explicit approaches that clearly articulate one's beliefs and goals for their classrooms. Emma, for example, described one component of their activist journey as a teacher as being "gradually more and more explicit, whether it's through my readings or now essential questions, like this is what we're going to talk about this semester. I'm going to put this right out here up front." Similarly, others shared how they task future teachers with planning and facilitating their own professional learning and growth to counter one-size-fits-all approaches to professional development. In his methods course, Noah tasks PSTs with exploring "self-directed approaches to professional learning." For teachers such as Emma and Noah, an orientation as a teacher-activist requires transparency and positioning equity and justice as the central focus of teaching rather than as an add-on and empowering students with meaningful choices and ownership of their educational journeys.

Others, like Charlotte, described the necessity of refusing norms and traditions as activist practices. Her focus on helping teachers let go of the way things have always been creates opportunity to examine the implications and consequences of the status quo and the ways a radical shift in how we teach and work alongside students disrupts taken-for-granted norms and fosters change from the classroom outward.

Perhaps the most clearly visible way these educators bring activism into their teacher preparation can be seen in assignments that explicitly ask PSTs to consider, design, and engage activism. Some offered social action or equity projects in their syllabi; others refused norms by designing antiracist and antibias teaching. And a few asked students to get out and be involved in their community. Blair and Nora shared quite a bit about their social action projects, which task students with researching a relevant social issue, most often drawn from the young adult literature they read in class, collaborating on a plan of action, and engaging the issue to effect change. Arthur shared how he goes one step further by making community involvement a component of his course. Arthur asks students to choose how they want to engage their communities, offering them examples such as "working for a political candidate who they believe is doing right by the climate," getting involved with organizations that support and settle refugees, or working with existing projects on campus that focus on sustainability or environmental justice in some way.

While we acknowledge the examples described here are far from a comprehensive list of the amazing work taking place in ELA teacher education, they help us further consider the range of ways activism and activist orientations can take shape within preparing future ELA teachers. To this end, we find it important for ELA teacher candidates to develop teaching materials that advance activist themes and justice, whether via content, method, or both. To assist PSTs with developing teaching materials, we recommend providing activist-themed courses. To make explicit connections to course readings, teacher candidates can craft narrative frames around the pedagogical decisions they make that account for their intellectual influences and the activist goals their lessons and units advance.

Navigating Barriers to Activism in ELA Teacher Education

The teacher educators we interviewed also shared a variety of barriers they encounter to their activist work and how they navigate those in order to be activists and teach in activist ways. At times, these were perceived barriers, and at others they were actual, but we were reminded speaking with them that perceived barriers are born of the real world and can hold as much sway.

Many participants noted the near omnipresence of anti-CRT legislation that has passed or threatens to pass in their states, which includes the de-professionalization of teachers and teaching. These bills loom as ambiguous warning signs that create ominous and unknown working conditions. However, many participants lean on disciplinary standards and practices in ELA, including the importance of preparing informed and critically literate students, to frame their activist teaching.

Other participants noted the importance of educating administrators, community members, and parents about their commitments to activist teaching in order to potentially forestall future obstacles. Still other participants navigated barriers in their institutions by participating in community a ctivism to remake their contexts. One educator advocated for GSA programming in her local school district while looking for ways her teacher education students and institution could support that work. Others described (1) the importance of forming teacher inquiry groups and collectives; (2) the need to "build all sorts of liminal spaces, where you can share power with students and radically imagine transformative communities," as Henry described; (3) the necessity of communication, trust building, and community forming, as Nora noted; and (4) calls to, as Elizabeth said, "help inform the parents and the communities around us what we're doing [and] to think about how to be proactive ... from the beginning of [our] teaching career."

Others shared their lack of belief in institutional commitment to change, challenges with balancing procedural portions of their jobs with their drive to be activist in and outside their classrooms, and the existing power dynamics within their departments, institutions, and teacher education more broadly. Henry, for example, noted that shared governance breaks down when white, male voices—and white supremacy by connection—dominate conversations and ideas. This barrier is clear in Ivy's experiences as a woman of color when she described the challenges she must navigate: "I get kind of tired of being, like, the go-to person on things, too. And that's really exhausting [. . .] it's exhausting to be in a profession that, you know, you get ten times more knocks on your door from people of like parallel programs at your university, of people who just need support in thinking through [equity]."

We believe it is also important for ELA teacher educators to use their classrooms to help PSTs anticipate the challenges they may encounter and begin to create opportunities for their activist teaching. In addition to reflecting on readings and engaging frequent discussion around barriers and challenges, we recommend inviting guest speakers—teachers, administrators, librarians, community educators—who do activist work with young people and in schools. Hearing directly from activist leaders can provide valuable perspective on working within systems and communities to accomplish a transformative vision for education.

Engaging Students in Activism in ELA Teacher Education

The barriers described above notwithstanding, many of these teacher educators continued making activism central to their coursework. Often, they connected student activism to critical literacy and the contours of their activist teaching. For instance, Blair and Nora used YAL to create awareness of social problems and injustice, and students then designed community-engaged projects to enact change. One student group, after reading a young adult novel about mental health, created a campaign to improve signage on campus for mental health services. Other groups designed and enacted projects that addressed gender-based violence on campus; affirmed members of the LGBTQ community; supported local community initiatives; and defended rights for those with hearing impairments in the community.

Other teacher educators in our work supplemented critical literacy teaching with the power of choice to encourage students to bring their interests and community needs together, such as a clean water campaign. Others laid a foundation for activist teaching that led PSTs to respond strategically to local issues. For instance, Hazel sponsored and led an after-school group focused on antiracism, which organized a protest walkout supportive of a student who suffered racial abuse online. Through these ELA teacher educators' courses, PSTs engaged in other forms of activism as well, such as protesting university testing policies, writing and performing social justice theatre installations, designing justice-based instruction for their internship placements, providing books to classrooms overseas, engaging in social media and letter-writing campaigns, joining existing and forming new community programs, and testifying before state legislators.

As part of efforts to engage students in course-related activism, we feel it's essential for ELA PSTs to practice *doing* activism in their coursework. Activist-focused projects can be connected to campus life, local community context, and/or instructional design. We stress, too, that this work must be thoughtful, well planned, and sensitive to context, needs, and positionality. In addition to the crucial role of practice and reflection, community involvement is essential as well. We encourage teacher educators to invite activist teachers and educators into their classrooms to share and mentor future teachers. Similarly, when possible, providing ELA PSTs opportunities to observe activist-oriented teachers in action (e.g., during internships or practicals) holds much promise for supporting future teachers' transfer of activist orientations into their future classrooms.

Where Do We Go from Here?

We found that these educators conceptualize activism in teacher education in a variety of ways and engage in activist teacher preparation in subtle and explicit ways. While such difference is to be expected, it is precisely those differences that stand out to us. Our experiences suggest that defining "activism" as it relates to teacher education in ELA is complicated, contextualized, and tied heavily to individual interests, beliefs, support, and so forth, and taken together, this offers a more nuanced view of the ways activism is employed within ELA teacher education. Our work also contributes a series of snapshots of how ELA teacher educators bring activism into their courses and the ways their students, through those courses, act on the world, which furthers our understanding of the field and, more practically, provides a broad view of instructional ideas from which to borrow and build.

The voices and perspectives of these teacher educators connect to the literature on teacher identity development (e.g., Franzak, 2002) and can offer ways to help PSTs grapple with the dissonance they may feel between their existing definitions and ideas of teaching—as deliverers of curriculum with little to no engagement outside of school—and the notion of activist teaching, in which they use their instruction to, alongside students, focus on futurity and civic learning and to interrogate and interrupt inequities in schools and communities (Picower, 2011). Part of the journey, as Hess and McAvoy (2015) suggest, is to help future teachers and their future students recognize the relationship between education and civic engagement. Equally important is helping PSTs recognize and carve out spaces within their standards and curricula for activist-focused teaching. The work English teacher educators are doing in their own classrooms serves as places to start and/or as inspiration for those looking for other ways to make activism central to their work.

Works Cited

Cook, M. P. (2021). Adopting hands-off approaches to activism: Examining PSTs' experiences navigating visibility and vulnerability as teacher-activists. *Journal of Teacher Education, 72*(5), 538–550. https://doi.org./10.1177/0022487120979110

Cook, M. P. (2022). ELA teachers & whiteness: Hesitancy as barrier to teacher agency development. *English Education, 54*(4), 273–293. https://doi.org/10.58680/ee202231979

Cook, M. P., & Yeilding, G. H. (2022). Conflict, politics, and self-censorship: PSTs and their struggles with writing as civic-engagement. *Teaching/Writing: The Journal of Writing Teacher Education, 11*(1), Article 1.

Blackburn, M.V., Clark, C.T., & Schey, R. (with Penn, J. P., Johnson, C., Williams, J., Sutton, D., Swensen, K., & Vanderhule, L.). (2018). *Stepping up! Teachers advocating for sexual and gender diversity in schools*. Routledge. https://doi.org/10.4324/9780203705209

Butler, T. T. (2016). "Stories behind their hands": The creative and collective "actionist" work of girls of color. *English Teaching: Practice & Critique, 15*(3), 313–332. https://doi.org/10.1108/ETPC-01-2016-0015

Franzak, J. K. (2002). Developing a teacher identity: The impact of critical friends practice on the student teacher. *English Education, 34*(4), 258–280. https://doi.org/10.58680/ee20021614

Haddix, M. (2015). Preparing community-engaged teachers. *Theory into Practice, 54*(1), 63–70. https://doi.org/10.1080/00405841.2015.977664

Haddix, M., & Price-Dennis, D. (2013). Urban fiction and multicultural literature as transformative tools for preparing English teachers for diverse classrooms. *English Education, 45*(3), 247–283. https://doi.org/10.58680/ee201323559

Hess, D. E. & McAvoy, P. (2015). *The political classroom: Evidence and ethics in democratic education*. Routledge. https://doi.org/10.4324/9781315738871

Morrell, E. (2005). Critical English education. *English Education, 37*(4), 312–321. https://doi.org/10.58680/ee20054133

Nieto, S. (2006). *Teaching as political work: Learning from courageous and caring teachers*. Child Development Institute (Occasional Paper Series). https://www.sarahlawrence.edu/media/cdi/pdf/Occasional%20Papers/CDI_Occasional_Paper_2006_Nieto.pdf

Picower, B. (2011). Resisting compliance: Learning to teach for social justice in a neoliberal context. *Teachers College Record, 113*(5), 1105–1134. https://doi.org/10.1177/016146811111300503

Of Loyalty, Freedom, and Agency: Framing Our Roles as Citizens in Literacy Teaching and Teacher Education

NICHOLAS DEPASCAL & MARY RICE

Support for engaging in literacy tasks is a crucial part of English language arts teachers' work (Mirra & Morrell, 2011). The Civic Mission of Schools Report (Patrick, 2004) highlighted this connection by connecting civic activities with obtaining information, initiating dialogue with others, and even acting politically through public speaking, petitioning, and protesting. All these activities require seeking, reading, and drawing from multiple sources of information, bringing ideas together into arguments, and determining audiences for work—per the Common Core State Standards (National Governors Association Center for Best Practices, Council of Chief State School Officers, 2010). Such knowledge, skills, and dispositions underscore what Scherff and Morrell (2015) argued when they wrote that "English is a discipline that helps prepare engaged citizens who use language and literacy to speak the truth to power" (p. ix).

In addition to the importance of language skills for civic thought and activity, civics education researchers have been able to make links between levels of overall academic achievement, political knowledge, and civic participation. These correlations hold, irrespective of whether civics education was formally included as part of the curriculum or not (Niemi & Junn, 2005). Thus, Lai (2018) noted that while there are strong connections made between learning the language and literacy of schooling and the knowledge and practices of civic participation, these connections are rarely acknowledged or investigated.

There is, of course, the potential for tensions and challenges to emerge within the definitions of *civics* within an institution such as school. For example, schools tend to value loyalty and obedience to the school over other considerations that might be components of citizenship (Raby, 2012; Thornberg, 2009). Moreover, schools tend to foster structured civic behavior as obedience to rules within the institution, even when this means that students with learning differences and emotional behavioral needs will not be able to meet these expectations and will therefore be labeled deviant (Rice & Dunn, 2023; Taylor, 2020). Finally, the infusion of technology and capitalism into schools has brought with it increased framing of civic behavior in schools as loyalty and enthusiasm for companies, products, and markets (Molnar & Boninger, 2015; Spring, 2003).

Considering the potential for problems and excesses, there is an ongoing need for teacher educators and teachers to remain in solidarity and to keep vigilance in order to ensure that civic learning and literacies remain focused on supporting students in developing critical literacies for asking questions about their circumstances, advocating for support in their communities, learning how political and social processes work, and becoming committed to lifelong participation in processes do more than merely maintain democratic principles. Instead, these literacies are continually reformed and reframed in ways that expand opportunities for participation by others. The purpose of this essay is to share examples of how we, as a teacher and teacher educators, have conceptualized civics in English language arts (ELA) in our setting. We are two white teachers in New Mexico—a state where nearly 75 percent of children claim a combination of Hispano, Latinx, Indigenous, and affiliations with Indigenous groups (New Mexico Voices for Children, 2020). There are also populations of Black/African American students and Asian students. Around 60 percent of teachers in New Mexico report being white like us, although that number is lower than the national average of closer to 80 percent (NMKidsCan.org, 2018).

Framing for Civic Praxis

There are several sources from which prospective and practicing teachers can draw ideas about civic practice for teaching. One source is John Dewey (1933, 1997), who wrote about the purpose of education being to help children participate in a transformational democracy. To Dewey, this meant more than voting, although voting is a crucial component, perhaps especially when exercising this right is accompanied by thoughtful study and an imagining about what is in the best interest of all the community and not just one's own household, family, or self. Another often considered perspective comes from Paulo Freire (1970, 2018), who wrote about education as the practice of freedom and suggested that educators needed to be proactive about using the structures of education to provide support for learners to throw off that which oppresses them. In a similar vein, Ivan Illich (1973) wrote of schools as advancing a radical monopoly over the technologies of education, which they used to do harm not just to individuals but to societies. Disrupting this harm would require a turn to understanding and using what he referred to as convivial tools that allowed people to form meaningful social ties for the purpose of solving the problems they faced in their current circumstances. More recently, scholars like Brayboy (2021) have highlighted the ways in which school and reform knowledges are Eurocentric and need to broaden to include Indigenous knowledges and scholarship. Nelson (2021) also highlighted how civic education that did not directly address social injustice failed to induce civic participation in Black/African American and Latinx youth. To this cause, Tuck and Yang (2018) considered what might constitute justice:

> There are social justice projects which we find compelling, which move us, which call our names; and there are those that flatten us. We tend to refuse the many projects with theories of change that rely upon the benevolence of the state or of the dominant in society. We refuse:

- Justice projects which require us to prove humanity or worth
- Justice projects which require us to frontload a lot of learning or consciousness-raising
- Justice projects which require us to appeal to the people who abuse us
- Justice projects which require us to gather an audience of white settlers who are presumed to have agency
- Justice projects that presume compromise as the main avenue for achieving solidarity (p. 8)

Within this thinking about justice more broadly, Tuck and Yang's (2014) definition might support thinking about what civic education could look like in a school setting.

To encompass and enact a civics education in ELA (and perhaps all) classrooms that concerns themselves with social justice, teachers must come to see that education is not neutral. Especially now—in an era of increasing book bans that seek nothing less than to further marginalize diverse groups and reinforce dominant historical narratives, as well as punitive laws that seek to silence teachers and students who would challenge these bans and narratives—the teacher's powerful role in promoting a broad and inclusive definition of civic activity must be emphasized in teacher collaboration, professional development, and teacher education. The definitions of civics and teachers' roles in supporting the exploration and practice of civics must also be expanded to include the ever changing and expanding technologies that are being funneled into and tested in classrooms and fostering a critical viewpoint as to their impact on citizens' abilities to engage civically in society and control their own lives.

Further, just as "history from below" (Thompson, 1966) focuses less on the traditional big names of history and more on the broad swathe of people who lived and made history, a similar focus on "civics from below" would look less at how democracy and social progress happen through loyalty and compliance and would instead examine how resistance and refusal often serve as the engines of effective civic participation, action, and justice (p. 1). Developing classroom settings and curricula with teachers and students that contend with and challenge the implied norms of civic participation in contemporary society would honor the long history of teaching and learning as subversive activities that often become necessary under the oppressive yoke of the state.

Questioning Daily Practices

As part of literacy teacher education course-work, teachers in courses where Mary teaches are encouraged to consider the everyday practices in schools, what literacies those practices assume are present or required, and then teachers can design projects that explore their questions and wonderings. Teachers can generate interesting questions about a variety of topics. One practice that teachers sometimes bring to courses for questioning is the Pledge of Allegiance to the United States flag. In New Mexico, schools are obliged to recite the Pledge of Allegiance (NM Stat § 22-5-4.5, 2023). As there are many speakers of Spanish(es) in our state, the English version is often followed by the Pledge of Allegiance in Spanish, but there is no requirement for this. When the issue arises, teachers express a diversity of very strong feelings on the issue (Bennett, 2005). Some teachers feel that saying the Pledge of Allegiance is a unifying part of civic life that ought to be taught and enforced in schools. Other teachers feel that saying the Pledge of Allegiance is a recitation of meaningless words to most students and that doing so endangers the type of unreflective patriotism that is problematic (Martin, 2012). Other teachers point out that teaching the Pledge of Allegiance on stolen, unceded land in a state with multiple Indigenous Pueblo and Apache Nations and the Navajo (or Diné) Nation without an accompanying acknowledgment of the injustices against these peoples and their ancestors is an assault on their identities, dignities, and freedoms.

Teachers can consider these various points of view and then make decisions about what they might do with their students. Mary and the students discuss various ways in which teachers might be able to consider how to start conversations with their students, design activities to learn more about where the Pledge of Allegiance comes from, how it came to be said in schools as a routine practice, and how it came to be a matter of state law to offer the Pledge of Allegiance to students (Ellis, 2005). Also, the teachers discuss what it means to be required to recite the Pledge of Allegiance to students and whether students have ever had a meaningful conversation about this routine. Many children may feel just fine; other children might have questions. Some young people realize that even though the Pledge of Allegiance must be recited, each person in the school is not required to recite it. They may join in reciting the Pledge of Allegiance, stand, sit, or perhaps do some other activity. Most district policies have elaborated that students are not allowed to disrupt without being subject to potential disciplinary procedures, although there are rarely definitions of *disruption*.

Some teachers enjoy the opportunity that class introduces for them to discuss these nuances with their students, and many enjoy helping the students understand what it is they are saying when they are reciting the Pledge of Allegiance. Sometimes the teachers even design activities for students to consider what else in their family and community deserves allegiance or various degrees of loyalty and why. Sometimes conversations ensue about whether there is a flipside to allegiance or such a thing as too much allegiance to one person or one idea. Also, sometimes teachers and children think of other ways to honor various groups in the state, their families, and their class communities as part of greeting the day. Additional school structures for critical interrogation as a class might include something like the use of the Dewey decimal system to organize books, the choice of a specific school mascot or even the practice of having one at all, or critiquing a classroom practice with students where it would be easy to change or give choice, like having students keep reading logs.

It is also true that some teachers express discomfort with the idea of informing the children that they have choices about whether and how to participate. This seems very disruptive to the regime of school, where if children realize they have a choice about the Pledge of Allegiance, what else might they realize or believe they should have choices about? Discomfort may stem from individual teacher perceptions of the purposes of schooling and be a possible effect of increased district and state book bans, with resultant threats to teacher autonomy and wellbeing. A 2023 RAND study of 8,000 teachers found that "roughly one-quarter of teachers reported that limitations placed on how teachers can address topics related to race and gender have influenced their choice of curriculum materials or instructional practices" (Woo et al., 2023, p. 2).

Social control is really at the heart of the matter. What is done to children in school settings in the name of social control when something more cooperative would do? If teachers do not want to address or (re)address the Pledge of Allegiance in any way, then of course, we cannot compel them to do that, but where are they making space so that youth can learn about civic engagement and not just practice obedience? What does it say about a school or school community that deliberately obfuscates opportunities for children's agencies? It is ironic as well that children might feel forced to behave a certain way to prove fealty to a symbol of freedom. Children and teachers in civic spaces should be premised on justice where their worth is assumed (Tuck & Yang, 2018). What roles are they being prepared for in different types of spaces?

Roleplaying as Civic Praxis

Roleplaying activities—during which students inhabit the personas of fictional characters or real-life people to make sense of the past, present, and future—have become increasingly popular ways to engage students in texts and events, experience and share multiple viewpoints on social issues, and create spaces that allow for affect and empathy in the classroom (Elegreet-DeSalvo & Levitsky, 1989; Hanson, 2009; Kersulov et al., 2021; Scarbrough et al., 2018; Schey, 2020; Seltzer, 2019). Often, these activities, especially in writing classrooms, ask students to read or conduct research on a particular group of people (Irish immigrants or high school principals, for example) and write a script or document that shares a representative individual's viewpoint from that group on a particular topic or event (migration or the request to remove a book from a school's library) and then to discuss, share, and debate the various reactions that different people or groups have about the event. The point is usually to introduce challenging or complex topics from history in a way that makes them feel more immediate and accessible to students, who may be quite removed in time and place from events that nevertheless have been formative. Roleplays can also be useful tools to study lesser-known historical and current events that have traditionally been whitewashed by the dominant historical narrative favored in textbooks or ignored or underplayed by mainstream media. Without sensitive modeling and sufficient time, though, roleplays risk reinforcing stereotypes or leaving students with an oversimplified view of complex events.

Roleplays are often favored in social studies classrooms, where attempting to engage students with history is of great importance. When roleplays are used in ELA classrooms, the focus is often on having students write creatively to engage with complex topics by having them imagine what fictional characters might say or do in a particular time or place. Yet using roleplays in ELA classrooms that include roles from real people encountering contemporary or historical events and conflicts is an excellent way to give engaging contextual background beyond slide presentations for class texts and can help answer the oft-asked question of *why* we read certain texts. What teachers and students read together in ELA classes cannot be untethered from the time and place in which it was written or which it is supposed to portray, just as it cannot be read as a dead text to be dissected only for its analyzable parts. Revealing the often unknown or lesser known or celebrated people of then and now who have shaped history and continue to shape the present can give students a view as to their agency in revealing truth and affecting change. Creating and using roleplays that demonstrate how people have and do define their roles and realities as citizens through resistance and revolt as opposed to strictly traditional methods of citizenship positions students as willing and able to challenge just the sort of strictly enforced methods of acceptable engagement typically favored in school and society. Given the threats that students, schools, and society face—gun violence, climate change, and the continued creep of fascism—engaging students not only to understand a text or a historical event but also to see themselves as historical and contemporary actors is of utmost importance. What follows is an explanation of how Nick has used roleplay activities in his own ELA classroom to engage students in the past and the present through fictional, historical, and personal experiences in hopes of helping them see themselves as forces of change.

Nick has used roleplay activities in general education and Advanced Placement classes alike with positive results. In his most recent AP language classes, he used a roleplay activity about environmental racism (published online by Zinn Education Project) as the introductory lesson to a unit on environmental writing that featured texts from international authors on various climatic and environmental issues. Roleplay activities require thoughtful and sensitive planning by the teacher, a safe and established classroom community for students, and clear communication of the expectation and goals of the activity. Zinn Education Project (https://www.zinnedproject.org/news/how-to-teach-role-plays/) offers a detailed and transparent consideration of roleplays and many useful tips for using them in the classroom.

Before the roleplay, Nick asked the students to define environmental racism in their own words—without much success. Nick and the students broke down the words together and came to an acceptable working definition but one without much nuance before launching into the roleplay activity. Students received written roles that featured the experiences and work of real people facing situations of undrinkable water—in Jackson, Mississippi; Newark, New Jersey; and Flint, Michigan—over the last decade or so. The roles included politicians but also doctors, researchers, citizens affected by undrinkable water and members of community organizations fighting for drinkable water and enacting community-oriented acts of self-reliance outside of the typical govern-mental sphere. After discussions that these roles represented real people and the responsibility to portray their stories meaningfully and respectfully, students (and Nick) circulated, shared, and listened to the stories we inhabited and looked for connections in what we heard.

In writing and discussions after the roleplay, Nick and the students considered the idea of a government's responsibility to provide safe, livable conditions for its citizens and how citizens can force change when that sense of responsibility from lawmakers and leaders is not forthcoming. At the end of class, each student wrote a new definition of environmental racism in their own words based on their experience of the roleplay. The results were more nuanced, and many of the definitions included the idea that economic development and resources are unevenly distributed and based on race, which is often tied to class and location. Students' new definitions also keyed into the idea that racism isn't always a person-to-person action but is also expressed through laws, policies, and budgets. Some students also shared connections to their own lives and how they had seen such uneven distribution and treatment of citizens based seemingly on their class and/or race. Conducting this lesson before embarking on the readings for the unit primed students' thinking about the concepts and ideas that would undergird many of the readings we would explore from writers like Wangarĩ Maathai, Robin Wall Kimmerer, Greta Thunberg, and more. Exploring a concept like environmental racism allowed students to approach the readings not as dry texts to be analyzed for their rhetorical purposes and then put away but rather as powerful, living texts, interconnected strands of a web that linked people all over the world in a common cause, and for students to include themselves in those connections as well. As part of teaching argument writing, the connections made between texts and larger concepts showed students that thinking and writing can *do* things and that their thinking and writing can become part of conversation and action beyond the classroom. The next step is to create authentic and actionable opportunities for students to use their thinking and writing skills to affect their world.

Conclusion

From the teacher education classroom to the high school classroom, the conversation about what civic participation does and can look like continues. An enlargement of what constitutes civic education is necessary to maintain, or better yet expand, our concepts of justice, freedom, and democracy. What is evident from the examples above is that both time and space are necessary for teachers to develop the knowledge and practices needed to enact meaningful and intentional civic education in ELA classrooms. Research, deliberation, discussion, and debate are the hallmarks of civic participation, and these same elements are required in the creation of classrooms and curricula that deal justly and openly with what it means to be a citizen in the US and globally. Finding time and space—in university courses, teacher collaborative communities, and educator professional development—for teachers to seriously see themselves as civic actors charged with helping to usher future generations into citizenhood is increasingly challenging. The pressures of a fractious and polarized American society is one reason. The continued deprofessionalization and intensification of teacher labor is another. Yet these challenges also provide opportunities for teachers to enact and model their own forms of civic engagement through the many ways they fight back against unjust laws and policies using activist positionings and the curricula and cultures they bring into their classrooms.

Works Cited

Bennett, L. J. (2004). Classroom recitation of the Pledge of Allegiance and its educational value: Analysis, review, and proposal. *Journal of Curriculum & Supervision, 20*(1), 56–75.

Brayboy, B. M. J. (2022). Tribal critical race theory: An origin story and future directions. In M. Lynn & A. D. Dixson (Eds.), *Handbook of critical race theory in education* (2nd ed., pp. 191–202). Routledge. https://doi.org/10.4324/9781351032223

Council of Chief State School Officers & National

Governors Association. (2010). *Common core state standards for English language arts & literacy in history/social studies, science, and technical subjects.* https://learning.ccsso.org/wp-content/uploads/2022/11/ADA-Compliant-ELA-Standards.pdf

Dewey, J. (1997). *Experience and education.* Touchstone.

Elegreet-DeSalvo, N., & Levitsky, R. (1989). "We left our homeland, a sad, sad day": An interdisciplinary approach. *The English Journal*, 78(6), 62–65. https://doi.org/10.2307/817927

Ellis, R. J. (2005). *To the flag: The unlikely history of the Pledge of Allegiance.* University Press of Kansas.

Freire, P. (with Macedo, D., & Shor, I.). (2018). *Pedagogy of the oppressed* (M. B. Ramos., Trans; 50th anniversary ed.). Bloomsbury Academic.

Hansen, J. (2009). Multiple literacies in the content classroom: High school students' connections to U.S. history. *Journal of Adolescent & Adult Literacy*, *52*(7), 597–606. https://doi.org/10.1598/JAAL.52.7.5

Illich, I. (1973). *Tools for conviviality.* Harper & Row.

Kersulov, M. L., Falch, K., & Hartwig, A. (2021). Classroom drama: Roleplaying fictional characters in a political debate. *English Journal*, *110*(3), 74–81. https://doi.org/10.58680/ej202131071

Lai, P. F. (2018). *Civics English: Integrating civics in middle school English language arts teaching* (Publication No. 10930491) [Doctoral dissertation, University of California, Berkeley]. ProQuest Dissertations and Theses Global.

Martin, L. A. (2012). Blind patriotism or active citizenship? How do students interpret the Pledge of Allegiance? *Action in Teacher Education*, *34*(1), 55–64. https://doi.org/10.1080/01626620.2012.642288

Mirra, N., & Morrell, E. (2011). Teachers as civic agents: Toward a critical democratic theory of urban teacher development. *Journal of Teacher Education*, *62*(4), 408–420. https://doi.org/10.1177/0022487111409417

Molnar, A., & Boninger, F. (2015). *Sold out: How marketing in school threatens children's well-being and undermines their education.* Rowman & Littlefield. https://doi.org/10.5771/9781475813623

Morrell, E., & Scherff, L. (Eds.). (2015). *New Directions in teaching English: Reimagining teaching, teacher education, and research.* Rowman & Littlefield.

Nelsen, M. D. (2021). Teaching citizenship: Race and the behavioral effects of American civic education. *The Journal of Race, Ethnicity, and Politics*, *6*(1), 157–186. https://doi.org/10.1017/rep.2019.19

New Mexico Voices for Children (2021). *2020 New Mexico kids count data book.* https://www.nmvoices.org/archives/15123

NewMexicoKidsCAN. (2018). *State of education in New Mexico 2018.* https://nmkidscan.org/wp-content/uploads/sites/15/2017/09/SoE-NM-WEB.pdf

Niemi, R. G., & Junn, J. (2005). *Civic education: What makes students learn.* Yale University Press.

Patrick, J. (2004). The civic mission of schools: Key ideas in a research-based report on civic education in the US. *Teacher Librarian*, *32*(2), 26–28.

Raby, R. (2012). *School rules: Obedience, discipline, and elusive democracy.* University of Toronto Press.

Rice, M. F., & Dunn, S. (2023). Challenging digital citizenship discourse through the lens of (dis)ability. In J. D. DeHart (Ed.), *Critical roles of digital citizenship and digital ethics* (pp. 61–75). IGI Global. https://doi.org/10.4018/978-1-6684-8934-5.ch005

Scarbrough, B., Pieper, B., & Vetsch, H. (2018). Engaging banned and challenged books through role-play simulation. *The English Journal, 108*(2), 74–83. https://doi.org/10.58680/ej201829880

Schey, R. (2020). Youths' literacy disidentifications in a secondary classroom: Contesting transphobia through humor in role-playing. *Teachers College Record, 122*(7), Article 070312. https://doi.org/10.1177/016146812012200712

Seltzer, K. (2019). Performing ideologies: Fostering raciolinguistic literacies through role-play in a high school English classroom. *Journal of Adolescent & Adult Literacy, 63*(2), 147–155. https://doi.org/10.1002/jaal.966

Spring, J. (2003). *Educating the consumer-citizen: A history of the marriage of schools, advertising, and media*. Routledge. https://doi.org/10.4324/9781410607591

Taylor, A. (2020). The metaphor of civic threat: Intellectual disability and education for citizenship. In L. Ware (Ed.), *Critical readings in interdisciplinary disability studies: (Dis) assemblages: Vol. 12. Critical studies of education* (pp. 53–68). Springer. https://doi.org/10.1007/978-3-030-35309-4_5

Thompson, E. P. (1966, April 7). History from below. *The Times Literary Supplement*, 3345, p. 279. https://link-gale-com.ezp.lib.rochester.edu/apps/doc/EX1200341290/TLSH?u=nysl_ro_rochstru&sid=bookmark-TLSH&xid=95569b2a

Thornberg, R. (2009). The moral construction of the good pupil embedded in school rules. *Education, Citizenship and Social Justice, 4*(3), 245–261. https://doi.org/10.1177/1746197909340874

Woo, A., Lee, S., Tuma, A. P., Kaufman, J. H., Lawrence, R. A., & Reed, N. (2023). *Walking on eggshells—Teachers' responses to classroom limitations on race- or gender-related topics: Findings from the 2022 American instructional resources survey*. RAND Corporation. https://www.rand.org/pubs/research_reports/RRA134-16.html

Educators Writing to Change the World

KRISTINE WILBER, KATE SJOSTROM,
NATHANIEL CHA, MARY ROSE O'SHEA,
ANDREA VAUGHAN & REBECCA WOODARD

Choosing love we also choose to live in community, and that means that we do not have to change by ourselves.

—bell hooks

Educators Writing to Change the World

This essay represents writing from participants in the Chicago Area Writing Project's (CAWP) EdWrite Collab, twenty-one educators who gathered to "write to change the world." Contemporary teaching is fraught with difficulty; teachers are underpaid, undervalued (Drudy, 2008), and highly scrutinized (Goldstein, 2014). We feel a lack of self-determination (Dunn, Farver, Guenther, & Wexler, 2017), and disrespect from elected officials and the media (American Federation of Teachers & Badass Teachers Association, 2015). Furthermore, while the majority of educators are women, key forums that drive public policy and opinions are led by men (Orenstein, n.d.). The EdWrite Collab believes that we need more educators to bring our identities, experiences, and desires into these spaces with a goal of shaping better educational systems.

Kristine, Andrea, and Becca—coauthors of this essay—are leaders of CAWP who designed, and/or facilitated the EdWrite Collab. We supported educators' *civically engaged writing* about education, which we defined as writing that employs a public voice, advocates civic engagement or action, argues a position based on reasoning and evidence, and employs a structure to support a position (National Writing Project, n.d.). Civic writing that supports interrogation and innovation can even foster a reimagination of public life in ways that "honor . . . experiences, relationships, and dreams for the future" (Mirra & Garcia, 2020, p. 297).

Our group included four university educators, one educational consultant, three elementary school teachers, six high school teachers, six graduate students of education (some of whom were also K–12 teachers), and one preservice teacher. We identified primarily as women but also included men and nonbinary educators. Approximately a quarter of the group identified as people of color. Our work included a series of workshops through The OpEd Project that focused on "changing who writes history" through elevating "the ideas and knowledge of underrepresented expert voices" (The OpEd Project, n.d.). We also met over Zoom four times for two hours each to think, talk, and write together. Our goal was for each member to craft an op-ed about education and submit it for publication.

For this project, we reviewed writing and videos from our meetings, identifying three themes: (1) Teachers are well-positioned to share our experiences and critically analyze significant problems in educational systems; (2) Gathering in writing communities empowers teachers to raise our voices on collective concerns; and (3) By gathering, teachers create connections and support that cannot be accessed in isolation, and that is sorely needed. Here, we share stories from EdWrite Collective members (all coauthors of this piece) reflecting on these themes—from Kate, an English professor; Mary Rose, a high school teacher and graduate student; and Nathaniel, a former middle school teacher and graduate student.

Kate: Courage to Reject Complacency

In January 2014, before I became a university supervisor of English language arts (ELA) student teachers, I interviewed my retired public school teacher father for my dissertation on teacher identity development. About to become responsible for evaluating teachers myself, I listened with interest as he described the ways he had been evaluated over the years. The most memorable was a tool for assessing his students' learning that would, in turn, be used to assess his teaching:

> [T]hese very elaborate . . . punch cards. Around the sides of them . . . they had skills—like forty on each side of the card—and there were little holes. And you would *punch* [to] enlarge the hole to the margin. [. . .] So that if you skewered them on a little rod and held them up, they would fall off if they had been punched, if that [skill] had been mastered.

Decades later, my dad was still shaking his head at this ineffective, byzantine system.

While my dad's story of the punchcard-and-rod evaluation seemed a tale of times long gone, I had learned enough through my own experience teaching to know we were still firmly in the accountability movement's clutches—if it wasn't one standardized test, it would be another. Perhaps it was the seeming inevitability of this cycle that lulled me into complacency, keeping me quiet for too long as I was caught in yet another evaluation system that contradicted common sense.

Indeed, my first semester supervising student teachers marked the introduction of the Educative Teacher Performance Assessment, or edTPA, required for initial licensure. That first semester was a trial run as we prepared for it to become law in our state the following year. My mentors, finding the edTPA ridiculously inappropriate (it required some fifty pages of writing, video clips, and graphs—much like the portfolio required of veteran teachers seeking National Board Certification—and had to be completed *while teaching for the very first time*), insisted it wouldn't stick and did nothing to prepare in case it did.

It stuck. And I, a graduate instructor getting evaluated on my *own* teaching without the protections of tenure, worked like crazy to support student teachers in passing the assessment. I attended voluntary professional development sessions, redesigned the student teaching seminar as an edTPA boot camp, and counseled my student teachers through exhaustion, curricular and instructional challenges, and financial struggles. Student teachers were spending late-night hours reviewing potential edTPA video clips after planning for two-to-three courses, and giving feedback on their 100+ students' work. Some couldn't afford the edTPA fee *and* meet rent while student teaching time-and-a-half for free. Almost all were neglecting sleep and relationships.

Deep down, I knew none of this made sense—and that the assessment's narrow curricular focus on reading instruction was potentially devaluing writing instruction for a whole generation of teachers. But I was tired and too afraid of institutional failure to do much about it. It wasn't until I found strength in and became accountable to a community that I spoke out.

When I was invited to join the EdWrite Collab, I said yes without knowing much about it; having reached what felt like the nadir of my frustrations with work, I made a resolution to say yes to anything writing related, as writing had once been my source of energy and inspiration. Until that point, though, writing had been a solitary act, and I wrote almost exclusively for myself.

But how to turn away from my new EdWrite colleagues as they said things I might have said myself? From Elizabeth, who asked, "How many of us in education are working against our own values on a daily basis?" As we shared stories of our personal yet interconnected teaching contexts, I sensed a web was forming and wondered if I could let it support me. At the very least, I could sign on for step two: attending the OpEd Project to write about an issue in education.

Yet it remained hard to imagine that my story mattered or would make any difference. (I comforted myself by thinking that I could *write* the op-ed but didn›t have to *do* anything with it.) Still, as others attending the OpEd Project struggled to find a focus, I immediately knew what I wanted to address: how the edTPA diverted student teachers' attention from the kids in front of them; how it made it harder for lower-income student teachers to be licensed; how it devalued the education programs and cooperating teachers already assessing student teachers' readiness for the profession; how it sent new teachers into their first year of work already stressed and demoralized. It took members of my new community to clarify for me that mine was an expert voice, that though I didn't have the final say in the current system, my lived experiences were worthy of being considered in creation of a new system.

And so I wrote for the members of the collaborative, for my students, for myself—and, frankly, for the assignment. When it came down to it, having the structure of an assignment and the designated time to complete it were two of the most important ingredients in finally speaking up on an issue that had mattered to me for so long. But I would never have completed the assignment on my own. Without engaging in civic learning with my community of colleagues and without those colleagues' encouragement and counsel, I would not have had the guts and know-how to submit the op-ed to papers. Nor would I have gone on to send, with confidence, copies of the op-ed (Sjostrom, 2023) to my state legislators, who are now considering discontinuation of the edTPA requirement in my state.

In my op-ed, I argued that enough is enough, that given all the hurdles student teachers and teacher education programs already have to clear, the edTPA is not necessary. I challenged readers to imagine a different future: one where student teachers were focused on students and not a test, one where a teacher shortage was not exacerbated by a costly assessment of questionable reliability. I'm under no illusion that my op-ed was the tipping point in this scenario. But I'm also under no illusion that it had no effect at all.

When I interviewed my dad ten years ago about his teaching life, he didn't just tell me of the inanities of bureaucracy. He told me, too, of his best teacher friends and the great school events they organized together—the Olympic games representing the many cultures of their first-generation students, the mock convention at which Adlai Stevenson gave a speech. I remember being envious as he smiled and reminisced, bogged down as I was by exhaustion and isolation, disheartened as I was by the state of education. I see now that sometimes we luck into a strong teacher community right in our own school building. Sometimes, however, we have to accept the invitation to join another—or to even create a collective to work with toward change.

Mary Rose: Why Community Matters in Amplifying Teacher Voices

I am a public high school English teacher, labor activist, and graduate student in education. While my work weaves across these different roles, I sometimes find it difficult to reconcile them. For example, during the 2012 and 2019 Chicago Teachers Union strikes, when I was a delegate and strike captain, social media provided a way to connect immediately with my communities. But the larger picture is hard to paint with only 140 characters, even when in a thread. Then, when I engage in academic writing, it is sometimes so full of specialized jargon that it fails to connect to wide audiences. The op-ed form was intriguing to me as a medium that is oriented toward a broad audience and can be grounded in theory and literature, thus explicitly bridging the gap between theory and practice.

So, in July 2020, a few years before the EdWrite Collab formed, I wrote an op-ed with my two brothers entitled "Irish Americans, We Must Stand Up for Black Lives Matter" that was published in the *Chicago Sun-Times*. My two brothers, Conor and Michael, and I wrote this piece out of deep concern about the dissonance between the values of the community in which we were raised and the words and actions of that same community—a dissonance that reached a fever pitch after the murder of George Floyd. Although we'd collaborated in various contexts over the years, we'd never written together nor had I ever published an op-ed. Michael had though, and he used his experience with collaborative writing to reassure us and to spearhead the initial draft ("the starter"). Our conversations and shared insights deepened our collective understanding of this uniquely American brand of racism in Chicago and our own complicity within various systems of oppression. We fell into a natural cadence of writing, revision, and commenting. As the English teacher, I reviewed final edits on our piece ("the closer"). I was nervous about how it might be received and also about how to actually get it published. Was this whole thing nothing more than a fool's errand?

Enter Gina, a school librarian, grad school friend, and fellow "proseminista"—one of a group of fiercely honest, loyal, and supportive women who bonded during an initial proseminar class and helped each other weather the storm of grad school and life. Gina is a real-life op-ed queen (over seventy in print!) and once wrote a piece on a flight to a conference while I looked on from across the aisle, awestruck (such confidence!) (Caneva, 2024). I shared our piece with her and, with Gina's encouragement and introduction, submitted our finished draft to the *Sun-Times*, where it was published a few weeks later.

I raised my voice through op-ed writing as a direct result of collaborative spaces and relationships—from my brothers as co-writers to the proseministas as supporters. These collaboratives were instrumental in developing my thinking, and they continue to inspire my work.

Success publishing an op-ed helped me find and use my voice in public spaces, but putting forth original ideas and opinions into the larger public sphere continued to be challenging. I've had a hundred ideas and written dozens of drafts, ultimately archiving them away. So, when I received the EdWrite Collab invitation from Kristine, I agreed to participate without hesitation. Here was another opportunity to engage in collaborative learning through a supportive writing community and to strengthen my voice in the public sphere. Furthermore, as a graduate student, I was being challenged to position myself as a public intellectual and to ensure that research makes it beyond the ivory tower. As it turns out, it's a lot easier to *talk* (who knew?) about these things in class or at conferences than to actually *do* something about them (see ongoing research-practice divide). Through our op-ed, we were able not only to raise concerns about anti-Blackness in our community but also to encourage action. In our closing, we recommended some "first steps" and challenged ourselves and our community to "take at least one action today" (e.g., educating ourselves, interrupting racist comments, attending cultural events beyond our own).

I did not ultimately publish any writing as a direct result of my participation in the OpEd Project, but my experiences strengthened my growing understanding of the power and, perhaps, necessity of collaborative writing. I've learned that collaborative spaces and relationships are necessary to enable teachers to find, develop, and share their voices. These spaces and the ways in which we engage within them, however, must be nurtured. My sibling collaboration was possible because of our existing understanding of and respect for one another, and we continue to refine our approach as we engage in more current projects. Last year, Michael and I used thematic analysis to analyze two years of agenda and meeting minutes of our virtual sibling meetings and identified the following values as characteristics of our so-called "Family Research Methodology": "community, acknowledging connections to land and its histories, kindness and patience, well-being, shared vulnerability, inter-sustaining relationships and research, agency and non-competitiveness, and time" (O'Shea & O'Shea, 2023). Similarly, the EdWrite Collaborative was and is a community of educators allowing themselves to be challenged, to be vulnerable, to support one another.

Without collaboration, the ideas we seek to write would not be the same or perhaps even exist. In a reflective memo on later collaborations with my brothers, I wrote, "our own collaborative research is a welcome respite from our regular, disciplinary topics and an endeavor in which no sibling is solely expert, novice, nor any other role" (O'Shea & O'Shea, 2023). More than just collaboration, it was the egalitarian nature of the group that allowed our ideas and writing to develop. Likewise, the shared community of the EdWrite Collab has provided the space, reassurance, and feedback that so many of us need to feel empowered enough to share our voices. We were university faculty alongside graduate students alongside practicing K–12 teachers, all sharing vulnerability and in need of community.

Collaboration allowed me to find my voice. Without it, I would not have found the right community through which to continue engagement in public discourse.

Nathaniel: Toward Teacher Belonging, Purpose, and Solidarity

Waiting for the Zoom room to open, I could not help feeling conflicted. On the one hand, it would be comforting to see old friends and professors—exciting to hear the stories of these teacher-veterans. Yet I felt out of place. Having left my sixth-grade classroom two years ago to attend graduate school, I worried about how I would relate to practicing teachers. And having just finished coursework, I felt disconnected from my colleagues and professors. I realized the potential power of the EdWrite space for fostering relationships, vulnerability, and civic connection.

I had a dual role as both a research assistant and co-facilitator with Kristine. We took seriously the work of fostering nurturing relationships, and each meeting began with time for participants to express their identities beyond the classroom. We learned how certain teachers were activists, runners, and lovers of poetry and punk. Kristine and Kayla—another EdWriter—stood out to me in the ways they made time to support teachers who were parenting younger kids, listening to their frustrations and offering resources and support. Others dropped food off for Judith as she shared her struggles with a family emergency. In witnessing each other's lives, we affirmed and enacted care for each other.

Our relationships also fostered a vulnerability that empowered us to grow as writers. At the beginning of each meeting, Kristine and Becca would center the group with the purpose and goals of our workshops. In one small-group breakout when we were charged to discuss our idea for an op-ed, I admitted to my partners how I could not meet my goals due to writer's block and time management. I was relieved by how my partners assured me that their drafts and progress were not perfect either. Judith encouraged me to consider how youth learn outside of schools. I heard about other topics folks were considering writing about, including teacher burnout, student homelessness, and the Reading Wars. In being vulnerable with each other, we were able to create empathetic moments that balanced grace with pushes for growth. These moments helped us share personal stories, connecting our identities with issues. However, by the end of the second workshop, I still felt out of place for lacking a topic for my own writing.

At the same time, I attended the annual meeting of the American Educational Research Association in Chicago. Thousands of people presented an overwhelming number of ideas about what should matter in education. Amid all the voices, it was the news of teen-agers "rampaging" or "rioting" blocks away that moved me. I took out my phone. Headlines shouted, "'Teen takeover' terrorizes Chicago as hundreds of teenagers destroy property, attack tourists" (Lee & Fox News, 2023) and "Next Chicago mayor excuses rioters: Expect more victims of violence" (Caldwell, 2023). The readers' comments were worse. People condemned South Side and West Side Chicago youth without considering that there was more to the story. The small victories in my South Side social studies classroom, like an engaging classroom debate on the Obama

Library, suddenly seemed irrelevant. But even worse, it felt like my students' growth had been discarded. I thought of Adrian, whom I had mentored, connecting over kung fu movies and *One Hundred Years of Solitude*. I also thought of Akhil, who had a temper and acted tough but secretly liked Beethoven and robotics. To think that my students were labeled as "thugs" made my blood boil. I called my teacher (and grad school) mentor for solace. Adrian and Akhil's progress suddenly seemed fragile, and the academic world I was in felt distant from them. But my mentor firmly reminded me that this was why our work as teachers is crucial.

The topic for my op-ed clicked as I began to ask what sort of restorative spaces teachers can create for Chicago students to both recover from violence and prevent future harm. This topic served as a bridge between my academic and teaching worlds. After years of trying to foster restorative moments for students like Adrian and Akhil during lunch and study hall, I felt compelled to use my voice and resist what mainstream media said. Determined to honor my students' progress and my allies' advice, I began to write.

Back within the collective, civic connections formed and solidarity gained momentum. While sharing ideas with my peers, I felt more settled and included. Melissa pushed me to consider how restorative spaces rely on policy so that any progress gained is sustained. Kristine reminded me to celebrate joyful moments, which sustain our civic engagement (and writing!). In the end, my writing never made it to a published op-ed. But it did lay the foundation for my dissertation. The spaces co-constructed at EdWrite pushed me to question what teachers can do to foster similar spaces for their students. How can teachers specifically sustain restorative spaces for students, allowing them to process and even interrogate the world? That question led me to reach out to another teacher collaborative that facilitated restorative circles. As a volunteer, I recall the end of my first week, when the director shared her plans for future events. When asking everyone about their weekend plans, I could not help but smile as I answered, "I feel like writing."

Reflection and Advice

Through Kate, Mary Rose, and Nathaniel's stories, we offer examples of what can happen when educators gather to write to change the world. They highlight important themes in our own work, including: the courage it takes to reimagine better educational systems; the necessity of collaborations to amplify teacher voices; and how community can reduce isolation, clarify purpose, build solidarity, and cultivate action. We found that whether or not our members published op-eds through the EdWrite Collab was not what mattered most. Rather, what moved us was our choice to change together as we lived and loved in community, enacting an echo of bell hooks. *This,* we believe, is how educators can practice transformative and just civic futures.

We know the last thing teachers need is another task on their already endless to-do list. Part of the power of our work, however, was in its simplicity: We wrote and talked together. We listened to each other and validated our respective experiences. We all felt as though this type of support was missing in our places of employment and in our national conversations about education. If you are looking to foster similar work, here are a few practical suggestions to get you started:

- Gathering can occur anywhere and with any number of people.

- Once you gather, support ways to inquire into and invest care into each other's non-teaching lives.
- Orient civically engaged writing about education toward *interrogation* and *innovation* for the future. Honor writers' identities, experiences, relationships, and dreams.
- "Assignments" with goals and deadlines can be helpful, but they need not limit or define the group's work together. Write for your students, for each other, for the educational systems we dream of.

Ultimately, teacher collectives that foster civic writing are about envisioning, articulating, and acting toward alternative futures for education—ones that are humane, loving, justice oriented, and grounded in the experiences and hopes of teachers, youth, families, and communities.

Acknowledgment

The EdWrite Collab was supported by the University of Illinois Chicago's Institute for Policy and Civic Engagement.

Works Cited

American Federation of Teachers & Badass Teachers Association. (2015). Quality of worklife survey. Retrieved from https://web.archive.org/web/20210410212235/https://www.aft.org/sites/default/files/worklifesurveyresults2015.pdf

Caldwell, G. (2023, April 18). Next Chicago mayor excuses rioters: Expect more victims of violence. *New York Post*. https://nypost.com/2023/04/18/next-chicago-mayor-excuses-rioters-expect-more-victims-of-violence/

Caneva, G. (2024). Finding my voice as a public scholar: A discourse self-analysis of my own opinion writing about education. [Doctoral dissertation, University of Illinois at Chicago]. UIC Library. https://doi.org/10.25417/uic.27152535.v1

Drudy, S. (2008). Gender balance/gender bias: The teaching profession and the impact of feminisation. *Gender and Education*, *20*(4), 309–323. https://doi.org/10.1080/09540250802190156

Dunn, A. H., Farver, S., Guenther, A., & Wexler, L. J. (2017). Activism through attrition?: An exploration of viral resignation letters and the teachers who wrote them. *Teaching and Teacher Education*, 64, 280–290. https://doi.org/10.1016/j.tate.2017.02.016

Goldstein, D. (2014). *The teacher wars: A history of America's most embattled profession.* Doubleday.

Herzog, G., O'Shea, M. R., O'Shea, C., & O'Shea, M. (2020, July 13). Irish-Americans, we must stand up for Black Lives Matter. *Chicago Sun-Times*. https://chicago.suntimes.com/2020/7/13/21322711/irish-americans-we-must-stand-against-white-supremacy-op-ed-mary-oshea-conor

Lee, M. (2023, April 16). *"Teen takeover" terrorizes Chicago as hundreds of teenagers destroy property, attack tourists.* Fox News. https://www.foxnews.com/us/teen-takeover-terrorizes-chicago-hundreds-children-destroy-property-attack-tourists

Mirra, N., & Garcia, A. (2020). "I hesitate but I do have hope": Youth speculative civic literacies for troubled times. *Harvard Educational Review*, *90*(2), 295–321. https://doi.org/10.17763/1943-5045-90.2.295

National Writing Project (n.d.). *Why civic writing?* https://cewac.nwp.org/why-civic-writing/

Op-Ed Project. (n.d.). How thought leaders rise [Write to Change the World Handout]

Orenstein, K. (n.d.) Change the world's conversations [Write to Change the World Handout]. The OpEd Project.

O'Shea, M. R. & O'Shea, M. (2023, April 13). *Around the kitchen table: Proposing a family research methodology* [Roundtable]. 2023 AERA Annual Meeting, Chicago, IL, United States. https://convention2.allacademic.com/one/aera/aera23/index.php?cmd=Online+Program+View+Paper&selected_paper_id=2017522&PHPSESSID=cutggji3gsh4dh325hreib410d

Sjostrom, K. (2023, March 31). *I teach future teachers. They don't need the EdTPA.* Chalkbeat Chicago. https://www.chalkbeat.org/chicago/2023/3/31/23662188/edtpa-teachers-license-covid-unnecessary/

Participatory Action in Higher Education: Empowering a Collective of Education Majors as Partners in Institutional Change

KRISTIAN B. DOUGLAS & DEMETRIUS DOVE

Without community, there is no liberation.
—Audre Lorde

Introduction

The traditional hierarchical model of decision making in educational institutions is gradually shifting to a more collaborative and inclusive approach. More specifically, colleges and universities are increasingly recognizing the significance of integrating student voices into governance structures and policy-making processes surrounding their programs of study. The imperative for student engagement and empowerment has gained prominence in the evolving landscape of higher education over the last decade (Hanson, 2022).

Taking into consideration this reality, this essay aims to accomplish a few things: First, it will explore the strategies and corresponding underpinnings employed by a forward-thinking HBCU, the School of Education at Clark Atlanta University, to promote meaningful student involvement in institutional decision making. In so doing, it will uplift the often-untapped power of integrating students in decision-making processes alongside their educational experiences within the higher education landscape, particularly relative to education majors, an area that is critically necessary to form a more socially conscious and justice-oriented society—which lies at the heart of the conceptual framework of the School of Education at Clark Atlanta University. Drawing on the work of Freire (1996) and other scholars advocating for critical literacy—that is, reading the word and reading the *world* (Cooper & White, 2006; Johnson & Vasudevan, 2012; Mayo, 1999)—this work emphasizes that students, recognizing issues affecting them, desire to engage in collective action through their voices to effect meaningful and innovative change and to do so as a community. The essay will also incorporate the work of scholars who emphasize the importance of centering student voice and creating space for them to embody their advocacy and autonomy (Bauer et al., 2022). In this way, it underscores the significance of what Noddings (1988) terms as "ethics of care," addressing the unique needs and desires of students.

An extensive corpus of scholarship has already highlighted the myriad ways that institutions have enacted harm on students. Love (2019) has termed some of this to be "spirit murdering." To this point, a growing body of scholarship highlights students of various age ranges engaging in student activism, especially amid the global health crisis of COVID-19, which continues to exacerbate social, civil, racial, and economic unrest (Douglas, 2022). Recognizing students as active partners in shaping their own learning journeys not only aligns with progressive educational paradigms in engaging the submission of this work for the NCTE's special call of a praxis of participatory action collective, but it also seeks to give attention to a more responsive and dynamic paradigm for students through the prism of democracy. For education majors, the opportunity to codesign curricula and programming enables them to begin their career in education before completing their undergraduate course of study. Allowing students to shape their education encourages them to connect and apply theory to praxis in real time, positioning them as thought partners and innovative leaders and work-ready talent. Ultimately, this essay advocates for a paradigm shift in the relationship between students and their institutions, particularly colleges/schools of education. By integrating students into decision-making processes and involving them in codesigning educational experiences, institutions can cultivate a culture of shared responsibility and innovation.

Context

Clark Atlanta University in Atlanta, Georgia, has a storied history deeply connected to the struggle for civil rights and educational equity. Established in 1988 through the consolidation of two Black institutions, Atlanta University (founded in 1865) and Clark College (founded in 1869), Clark Atlanta University champions a legacy of resilience and academic excellence amid the sordid past of the American legacies of chattel slavocracy, segregation, Jim Crow, and modern-day crusades against diversity, equity, and inclusion (DEI)—both within and outside traditional learning spaces. A cursory review of history reveals that Atlanta University stood at the forefront of Black scholarship in the United States, producing influential intellectuals like W.E.B. Du Bois, while Clark College provided crucial educational opportunities for Black students in the post-Civil War South: Atlanta, Georgia. Together, they formed Clark Atlanta University, ultimately combining their resources to continue their shared missions of curating deep intellectual inquiry, social justice, and robust community engagement. Clark Atlanta University has been and continues to be a site of hope for Black persons throughout the United States and, likewise, the diaspora. The institution is also a place where students, faculty and administration are continuously empowered to "fight the good fight."

It would be remiss not to mention that Clark Atlanta University shares a campus with its two notable sister schools, Morehouse College and Spelman College. Morehouse College, founded in 1867, is a liberal men's college that has been the home to notable alumni such as the Reverend Dr. Martin Luther King Jr.; Senator Raphael G. Warnock, PhD; and Spike Lee. Spelman College, founded in 1881, is a women's liberal arts college home to alumnae such as Alice Walker, Marian Wright Edelman, and Stacey Abrams. Together, these three schools make up the Atlanta University Consortium (AUC), which has been colloquially termed the "hub of Black education." This context matters because it foregrounds the work that students in the School of Education at Clark Atlanta University are engaged in. Students and faculty alike have a commitment to the social uplift of those who have been marginalized and to social justice, largely through education.

We now turn our attention to literature that offers additional context around this essay and concomitant student work, particularly in pointing out the ways that critical literacy (Freire, 2017) engages students and calls into question [institutional] structures of power. This literature will provide integral framing around the work of resistance and reimagining students majoring in education. In following sections, we engage around the ways this work might be championed and continued in the future, understanding the powerful role that education plays within contemporary society, particularly as it relates to divesting from antiquated paradigms and ideologies that disproportionately harm those from underserved populations. This closely relates to civics education, particularly through the prism of English language arts, given the myriad connections that can be made between text—both written and experienced—and contemporary realities.

Literature Review

An extensive corpus of scholarship has highlighted the ways that social institutions have enacted harm on students. Originally drawing from legal scholar Patricia Williams, Love (2019) popularly brought attention to this reality in her work known as "spirit murdering." Speaking directly to this, a growing body of scholarship highlights students of various age ranges increasingly engaging in student activism, especially amid the global health crisis of COVID-19, which continues to exacerbate social, civil, racial, and economic unrest (Douglas, 2022). As a tool of interest, critical literacy portends that there is, amid trouble, trials, and tribulations, a way forward.

Freire (2017) is often credited as being one of the progenitors of critical literacy, which is oriented to not only reading the word (i.e., printed text) but reading the world (i.e., lived experience). In this way, critical literacy not only expects the one who engages it to merely read these two elements but also to consider their meaning(s) and implications, particularly as these relate to inequality, injustice, marginalization, oppression, and other societal ills, wherever they may be found. The chief goal of critical literacy is to *respond* to injustice and myriad oppression. Critical literacy can be used with a range of texts (multimodal, experience, print, etc.). Adams (2020) points out how young adult (YA) literature has been a viable tool in uplifting experiences that beget critical stances. In this way, students can use what is learned within traditional classroom spaces in the real world. Adams (2020) also highlighted the important role that group discussions play concerning critical literacy stances and student activism.

The reality is that not only does critical literacy encourage and cultivate student engagement within democratic processes, but Hadley et al. (2019) point out that it can also be a mechanism of restoration for youth. That is, through its usage, it can call necessary attention to the social ills and offer a path forward toward wholeness. In addition, Douglas (2022) briefly highlighted how YA can be positioned as a mechanism of curating empathy concerning the experiences and plights of subjugated cultures and racial groups and how critical literacy might be taken up from such stances.

What is clear, however, is that across critical literacy, student activism, and social justice pursuits, there is not a clearly defined and agreed upon definition of the term that may limit the full scope of centering relevant literature. Blixen and Pannell (2020) found that teachers in their work were not exactly able to pinpoint the relevance of critical literacy—they remained open to the concept/idea—and that while teachers in their study were accustomed to their own pedagogical practices, they are also credited with being creative and receptive to learning and unlearning. Scholarship concerning student activism, critical literacy, and social justice continues to grow, particularly within the context of the twenty-first century. A number of scholars have taken up social justice work within the confines of traditional and nontraditional learning spaces. While educators, particularly those who are untenured, often express a sense of hesitancy in dealing with difficult topics, there remains hope the work will be taken up with more fervor. In addition to this, Lewis and Tierney (2013) note that while teachers may be committed to educational equity, they are often preoccupied with other daily demands required of the profession.

Methodological Approach

In this essay, we draw from the work of Santa-Ramirez et al. (2024) in the layout, particularly in centering our counterstories. One of the main tenets of critical race theory (CRT) is counterstory, which endeavors to uplift the voices of those who have been marginalized and disenfranchised throughout time and space. Scholarship around counterstories often includes those who are racialized as Black and Brown within the context of the United States, but so often other group and personal narratives are discarded from this critical dialogue. To that end, it is absolutely essential to remember that counterstories can also be extended to groups outside of racialized binaries to include, for example, those who are members of ethnolinguistic minority groups, those who self-identify as nonbinary, those who live in poverty, and those who are members of the LGBTQ community. Indeed, we recognize that this list is nonexhaustive, but it matters, in our estimation, to provide examples of such groups so as to give space to experiences that otherwise might be invisible in academic scholarship and public discourse. In so doing, we bring to attention the intersections (Crenshaw, 2013) of identities and the concomitant struggles for justice.

According to Delgado and Stafancic (2023),

> critical race theory builds on the insights of two previous movements, critical legal studies and radical feminism, to both of which it owes a large debt. It also draws from certain European philosophers and theorists, such as Antonio Gramsci and Jacques Derrida, as well as from the American radical tradition exemplified by such figures as Sojourner Truth, Frederick Douglass, W.E.B. Du Bois, Cesar Chavez, Martin Luther King, Jr., and the Black Power and Chicano movements of the sixties and early seventies" (p. 4).

It is necessary to foreground the idea of intersectionality to acknowledge the rapacious and interlocking systems of oppression that still impact contemporary society. Throughout this essay, we aim to provide the "roses and thorns" (Santa-Ramirez et al., 2024) of engaging in critical literacy (Freire, 2017), understanding the power that students can have in not only speaking truth to power but in envisioning a society in which all voices are heard and tended to.

We begin sharing our counterstories rooted in our own identities and positionalities, which provide a cognitive and social schema of the ways we make sense of the world and as a point of reference. It is important to remember, however, that although we are foregrounding our own counterstories, there are others that cannot be included in this iteration due to textual space constraints, but they matter equally. In highlighting similarities of experience, we remember the work of Williams and Evans-Winters (2005) who eloquently state, "We were usually the smartest when white was not present, visible when testosterone was not present, and usually revered when class privilege was ignored. Our similar but separate experiences have developed in us a multiple consciousness that is shared" (p. 203).

Kristian's Counterstory

As a junior faculty member coming to a notable institution that has historically been oriented toward social justice and civil rights, what became clear quite early on in my journey is the fact that the institution is fertile ground to continue to work toward social justice and to equip students with the necessary tools to join this struggle. The elements of the conceptual framework of the School of Education at Clark Atlanta University include: (1) critical inquiry; (2) critical theories; and (3) critical reflection (see Figure 1). It is through each of these components that students are provided with space to engage them. Across courses in their program of study, field placement experiences, and mentoring opportunities, students have been encouraged in word to take up the aforementioned components. From my understanding, the overwhelming majority of this work has been engaged via student surveys that gauge faculty instruction and class management following the end of each semester. After my first semester of teaching in my department, what became clear to me is the need to position student voice as a viable avenue to lean more rigorously into the mission of shared governance that the university upholds (and does well concerning faculty and staff affairs), particularly for undergraduate students—the largest demographic on campus. The reality, as I understood it, was that students had something to say about their learning, and I believed their voices needed to be not only heard but amplified.

My own work as an early-career scholar has been deeply influenced by my own lived experience as a Black, queer, Christian man who grew up in the Jim Crow South, was largely educated in the Northeast, and returned back to the South after teaching for a number of years in New York City Public Schools. My own background and the concomitant identities both provide insights into the reasons why I believe amplifying voices that are easy to overlook is important. Centering such voices is important so as to not sanction epistemic erasure. Not only is leaning into critical literacy—that is, reading the word and the world—important, it is necessary as society continues to become more diverse against the backdrop of increased attacks on such diversity. Understanding my own identities and positionalities enables me to curate change rooted in equity and social justice. This remains one of the most important lessons that I endeavor to teach my students today.

Across a number of my courses, I endeavor to incorporate the work of sociocultural theorists such as Paulo Freire into what I am teaching. In addition, I make it a point to include more contemporary scholars and writers whose work is oriented toward social justice pursuits and disrupting intersectional oppression in its myriad forms and contexts. Across my courses, both undergraduate and graduate students have gravitated toward the works of Bettina Love, Chris Emdin, and Gholdy Muhammad. Not only must students have skills that transfer into pedagogical approaches, but students who will soon stand before impressionable minds must also work on refining their own social and critical consciousness. Similar to Crawford-Garrett and Riley (2019), I work to "reconcile pressures from federal, state and institutional policy-makers to provide preservice teachers with neutral, skills-based approaches to [redacted] instruction (. . .) and aim to encourage pre-service teachers to question taken-for-granted practices in schools and consider the ways in which race, class, gender, and social class influence [redacted] teaching and learning" (p. 32). Students need to be clear on that which impacts peK–12 teaching and learning today—it is society. It was John Dewey who argued across his corpus that schools merely

Figure 1: Conceptual framework, Clark Atlanta University, School of Education

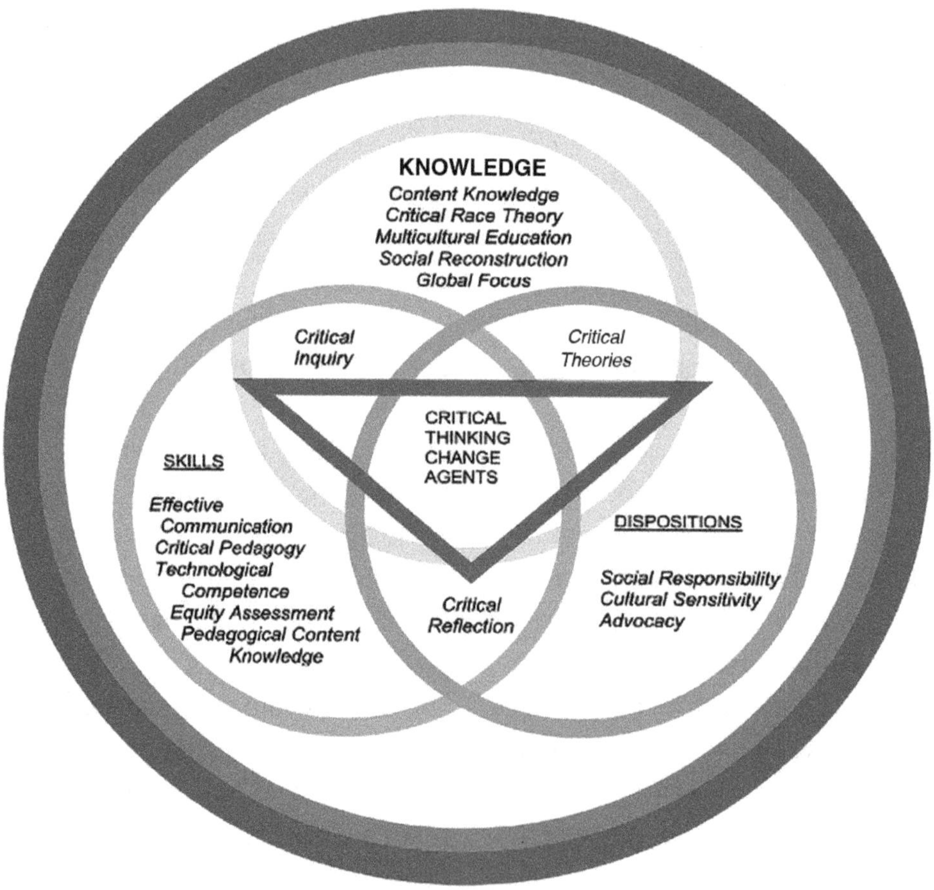

Theme: Preparing Critical Thinking Change Agents for Social Justice in Urban Schools and Communities

reflect and reproduce what is seen in society. Unfortunately, schools have often reproduced, knowingly or unknowingly, social ills instead of disrupting the narrative. The response to this integration has been overwhelmingly positive with students understanding that not only are they embracing our conceptual framework, they are being empowered to become viable members of society and engage democratic processes.

Demetrius's Counterstory

I could no more escape than I could think of my identity. Perhaps, I thought, the two things are involved with each other. When I discover who I am, I'll be free.

—Ralph Ellison

In my young adulthood, one thing has become certain—not every truth is found on purpose. And your calling lies in your truth. As I came to Clark Atlanta University from a small town called Spanaway, Washington, it was evident that I was in search of something more expansive than I was used to, something more culturally relevant to me, but more importantly, something purpose driven. At the time, I didn't know what my purpose was. I originally enrolled in Clark Atlanta as a business administration major. But inwardly, I felt deeply disconnected from business.

On the heels of the racial reckoning that took place in 2020, I was in search of community and somewhere where I could be unashamedly and unequivocally Black. This craving for justice and calling was something that business wasn't giving me. As a Black Christian young man from the Pacific Northwest, justice and purpose have always been central to my personhood. During the first semester of my sophomore year, I thought extensively about dropping out of college and going back home because the business major wasn't working out, and I knew home would be a constant. But I couldn't let the only thing I'd ever known dictate the possibility of a future I could shape for myself. I began to critically reflect on the past, my schooling experiences, and my rearing—only to realize that I hadn't had a Black teacher until I got to Clark Atlanta University. After much research and thought, it was then that I became an education major.

Since then, I have become the Aspiring Educators President of the Georgia Association of Educators and have a seat on the National Education's Association Board of Directors. My experiences navigating the pitfalls of never being adequately seen or advocated for in schools has profoundly contoured how I show up as an educator and leader. My work always begins with critical reflection. In order to lead well, you must have a clear understanding of your interior self—your beliefs, values, and convictions. My deepest conviction is to transform education into a system that works for those whom it wasn't intended to work for. I exercise my conviction through advocacy and organizing. Advocacy, for me, is more than a means of overcoming opposition. It is liberating self and others through taking up necessary space. My passion for advocacy has blossomed through the NEA and at Clark Atlanta. Advocacy, however, is not a singular action. It requires community coalitions. Building community is the primary tool for organizing. Through the Georgia Association of Educators Clark Atlanta University Chapter, we have created community through rallying around common issues in education and within our department. The sense of community coupled with care is what fuels my organizing and advocacy. Community care, organizing, and advocacy is the way to true freedom.

Rebellion in Uniform: Students and the Politics of Dress Codes

But almost always, during the initial stage of the struggle, the oppressed, instead of striving for liberation, tend themselves to become oppressors, or "sub-oppressors."

—Paulo Freire, *Pedagogy of the Oppressed*

Across a series of courses that are offered within the School of Education at our university, what became increasingly clear was that students are more readily making connections between course readings and their own lived experiences. As they work to transgress the boundaries of the label "aspiring educator," graduate, acquire their first teaching contracts, and be officially recognized as P–12 educators, they are actively paying attention to the ways that the theoretical connects to the practical and the corresponding impacts. It is not odd to hear interjections across classes with students highlighting their own lived experiences in relation to the subject matter being discussed within class lectures. For example, students have stated the following:

> "This applies directly to me."
> "Wow—I need to carry this with me to my future classroom."
> "I know someone who needs to read this."

These statements echo a resounding truth: students are ready, able and willing to do hard but necessary and meaningful work. While there are "roses and thorns" (Santa-Ramirez et al., 2024) associated with engaging critical literacy such as fear of retaliation, uncertainty around planning, etc., we believe it is absolutely imperative that students continue to make relevant connections between the theoretical and practical concerning social justice in education, particularly because they will be standing in front of young, impressionable students—ultimately, shaping their minds and the ways they, too, engage with the world. Students within the teacher education program began to, admirably, take their critical thinking back to the very faculty from which they were positioned to learn, faculty who introduced them to robust scholarship on critical literacy and social justice (i.e., Gloria Ladson Billings, Paulo Freire, Linda Darling-Hammond, etc.).

One of the chief arguments that students brought forth via written letter was their disdain for "respectability politics," particularly as it is practiced via dress codes that were championed during the 1950s and 1960s' Civil Rights Movements, especially for those who held prominent roles that were seen as a vehicle for social uplift of the Black middle class—namely, teachers and preachers. American sociologist W.E.B. Du Bois, who taught on the campus of what is now known as Clark Atlanta University, brought forth the idea of double consciousness, which argues that Black Americans are not necessarily tethered to one social identity—that they must, in order to improve the lot of the race as a whole and themselves, consider not just how they might view themselves but how hegemonic members of society, namely white people, view them. In this way, Black Americans are uniquely burdened with the difficult task of balancing and reshaping multiple identities. That is, those who ascribed to this positioning, knowingly or otherwise, were not able to fully be themselves. While during the 1960s, the Black middle class made significant strides and were positioned on an upward trajectory of social mobility, the following point, as highlighted by education majors to faculty and leadership in discourse, can't be underscored enough: The day and time has changed. Moreover, writer and social activist Audre Lorde reminds us that the master's tools will never dismantle the master's house.

In thinking about how to best support students and prepare them to enter the field of education, particularly during their student teaching experiences, students were provided with blazers that they were able to wear and keep during more business-oriented occasions. While some faculty members strongly encouraged students to wear these blazers during university-related events and off-campus convenings (i.e., conferences, field meetings, etc.), students began to feel as though this was an explicit directive from leadership. In understanding their concerns, faculty members encouraged them to organize and to voice their opinions regarding the matter and to share with departmental and school leadership. Students were able to compose a letter that spoke to their sentiments. Below is a snapshot of that letter:

> These dress codes force our Aspiring Educators to conform to a Eurocentric standard of "professional" dress and "professionalism," which is asinine at a Black university. As an HBCU, specifically the first doctoral degree granting institution for Black folx in this country, we should not look at Eurocentricity as a standard and ideal—this further upholds the colonist mindset that we need to disrupt. Furthermore, these dress codes challenge and force conformity upon those who express their gender identity in a myriad of ways. With these dress codes we are, as legal scholar Patricia Williams describes, engaging in an act of spirit murdering. Everyone will not present and express their gender in the traditional manner that some are used to—and that is okay, it should be celebrated. One who is comfortable enough to express their gender how they want to should not only be allowed, but should be encouraged and accepted. The current implementation of this dress code does not allow this. (Written communication, January 30, 2024)

In this letter, what is made clear is that students deeply understood class readings and the works of scholars such as bell hooks, Patricia Williams, Bettina Love, Kimberlé Crenshaw, and Angela Davis. They made connections to their own lived experience and leaned into the work of critical literacy and student activism to make their qualms heard (Freire, 2017). Ultimately, students' concerns were heard and addressed. Faculty and leadership understood their sentiments and made it clear that the wearing of blazers was not a directive but a possibility they could take up if they decided to. In this sense, students were able to become change agents and actively take up critical literacy in not only reading the word (i.e., class texts) but also in reading the world—both their current world and a world in the constant pursuit of liberation and social justice for all who have been subjugated by the dominant apparatuses of society. Integrating student voices into governance structures and policymaking processes surrounding their programs of study is a wise decision that honors and cultivates student voice and democratic pursuits. Moreover, allowing students to shape their education empowers them to connect and apply theory to praxis in real time, positioning them as thought partners and innovative leaders.

As a faculty member/departmental leader and senior education major, I feel it is important for us to reflect on our own lived experiences that have been marked by subjugation, oppression, and marginalization so as to not repeat this cycle within a space that historically has been oriented toward freedom and its ongoing struggle. Our unique roles in student and faculty leadership afford us space to speak truth to power, to organize, to advocate for change, and to offer critiques that push toward anti-oppression in all its forms. Dress codes, well intentioned or not, are rooted in centering a particular type of acceptability. It negates the myriad realities that aspiring educators and in-field practitioners must contend with daily and positions bodies as sites of policing. To this point, Jenkins and Warren (2024) point out that schools are often carceral spaces due to a range of policies, practices, and procedures, written or simply the status quo, that continue to perpetuate oppression. In this way, we further lean into CRT and the relevance of highlighting the necessity of the counterstory (Delgado & Stefanic, 2000) because such understandings are frequently unattended to at best and discarded/invisibilized at worst. In tending to the counterstories of students, students are disrupting the trend of the oppressed becoming oppressors, which Freire (2017) called attention to in his seminal work *Pedagogy of the Oppressed*, and doing so within a historically Black space in which the white gaze (Morrison, 1994) is still often aspired to as an ideal. Further, as Grundy (2022) highlights, "A plethora of tensions and cross cutting issues within Black spaces produce racialization beyond the physical presence of whites. Blackness is an active process that is made within our interactions with whites or dominant social institutions but also well beyond the reach of members of these dominant groups" (p. 19). This is critical to highlight due to the ways that respectability politics are still championed as a form of social uplift well into the twenty-first century and the epistemic erasure of those who refuse to conform. Below, we move to underscore work that the School of Education at Clark Atlanta University has engaged in and what others must do.

Discussion

Addressing Social Identities and Justice in Teacher Education

Early on in this essay, we centered our own identities and positionalities in an effort to draw attention to the ways that our own experiences situated us in the context of the work we do. For example, our shared identities of being Black men informs our perspectives and beliefs, particularly as it relates to the function(s) and responsibilities of education. Correspondingly, we believe that robustly engaging conversation about social markers in teacher education continues to be of great importance, particularly as ongoing data from the United States Census highlights that schools continue to rapidly diversify. Our counterstories emphasize our belief in and commitment to social justice in this regard and reminds the field of teacher education of its responsibility. Relative to this, Williams and Evans-Winters (2005) state, "Traditionally, thought to be liberals and open-minded citizens, future educators (and veterans) believe they know enough about race, class, and gender discrimination, and want to leave discussions about race and racism out of discussions about education" (p. 212). Ultimately, this has implications for the field and for students concerning what is valued and what is discarded.

Sleeter (2016) points out that only a small percentage of teachers in preK–12 schools today are Black males, and the overwhelming majority are white middle-class women. This matters in terms of student achievement, certainly, but it also matters in considering what ideals and beliefs are upheld, centered, and championed. As two white middle-class women, Crawford-Garrett and Riley (2019) remind us that far too frequently, teacher education spaces are incubators of not only implicit bias but also spaces of least resistance in favor of a culture of "niceness" (Bissonnette, 2016). This has implications for students who are subjugated by multiple matrices of oppression. Within teacher education programs, there is often significant discussion around teacher educator disposition, but such discourse has largely gone unexamined, particularly the implications it has on preservice teachers and new teachers to the field and their desire to remain in the profession. We contend that disposition has been used in the teacher education space as a form of "professionalism"—or a striving toward a particular ideal that forces students in teacher preparation programs to not only police their unique identities but also to fit into a mold subject to change and is conditional depending on a range of contextual circumstances. More attention should be focused within teacher education programs to interrogating coursework, policies that impact students holistically, and the implications this has for the field at large. We contend that students and faculty alike should be afforded space to advocate for change—to address issues that affect not only society at large but classrooms and schools. Such work takes seriously the arguments made decades ago by the late American philosopher John Dewey, who argued that schools not only mirror society but reinforce and reproduce it both within the confines of the school, which ultimately transgresses these parameters back into broader society.

Positioning Students as Leaders and Change Agents

The traditional hierarchical model of decision making in educational institutions is gradually shifting to a more collaborative and inclusive approach. As evidenced during the COVID-19 pandemic, leadership across both historically Black colleges and universities (HBCUs) and primarily white institutions have shifted to focus more on student experience and voice. That is, leadership across a number of institutions of higher learning understand that students enrolled in academic programs have something to say and are actively moving toward integrating student feedback across these programs, policies, procedures, faculty recruitment, and retention efforts. For HBCUs, however, this is not new. Historically, students have been changemakers within the ongoing pursuit of justice. In looking specifically at the history of the Atlanta University Center (AUC), notable students who have advocated for change include Martin Luther King Jr., Julian Bond, Otis Moss Jr., and Marian Wright Edelman, to name a few.

The conceptual framework in the School of Education at Clark Atlanta University recognizes the significance of social responsibility as a hallmark of a good disposition. Interestingly, this element is often unnamed and unattended in other spaces, especially outside of Atlanta, Georgia, and the AUC. To curate space for students to critically think, reflect, and act in ways that support community and social justice pursuits prepares them to go into the world and effect change in positive ways. The student and faculty handbook, unlike those of many institutions throughout the United States, explicitly advocates for preparing critical thinking change agents for social justice in urban schools and communities. For education majors, the opportunity to codesign curricula and programming enables students to begin their careers in education before completing their undergraduate degrees. Allowing students to shape their education empowers them to connect and apply theory to praxis in real time, positioning them as thought partners and innovative leaders.

Implications and Conclusion

As we conclude this essay that speaks to critical literacy within the context of education, it is important to underscore, yet again, the necessity of positioning students as active participants in their learning journeys and the need to integrate student voices into the processes of educational decision making. By curating spaces for students to critically engage with both theoretical frameworks and their lived experiences, we empower them to become agents of change who can navigate and challenge the myriad societal inequities that plague our society.

As highlighted earlier, students' resistance to traditional dress codes and their advocacy for more inclusive policies and practices also illustrate the ways that critical literacy can serve as a tool for challenging oppressive structures and promoting equity. This engagement not only enhances their personal and professional growth but also prepares them to cultivate similar critical consciousness in their own future classrooms, ultimately contributing to the broader pursuit of social justice through the centering of their own voices, perspectives, and experiences (Hanson, 2022). In considering the broader implications of this work, it becomes clear that the integration of student voices and critical literacy practices is not merely an educational strategy but a vital element in the forming of a just and equitable society. We believe that as future educators, students must be equipped not only with pedagogical skills but also with a deep understanding of the social and political contexts that shape education. By embracing this approach, institutions can bring up and support a new generation of educators who are not only effective pedagogues but also committed advocates for change.

Works Cited

Adams, B. (2020). "I didn't feel confident talking about this issue . . . but I knew I could talk about a book": Using young adult literature to make sense of #MeToo. *Journal of Literacy Research*, *52*(2), 209–230. https://doi.org/10.1177/1086296X20915489

Bauer, E., Razfar, A., Skerrett, A., Dobbs, C. L., Jang, B. G., & Parsons, S. A. (2022). Centering student voice in literacy research [Editorial]. *Journal of Literacy Research*, *54*(3), 219–221. https://doi.org/10.1177/1086296X221117204

Bissonnette, J. D. (2016). The trouble with niceness: How a preference for pleasantry sabotages culturally responsive teacher preparation. *Journal of Language and Literacy Education*, *12*(2), 9–32.

Blixen, T. B., & Pannell, J. (2020). Teachers' understanding and enactment of critical literacy – A lack of unified teaching method. *Cogent Education*, *7*(1), Article 1826073. https://doi.org/10.1080/2331186X.2020.1826073

Cooper, K., & White, R. (2006). Critical literacy in action. In K. Cooper & R. White (Eds.), *The practical critical educator: Critical inquiry and educational practice* (pp. 3–16). Springer. https://doi.org/10.1007/1-4020-4473-9_1

Crawford-Garrett, K., & Riley, K. (2019). Race and class silences in teacher education: Resisting strategy-based approaches to literacy methods instruction. *Teaching Education*, *30*(1), 31–51. https://doi.org/10.1080/10476210.2018.1443065

Crenshaw, K. (1997). Demarginalizing the intersection of race and sex: A Black feminist critique of antidiscrimination doctrine, feminist theory and antiracist politics. In K. J. Maschke (Ed.), *Feminist legal theories* (pp. 23–51). Routledge. https://doi.org/10.4324/9781315051536

Delgado, R., & Stefancic, J. (Eds.). (2000). *Critical race theory: The cutting edge* (2nd ed.). Temple University Press.

Delgado, R., & Stefancic, J. (2023). *Critical race theory: An introduction* (4th ed.): *Vol. 87. Critical America.* NYU press.

Douglas, K. B. (2022). *Exploring critical literacy pursuits through teacher narratives and critical race theory* (Publication No. 29327760) [Doctoral dissertation, State University of New York at Buffalo]. ProQuest Dissertations and Theses Global.

Freire, P. (2017). *Pedagogy of the oppressed.* Penguin Classics.

Grundy, S. (2022). *Respectable: Politics and paradox in making the Morehouse Man.* University of California Press.

Hadley, H. L., Burke, K. J., & Wright, W. T. (2020). Opening spaces of restoration for youth through community-engaged critical literacy practices. *English Teaching: Practice & Critique*, *19*(1), 95–106. https://doi.org/10.1108/ETPC-05-2019-0068

Hanson, A. J. (2022). *Centering student voice as a foundation of systems-level transformative leadership* [Doctoral dissertation, Iowa State University]. Iowa State University Digital Repository. https://doi.org/10.31274/td-20240329-128

Jenkins, D. A., & Warren, C. A. (2024). Towards anti-carceral leadership: Remaking public schools to refuse Black students' surveillance, containment, and control. *Educational Policy*, *38*(3), 624–641. https://doi-org.ezp.lib.rochester.edu/10.1177/08959048231220024

Johnson, E., & Vasudevan, L. (2012). Seeing and hearing students' lived and embodied critical literacy practices. *Theory into Practice*, *51*(1), 34–41. https://doi.org/10.1080/00405841.2012.636333

Lewis, C., & Tierney, J. D. (2013). Mobilizing emotion in an urban classroom: Producing identities and transforming signs in a race-related discussion. *Linguistics and Education*, *24*(3), 289–304. https://doi.org/10.1016/j.linged.2013.03.003

Love, B. L. (2019). *We want to do more than survive: Abolitionist teaching and the pursuit of educational freedom.* Beacon Press.

Mayo, P. (1995). Critical literacy and emancipatory politics: The work of Paulo Freire. *International Journal of Educational Development*, *15*(4), 363–379. https://doi.org/10.1016/0738-0593(95)00021-T

Morrison, T. (1994). *The bluest eye.* Plume.

Noddings, N. (1988). An ethic of caring and its implications for instructional arrangements. *American Journal of Education*, *96*(2), 215–230. https://doi.org/10.1086/443894

Santa-Ramirez, S., Vega, N., Hernández, R. D., & Montelongo, R. (2024). Roses and thorns: Counterstories of first-generation Latinx faculty pathways to and through doctoral education and into the professoriate. *Journal of First-*

generation Student Success, *4*(2) 1–17. https://doi.org/10.1080/26906015.2024.2313412

Skerrett, A. (2010). Teaching critical literacy for social justice. *Action in Teacher Education*, *31*(4), 54–65. https://doi.org/10.1080/01626620.2010.10463535

Sleeter, C. (2016). Wrestling with problematics of Whiteness in teacher education. *International Journal of Qualitative Studies in Education*, *29*(8), 1065–1068. https://doi.org/10.1080/09518398.2016.1174904

Van Sluys, K., Lewison, M., & Flint, A. S. (2006). Researching critical literacy: A critical study of analysis of classroom discourse. *Journal of Literacy Research*, *38*(2), 197–233. https://doi.org/10.1207/s15548430jlr3802_4

Williams, D. G., & Evans-Winters, V. (2005). The burden of teaching teachers: Memoirs of race discourse in teacher education. *The Urban Review*, *37*(3), 201–219. https://doi.org/10.1007/s11256-005-0009-z

Cultivating a Pedagogy of *Comunidad* through Youth Participatory Action Research in Classrooms and Schools in Cleveland

MARY FRANCES (MOLLY) BUCKLEY-MARUDAS, ROSALINDA GODINEZ, KARMEL ABUTALEB & DREW RETHERFORD

Introduction

I dream a world where students can fearlessly share their voice.

I dream a world where young people are loved and encouraged to be the changes they want to see in the world.

I dream a world in which students feel confident to step out, learn more, and make a difference.

I dream a world where YPAR helps steer and maintain our moral compasses to finally achieve freedom and peace.

I dream a world where YPAR helps raise generations of social justice advocates.

I dream a world where YPAR helps erase racism, prejudice, and bigotry from all hearts.

I dream a world where YPAR plants the seeds for creating and enforcing just laws that serve ALL humans equitably.

I dream a world where YPAR helps everyone see that they are not inferior or superior to others, simply equal.

I dream of a world where speaking back to power is normalized.

I dream a world where YPAR allows young people to generate new knowledge and to confidently share that knowledge with decision-makers and relevant stakeholders.

I dream of a world where students get to be themselves freely.

I dream of a world where we are all seen as human.

Inspired by National Public Radio's and the Colorado State Sustainable Teaching & Learning Collaborative's "I Dream a World" crowd-sourced poem challenge, we open this essay with the poem our Ohio-based *comunidad*[1] wrote in response to Langston Hughes's "I Dream a World." Our *comunidad* includes teachers, university-based researchers, high school students, and graduate students working together to design and implement youth participatory action research (YPAR) in public high schools in Cleveland. This YPAR team includes six full-time teachers in five content areas (English language arts, mathematics, computer science, social studies, and Spanish) and four

1. We intentionally use the Spanish word "comunidad" (community) because it captures the dynamic and interconnected relationships that go beyond simple commonalities among our HighKEY team, teachers, and students.

different schools. All the teachers on the team have designed and implemented YPAR in their school contexts, either in their content area as an elective or as an extracurricular. Our teacher and researcher team coauthored this poem on November 3, 2023, during one of our regular monthly meetings. Drawing on the National Writing Project's "Writing into the Meeting" protocol, we make room for reflective writing at nearly all of our meetings. At this particular meeting, in preparation for our upcoming presentation at the NCTE 2023 Annual Convention, teacher team members were invited to respond to the prompt: "Even in trying times, how does YPAR give you hope? Write just one line that begins with the phrase 'I dream a world . . .' and describe a change you hope for." The teachers and university-based design team members wrote their responses in a shared Google Document.

We open with this poem because it articulates our team of teachers and researchers' vision for a transformed world nurtured by YPAR principles and practice. It portrays a realm where students are empowered to fearlessly express their voices, where love and encouragement foster young individuals as catalysts for positive change. It speaks to the need to normalize speaking truth to power, foster confidence in generating and sharing knowledge with decisionmakers, and allow students to be themselves without constraints, contributing to a collective dream of unity and recognition of our shared humanity. The poem speaks to our efforts to work within and against the systems and structures of power and schooling by designing learning spaces that honor and cultivate critical literacies, youth voices, and civic engagement through YPAR. Finally, this poem invokes the long history of Langston Hughes's commitment to advocacy and social justice work, especially in and through the arts.

Importantly, given this volume's focus on practicing civic futures through teacher/adult learning, we believe that this collaborative poem illustrates how our group's formation, the result of each member individually agreeing to integrate a version of YPAR in their individual school context, led to us building a coalition of social justice-oriented educators. This coalition has cultivated meaningful professional relationships and fostered adult learning centered around our shared commitment to teaching for social justice. By coming together around our belief in young people's capacity to generate knowledge and fight for social change, our coalition has developed what we now call a *pedagogy of comunidad*. In this essay, we will share how our group evolved over time to build a professional coalition in the service of practicing civic futures. Drawing on specific examples from our team's work both designing and integrating YPAR in schools, we will introduce four key tenets of our *pedagogy of comunidad* framework. This *pedagogy of comunidad* is offered as a response to the call for "creative and liberatory possibilities for civic praxis in classrooms and communities."

Background on YPAR & Project HighKEY

Youth participatory action research is one way to support youth in confronting pressing social issues (Cammarata & Fine, 2008; Duncan-Andrade & Morrell, 2008; Mirra et al., 2016; Ozer & Wright, 2012). YPAR systematically guides students to deepen their understanding of issues and leverage their newfound knowledge to drive social change. YPAR stands out from other modes of youth involvement due to its emphasis on leadership, research, and effecting change by tackling root causes (Diemer, Voight,

& Mark, 2011) and is documented to support youth voice and agency as well as student attendance and engagement in school. In the last decade, Kimberlé Crenshaw and other antiracist and feminist researchers have drawn explicitly on YPAR to interrupt some of the implicit racial and gender bias in institutional research. The aim of this group's work is to center Black girls' voices, "by positioning them as inquirers, seekers of knowledge, theoreticians, data collectors, and presenters of research" (Crenshaw & Evans-Winters, 2024). In this work and others, YPAR is positioned as a theoretical and pedagogical tool for raising young people's critical consciousness and challenging existing systems and structures of power and control in school (Buckley-Marudas et al., 2024; Carl & Ravitch, 2018; Crenshaw, Ocen, & Nanda, 2015). YPAR is most commonly implemented in the context of out-of-school programs and activities for youth, but there are more and more instances of YPAR methodologies being implemented in schools, at times in core content classes but typically as an extracurricular (e.g., Buckley-Marudas & Soltis, 2018; Ozer et al., 2008; Voight, 2015; Voight & Velez, 2018).

Given the potential of YPAR, our school-university research team is engaged in a multiyear development and innovation project titled Project HighKEY. Project HighKEY, a research-practice partnership between Cleveland State University (CSU) and the Cleveland Metropolitan School District (CMSD), is a multiyear project focused on designing, integrating, and evaluating YPAR in four public high schools in Cleveland. On the university side of the partnership, this project is led by PI Adam Voight, co-PI Molly Buckley-Marudas, postdoctoral fellow Rosalinda Godinez, and several CSU doctoral students. On the school side, YPAR is being facilitated by teachers of various content areas (English, social science, Spanish, math, and computer science) in four different CMSD schools. Project HighKEY aims to explore how YPAR, which involves student-led cycles of issue identification, research, and action to improve real-world problems, can be adapted to high school classrooms in Cleveland. The goal of the larger research project is to explore ways in which YPAR can be built into the high school curriculum. Our collaborative research and author team has extensive experience designing, implementing, and evaluating YPAR in both in-school and out-of-school contexts.

At the time of this writing, our coauthors (Molly, Rosalinda, Karmel, and Drew) have been working together on YPAR-focused de-sign and school-based implementation for three years with CSU colleague Adam Voight, four other HighKEY teachers (Sarah, Taylor, Maggie, and Emily), and over twenty high school students. As members of the project's "Design Team," we have come together at least once a month to imagine what YPAR could be like in different classrooms, schools, and content areas, to develop YPAR units and lesson plans to reflect on implementation successes and challenges, and to revise and refine our approaches to YPAR. In light of the COVID-19 pandemic, all monthly meetings in the project's first year were hosted on Zoom. For years two and three, we moved to a hybrid rotation in which we alternated the monthly meetings between Zoom and in person. The Zoom meetings take place after school and are seventy-five minutes long whereas the in-person meetings take place during the day at CSU and are three hours in duration. Although this essay focuses on teacher and adult learning, the meetings include high school teachers, high school students, graduate students, and university-based researchers.

Researcher/Teacher Positionalities

We recognize that our positionality plays a significant role in what we bring to this work and how we approach the YPAR work. We also recognize that our varying identities and social locations inform the selection of YPAR topics and research questions and shape our perspectives on different social issues. Two of us (Drew and Karmel) are high school teachers in CMSD, and two of us (Molly and Rosalinda) are university-based researchers.

Hailing originally from Palestine but born and raised in Jordan, Karmel is currently a secondary math educator at Natividad Pagan International Newcomers Academy. Prior to her current position, she was a math educator at Facing History New Tech (FHNT), also in CMSD. Karmel takes pride in being a bilingual role model, deeply committed to fostering integrity and resourcefulness within the dynamic back-drop of diversity. She has implemented YPAR in her classes at FHNT for the past three years with a focus on social justice. Hoping for a more equitable world for all humanity, she helps students find their voices and challenge the system through research and actions. She believes in the invaluable tool that is YPAR to pursue her research interests: social justice in education, student engagement and motivation, and school attendance and its impact on performance.

Drew is a Jewish educator, teaches US history, world history, and public health at a public high school in Cleveland. He has four years of experience teaching YPAR in extracurricular clubs, cross-curricular government classes, and his public health course. He is committed to supporting youth to learn about the intersections between power, privilege, and systematic oppression from a historical and sociological lens. As an organizer and advocate in the broader Cleveland community, he is in solidarity with various struggles by translating his advocacy to work with youth, teaching them the tools necessary for collective and strategic action. His goal is to support students in becoming informed, strategic organizers who can drive meaningful change, embodying the principles of justice and dignity for all people.

Molly identifies as a white woman. As part of her work as an associate professor at Cleveland State University, she serves as Faculty-in-Residence at a public high school on CSU's campus that opened in 2017. In collaboration with the school's founding team of teachers and administrators, Molly designed a YPAR course that was integrated into the curriculum for all ninth-grade students. Seven years later, the YPAR course remains a required course for all ninth graders. Molly is co-PI with CSU colleague and PI Adam Voight of Project HighKEY and SchYPAR. Molly has been part of the HighKEY design team since the beginning of the project.

Rosalinda Godínez identifies as a Chicana/Latina of Nahuas ancestry in Sierra-Costa de Michoacán, Mexico, and of Spanish settlers to the area. Her life's work and research have focused on documenting the everyday experiences of non-dominant communities through the language of education and resistant practices. The theories of pedagogy, *cariño*, and coalition building used in this essay continue her previous scholarship (see Godínez, 2023; Godínez, 2022; Godínez & Baquedano-López, 2022). In her postdoctoral role at the Center for Urban Education at Cleveland State University, she has supported teachers like Karmel and Drew, both during the HighKEY meetings and in school, to plan and implement YPAR in schools.

Key Learnings: Pedagogies of *Comunidad*

To elucidate *pedagogies of comunidad,* we intentionally use the Spanish word "comunidad" (community) because it encapsulates the evolving relationships between our HighKEY team, teachers, and students. In Spanish, "comunidad" carries cultural connotations rooted in Latinx traditions and values, emphasizing familial bonds, solidarity, and a profound sense of belonging. Although our HighKEY teachers do not identify as Latinx, the value of relationships takes on an interconnectedness that transcends mere association around commonalities. As a collective community, we have developed strong relationships and emotional ties that bind us through our collective care/love for each other, our students, and our commitment to social justice. We harness our agency and share responsibility to support one another in working toward a common goal through YPAR. These relationships have been, and continue to be, nurtured over time through mutual *cariño* (care/love), strategic thinking and action, and collective partnerships. Below, we unpack the four fundamental tenets of *pedagogies of comunidad*: 1) relational learning, 2) mutual *cariño*, 3) strategic thinking and action, and 4) collective partnerships.

Relational Learning

Pedagogy of comunidad centers on relational learning, in which we all engage as learners and collaborators in the educational process. As university researchers, we have gained valuable insights into teachers' challenges, including adhering to standards while implementing youth participatory action research (YPAR), managing administrative pressures, grading YPAR projects, and preparing students for standardized tests. Teachers do the critical work on the ground, navigating these complexities daily. Simultaneously, they learn from our research team, deepening their understanding of YPAR tenets and theories and exploring new writing opportunities. This mutual exchange of knowledge and experience has fostered a collaborative environment where we continuously learn from one another. We have created websites such as YPARinschool.org and schypar.org to support this ongoing collaboration, documenting student resources and lesson plans. The websites exemplify our team's commitment to relational learning in

Figure 1. A picture of the "Doing SchYPAR" section of the SchYPAR online resource hub

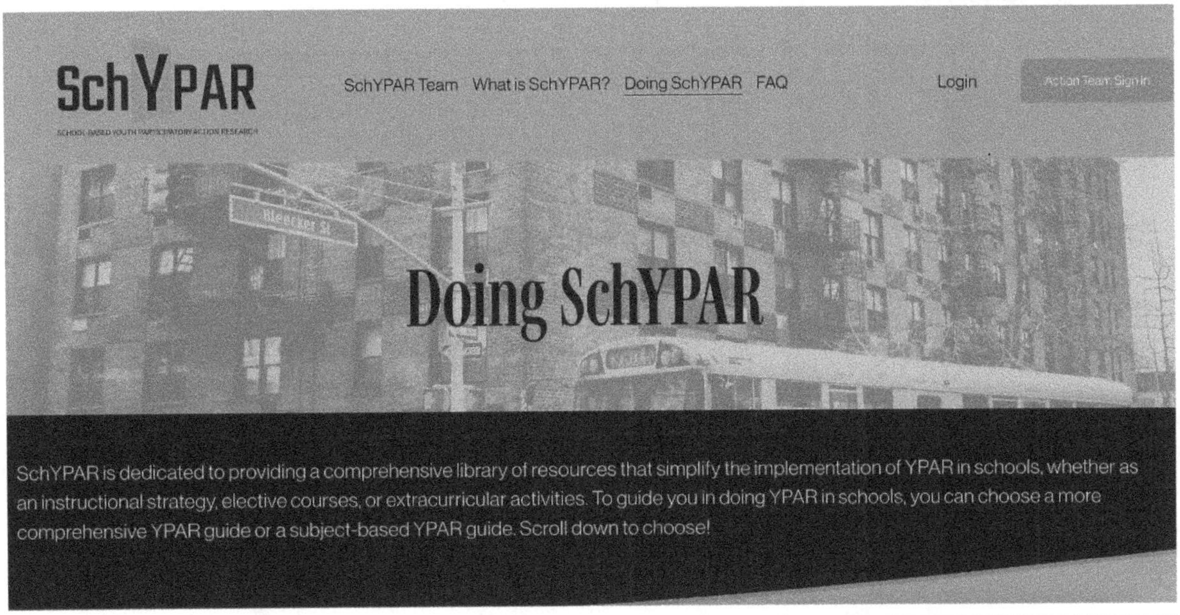

Figure 2. A picture of two of the teacher-authored YPAR content guides and crosswalks available in the "Doing YPAR" section of the SchYPAR online resource hub

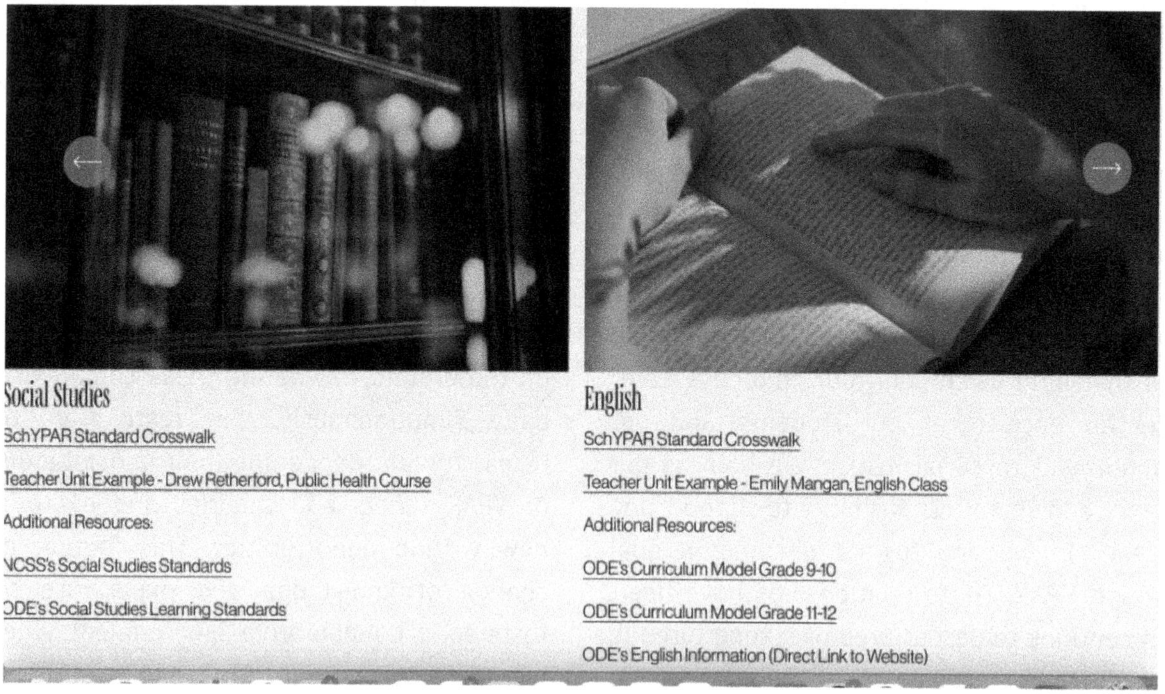

Figure 3: A picture of the "Resources" tab available on the YPARinSchool online resource hub

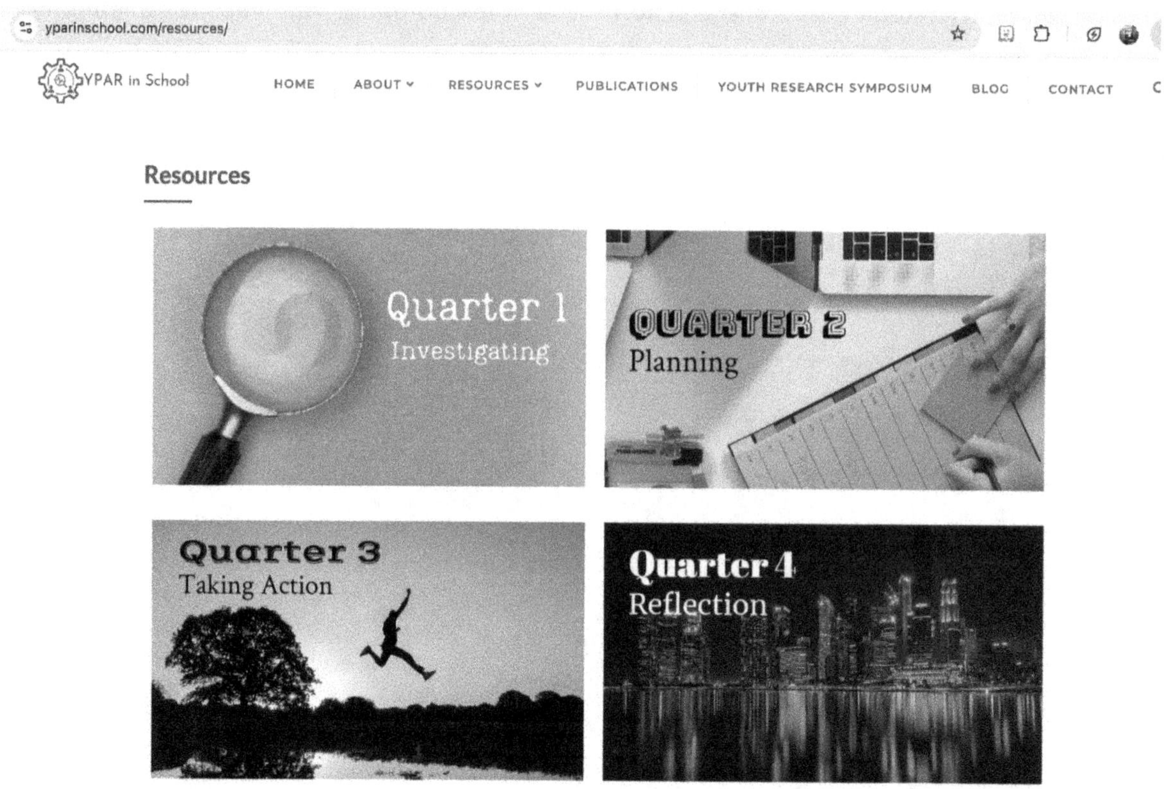

that they are fluid and ever changing. The sites include pages dedicated to teachers' contributions as well as pages that share the ways in which teachers and young people are finding ways to integrate YPAR in their classrooms and schools. These sites are also a space to connect with and share resources with other YPAR teachers. This includes resources designed by teacher team members as well as university researcher team members. As you can see in the images below, the resources reflect the content areas of different team members and the educational standards and expectations of our team's home state of Ohio.

Mutual *Cariño* by "Becoming-with"

Cariño is a Spanish term that encompasses a range of affectionate feelings, caring deeper emotional and cultural nuances that distinguish it from the English words "care" and "love." Here, we take on the word and its meaning to emphasize the quality of the relationship and the emotional investment in the wellbeing of others. It is about performing acts of care and fostering deep, personal connections. To explain how we witness the use of *cariño* in our team, we draw upon Mariana Ortega's (2016) notion of "becoming-with," which is a central idea of coalition building against oppression. Mariana Ortega stresses the interconnectedness of multiple selves through relationality for collective action. For our team, YPAR profoundly resonates with our social justice philosophies, which are inherently tied to uplifting and cultivating *affective* relationships with each other, teachers, and students. We aim to "becoming-with" and traveling to understand and work together to create change. For instance, Drew shares his intentions:

> I became a social studies teacher because I want to save the world. I mean that sincerely. I want to instill a value of citizenship in kids beyond the superficial activities of voting and watching the news; I want to give students the skills and the desire to organize and take action around issues that affect them on their own behalf. I wouldn't say I succeeded in doing those things before I started YPAR. In fact, the two most impactful moments of my career occurred this year, and both came from students who participated in YPAR [. . .] These two instances were the first time in my seven years as a social studies teacher that I felt like I'd done my job successfully, the first-ever confirmation that I may be able to save the world, and I think YPAR has tremendously helped me have that impact on kids. (November 2023)

Like Drew, our team is profoundly aware of the stark realities of poverty and structural inequalities for students and the challenges of teaching in schools with limited resources. To support us in this work and the complexities of situating this work within the context of public schools, we lean into Freire's (1987) and bell hooks's (1994) understanding of education as the practice of freedom and their attention to the vital role of critical consciousness in their construction of "engaged pedagogy." In keeping with their work and scholarship, we recognize educational contexts as inherently political and see YPAR as a valuable tool not only for critiquing inequities in schools and education but also acting on those inequities (hooks, 1994, 2003, 2009).

As guided by students, we are dedicated to effecting tangible change in students' lives.

Embracing "world traveling" and "becoming-with" theories, we actualize our intentions through actions and feeling for students as they engage in conversations about issues affecting their lives: poverty, gun violence, mental health, motivation, school attendance and performance, school cleanliness, and social media. We seek to establish relationships where open, candid dialogues can thrive, empowering students to articulate their concerns and providing a platform for students' genuine expression of their perspectives on various social and school-based issues.

Coalition Building: Strategic Thinking and Action

Pedagogies of comunidad provide the relational and cultural foundation that makes coalition building central, as noted above in our discussion of *cariño*. We want to highlight how coalition building is also about being strategic in our thinking and actions to make sustainable changes in various schools and across diverse groups. We understand schools as complex institutions that come with various realities that, inevitably, shape teachers' lived experiences as professionals and inform many of their pedagogical approaches and decisions. Project HighKEY teachers, like teachers across the country, are working within social contexts that come with diverse philosophies of teaching and learning, distinct power structures, and varying degrees of professional autonomy for curricular design. For our YPAR teachers, many of these realities surfaced as constraints and/or tensions for their everyday teaching practice. For example, during the 2023–2024 academic year, HighKEY teachers encountered book banning and text censorship, increased testing prioritization, and significant administrator and teacher turnover. Two of our four HighKEY teachers experienced multiple principal changes in one academic year, making it hard to feel connected to a unified mission and vision for the school.

Teachers who bring a social justice orientation to their teaching need to find ways to work within the existing systems of power and work against and beyond those systems to create opportunities for practicing civic futures for their learning and students' learning. One of the ways HighKEY teachers did this was by becoming a coalition. Our coalition can be characterized as a professional learning network that supports teachers to name and push back against some of the constraints and injustices they face in their schools. Although YPAR and the commitment to youth voice and action brought this disparate group of teachers together, we became allies over time to one another's efforts to challenge inequities and advocate for school-level changes.

We built this coalition by practicing civic futures together. Specifically, we met once a month for three years to collaboratively imagine, design, and implement opportunities for youth to practice civic futures in high school classrooms. During our HighKEY meetings and other collaborations, we ensure that strategies are developed and implemented to reflect the community's collective interests, values, and goals, fostering a sense of unity and purpose. Given that our pedagogy is social justice oriented, we often disrupt school norms that perpetuate dominant ideologies and ways of being. For example, during our November 2023 meeting, we engaged in an emotional conversation about the genocidal violence in Palestine, with one of our YPAR teachers courageously wearing a Free Palestine T-shirt on our university campus. This prompted a heartfelt discussion around oppression and freedom and later led to a lesson plan collaboration between two YPAR teachers (coauthors of this paper) that we will share later in this essay. We recognize that creating time and space for teachers to talk across differences and practice engaging with often divisive issues, beliefs, and worldviews is critical to this coalition.

Although YPAR teachers are doing this resistance work in their individual schools, this evolving coalition has provided teachers a sense of support and accountability to trusted peers who are doing similar kinds of resistance work in their schools. The teachers are building both community and confidence in and through their YPAR efforts with HighKEY, and we noticed how this has implications for their work in schools, both in terms of pushing back and making a difference in students' lives.

Collective Partnerships

In our educational settings, *comunidad* reflects a pedagogy that prioritizes collaborative learning, mutual respect, and the co-construction of knowledge. It highlights a partnership model that values every participant's input and experience, with decisions made through dialogue, consensus building, and reflection. This priority is evident in several aspects of Project HighKEY. It is evident in the design team, the group responsible for designing school-specific approaches to YPAR, composed of teachers, students, and university-based researchers. Although this composition poses some organizational and logistical challenges, especially with regards to meeting with students and teachers during the school day, the partnerships have been strengthened by bringing all stakeholders together on a regular basis. This approach is also evident in our larger team's multiple, overlapping projects, where cross-collaboration flourishes as teachers partner and share their expertise. For instance, our teachers have created long-term research sequences and alternative projects. One of our HighKEY teachers, Maggie, developed a comprehensive book project in her ELA classroom and in the school of another HighKEY teacher, Sarah; YPAR is now positioned as year one of a four-year research-sequence for all students. Finally, in a different school, Drew and his ELA colleague, Taylor, developed a mini-YPAR unit. These collaborative efforts enrich the learning experience and create a sustainable framework for ongoing educational innovation and mutual growth, and they offer evidence for integrating YPAR in ways that fit the specific classroom and/or school context and goals. The overlapping projects are also evident in the connections and relationships created between HighKEY and other similar projects. For example, HighKEY teachers have joined some of the monthly meetings for SchYPAR, a multiyear research-practice partnership between CSU and the Educational Service Centers (ESC) of Northeast and Central Ohio focused on implementing YPAR in thirty districts in Ohio.

As a research-practice partnership, Project HighKEY was designed with the intent to foster school-university partnerships. Although we knew that team members would share a commitment to YPAR, we did not know what this partnership would look like or how team members would connect with one another. After three years of working as a team, we have found that a key strength of the project design is that it invites teachers to collaborate with peers, consistently and over time, around a shared commitment to YPAR. This professional network serves as a compelling alternative to some of the more typical professional learning and development sessions that are offered by a school and/or district in that it creates opportunities to not only build a YPAR curriculum but also to build professional relationships. One of the most essential elements of this partnership is creating space and time for teachers to come together around meaningful work. For us, this means the regular all-team meetings the first Wednesday of every month but also regular school and classroom visits that could involve co-teaching, observing, planning, or debriefing a recent lesson. In this way, there is a strong commitment to being present and showing up in schools, supporting space for ongoing conversations between teachers, students, and researchers around the YPAR implementation process. Our teachers are situated as knowledge holders, knowing their teaching experience, their subject content, and the culture and social practices of schools.

The Application of Pedagogies of *Comunidad* in Schools

We want to provide an illustrative example of two HighKEY teachers, Karmel and Drew (both coauthors of this paper), coming together to build a coalition and create space to discuss and take part in social justice in schools. To preface the example in schools, we want to provide context to one of the HighKEY meetings that prompted the collaboration between Karmel and Drew. One of our HighKEY meetings in November 2023 took place soon after October 7, 2023, a socially and culturally tense moment that resurfaced (to our collective awareness) the Israel-Palestine conflict. On the day of the meeting at Cleveland State University, we were all feeling raw, quiet, and hesitant to be in such an ambivalent world climate. Karmel, whose grandparents and many relatives became refugees from Palestine to Jordan in 1948 and 1967 due to the Zionist occupation, and whose uncle has been internally displaced in Gaza since October 7, 2023, wore a shirt that read "Free Palestine." This clearly expressed opposition to the displacement of Palestinians, denying them the hope and possibility of returning to their homes. Drew commented, "I like your shirt," and expressed his desire to engage in such discussions without fearing potential job repercussions in schools. He emphasized the importance of instilling moral courage in students, allowing them to do what's right even in the face of negative consequences, and he pondered the extent to which one should be willing to take risks. Karmel acknowledged the inherent risks involved in these discussions. Some may accuse educators of indoctrinating students and creating discomfort among others. She discussed her efforts to incorporate Palestinian students' perspectives into her computer science classes to raise awareness and to educate others, all while staying within the guidelines to avoid trouble. She said, "I want to ensure that I present this lesson in a way that allows students to form their own decisions based on their research. It would be a crime to dictate what they ought to think." Karmel emphasized the importance of having a moral compass, encouraging students to investigate, research, collect data, and analyze that data. This approach allows the students to make unbiased decisions and contribute to creating a just world for all humanity. The conversation continued, and all teachers discussed their role in creating spaces for difficult conversations in schools and how YPAR is an invaluable avenue for it.

Inspired by the conversation and planning for the NCTE conference where HighKEY teachers would present, Molly ended the meeting with the prompt, "Even in trying times, how does YPAR give you hope? Write just one line that begins with the phrase 'I dream a world . . .' and describe a change you hope for," which created the opening poem in this paper. After this HighKEY meeting, various events occurred, such as the NCTE conference, YPAR work in the classrooms from Karmel and Drew and other HighKEY teachers, and a student YPAR conference at CSU organized by Molly. In particular, Karmel worked hard to create a detailed YPAR unit aligned with the content standards, using the computer science curriculum. The project addressed the research question, "How would you evaluate the situation in Gaza involving the Israeli military? What factors would you consider in determining whether it constitutes genocide?" and encompassed computer science applications developed by the students to address the research question and implement actions they proposed. Our HighKEY team members Rosalinda and Adam supported the project planning and delivery. The YPAR project occurred from February 26 to March 6, 2024, and students prepared a presentation for the student YPAR conference at CSU. Karmel's and Drew's students both participated. Drew, seeing Karmel's students present, mentioned to Karmel that he would love for her students to

Figure 4: Student presentations

4a. Students presenting. 4b. Audience of students on their phones exploring the applications Karmel's students did for the project. 4c. All participants enjoying cheese blintzes provided by Drew.

present at his school. Drew was impressed by her students' presentation, highlighting their deep understanding of the subject, thorough research, accurate information, creative application designs, and the significant impact of addressing it as a contemporary social justice issue. Additionally, the students' confidence and commitment to raising awareness about the topic were truly inspiring.

On June 12, 2024, Karmel's student, Dee (pseudonym), presented the computer science YPAR project in Drew's classroom. Dee copresented with two of Drew's students, who joined her on the presentation day. Two presentations took place; the first at 10 a.m. and the second at 1:40 p.m. Drew coordinated with ninth- and tenth-grade teachers to bring their students for the morning session and eleventh- and twelfth-grade teachers for the afternoon session. Dee and her copresenters provided an overview of their topic during both sessions, sharing their research questions, methods, and findings. After the presentations, attendees explored the applications created by the students. Drew and Karmel then facilitated a discussion on the importance of the project, highlighting the economic impacts of war and the allocation of resources. Drew explained how US tax dollars fund wars while domestic needs, like healthcare and education, remain underfunded. An English teacher remarked on the emotional impact of the conversation, emphasizing the need to channel those feelings into solidarity and action. Karmel concluded by emphasizing the importance of scrutinizing, researching, and questioning biased media while also advocating against all forms of dehumanization, oppression, unfairness, and mistreatment of prisoners on all sides of the conflict. Throughout both presentations, all participants savored cheese blintzes provided by Drew in celebration of the Jewish holiday, Shavuot.

This example of *pedagogy of comunidad* illustrates a powerful form of coalition building, bridging the gap between teachers and students across different schools to foster social justice education. Karmel and Drew, two HighKEY teachers, created a space for discussing and addressing socially and culturally sensitive issues, such as the Israel-Palestine conflict, in mutual *cariño* environments. This relational learning was sparked during a HighKEY meeting, leading to joint lesson planning and support from the entire team. The partnership enabled students to engage deeply with YPAR projects, culminating in shared presentations and discussions that connected Karmel's and Drew's students. This cross-collaboration empowered students to explore complex social issues and highlighted the importance of moral courage and critical thinking. Karmel and Drew demonstrated how coalition building in education can bridge diverse perspectives, create solidarity, and foster a collective partnership and commitment to social justice by facilitating these discussions and providing a platform for students' voices.

Thoughts Moving Forward: Growing the Coalition

Central to a *pedagogy of comunidad* is sharing the work with others and creating opportunities to expand the coalition. This work can't be done alone or in isolation. We need to shore each other up and find ways to extend our networks. We believe that our HighKEY team is engaged in this coalition building nearly every day. We know it happens in HighKEY teachers' classrooms but also with other teachers and administrators. In November 2023, our team was able to travel together to the NCTE Annual Convention to share part of this ongoing work with other educators. At the end of our presentation, after teachers' shared more about their experiences teaching

YPAR and why they are motivated to teach YPAR, we invited the audience to contribute to a new coauthored poem, inspired by the same Langston Hughes prompt: *Even in trying times, how does YPAR give you hope? Write just one line that begins with the phrase "I dream a world . . ." and describe a change you hope for.* This second coauthored poem reflects how important it is to extend the work and grow the coalition. It brings in new voices speaking to their hopes for education and how fostering youth voice and youth action can provide hope for our future.

Crowd-Sourced Poem
Inspired by Langston Hughes
Collaboratively Authored by Participants at NCTE's Annual Convention
November 18, 2023

I dream a world where our youth have the ability to change our future.

A world that provides a foundation for all youth to be leaders

Where ideas don't get criticized, no matter how big or small they might be

And students are engaged with their learning

because they are authentically interested

I dream of a world in which students become changemakers who actively shape the world around them for the betterment of all.

Where young people know they have power and voice

And a world where all students are valued, known, and respected

I dream a world full of people that know how to fight for joy

In which agency and voice are available to everyone, always

A world where everyone has agency to get their human needs met

I dream a world where we recognize each other in our full potential

I dream a world where people are aware of what they are

and what they can be

Concluding Thoughts

We hope that by sharing how we have cultivated a *pedagogy of comunidad* with YPAR teachers illustrates the value of relationship building around a shared commitment for adult learning and its implications for adults practicing civic futures. This work supports YPAR educators and YPAR researchers to be critical and intentional as we continue to understand the possibilities and challenges of situating a liberatory pedagogy such as YPAR in US public schools (Brion-Meisels & Alter, 2018; Caraballo et al., 2017; Rubin et al., 2017). Our collective work is deeply informed by our distinct positionalities, yet it is through these differences that we come together to co-create, embodying Ortega's theory of "becoming-with." By embracing our unique identities—whether as educators, researchers, or advocates—we cultivate a shared sense of purpose and a feeling for one another and an intent to uplift our collective struggle for dignity and justice. This essay contributes to an evolving conversation around what it looks like for teachers to be committed to this activist-oriented work in schools and how YPAR teaching might inform teachers' own adult learning and advocacy in their schools. Building a network and communities for teachers is extremely important when civil discourse is highly polarized. Through our *pedagogies of comunidad*, we aim to create hopeful and meaningful impacts for youth, for our teaching lives, and for the world at large.

Works Cited

Buckley-Marudas, M. F., Godínez, R., Abutaleb, K., Cooper, G., Rahill, M., Retherford, D., Schwab, S., Zepp, T., & Voight, A. (2024). Why teachers integrate YPAR in their teaching: Cultivating youth wellbeing, student voice, and social justice. *LEARNing Landscapes, 17*(1), 63–82. https://doi.org/10.36510/learnland.v17i1.1120

Buckley-Marudas, M. F., & Soltis, S. (2020). What youth care about: Exploring topic identification for youth-led research in school. *The Urban Review, 52*(2), 331–350. https://doi.org/10.1007/s11256-019-00530-5

Cammarota, J., & Fine, M. (Eds.). (2008). *Revolutionizing education: Youth participatory action research in motion.* Routledge. https://doi.org/10.4324/9780203932100

Carl, N. M., & Ravitch, S. M. (2021). Addressing inequity through youth participatory action research: Toward a critically hopeful approach to more equitable schools. *Action Research, 19*(2), 433–448. https://doi.org/10.1177/1476750318804623

Crenshaw, K. W., & Evans-Winters, V. E. (2024). Black girls youth participatory action research & pedagogies. *Journal of African America Women and Girls in Education, 4*(1), 1–6. https://doi.org/10.21423/jaawge-v3i2a165

Crenshaw, K. W., Ocen, P., & Nanda, J. (2015). *Black girls matter: Pushed out, overpoliced and underprotected.* African American Policy Forum & Center for Intersectionality and Social Policy Studies. https://scholarship.law.columbia.edu/faculty_scholarship/3227

Diemer, M. A., Voight, A. M., & Mark, C. (2011). Youth development in traditional and transformational service-learning programs. In T. Stewart & N. Webster (Eds.), *Problematizing service-learning: Critical reflections for development and action* (pp. 155–173). Information Age Publishing.

Duncan-Andrade, J. M. R., & Morrell, E. (2008). *The art of critical pedagogy: Possibilities for moving from theory to practice in urban schools: Vol. 285. Counterpoints: Studies in*

Coalition-Building Tips

- **Leverage Alternative Professional Development.** Recognize the power of coming together around a shared goal or intention as an effective alternative to typical district-sanctioned professional learning opportunities.
- **Create Space.** Ensure designated spaces for regular meetings, visits, sharing work, professional learning, and connection. These spaces should include time for reflective practices and open dialogue.
- **Foster Organic Design.** Embrace organic, by-design development opportunities rather than relying solely on traditional, formal ones.
- **Utilize Unexpected Spaces.** Understand that coalition building can happen in unexpected spaces. Harness the power of coming together to build a community of practice around a shared goal, such as YPAR.
- **Address Existing Tensions and Constraints.** Acknowledge the intensified school tensions and constraints, especially post-COVID-19. Recognize that while you may not have support and mentorship within your school, building a network outside of it is possible.

the postmodern theory of education. Peter Lang. https://doi.org/10.3726/b12771

Freire, P. (1987). *Pedagogia do oprimido* (17th ed.). Paz e Terra.

Godinez, R. (2022). *Mexicana/Latina campesinas cultivating knowledge: A collective agricultural land-based education in Central Washington state in the homelands of Yakama Nation* (Publication No. 29210540) [Doctoral dissertation, University of California, Berkeley]. ProQuest Dissertations and Theses Global.

Godinez, R. (2024). Manos que enseñan [hands that teach]: Mexicana/Latina campesina mothers and their children enacting the pedagogies of barbear. In M. J. Villaseñor & H. Jiménez (Eds.), *Latinx experiences: Interdisciplinary perspectives* (pp. 255–267). Sage.

Godinez, R., & Baquedano-López, P. (2022). Mother pedagogies of migration: Multiplicitous identities and pedagogies. *Diaspora, Indigenous, and Minority Education, 16*(3), 185–199. https://doi.org/10.1080/15595692.2021.2007074

hooks, bell. (1994). *Teaching to transgress: Education as the practice of freedom*. Routledge. https://doi.org/10.4324/9780203700280

hooks, bell. (2003). *Teaching community: A pedagogy of hope*. Routledge. https://doi.org/10.4324/9780203957769

hooks, bell. (2009). *Teaching critical thinking: Practical wisdom*. Routledge. https://doi.org/10.4324/9780203869192

Mirra, N., Garcia, A., & Morrell, E. (2016). Doing youth participatory action research: Transforming inquiry with researchers, educators, and students. Routledge. https://doi.org/10.4324/9781315748047

Ortega, M. (2016) *In-between: Latina feminist phenomenology, multiplicity, and the self*. SUNY Press. https://doi.org/10.2307/jj.18253458

Ozer, E. J., Cantor, J. P., Cruz, G. W., Fox, B., Hubbard, E., & Moret, L. (2008). The diffusion of youth-led participatory research in urban schools: The role of the prevention support system in implementation and sustainability. *American Journal of Community Psychology, 41*(3–4), 278–289. https://doi.org/10.1007/s10464-008-9173-0

Ozer, E. J., & Wright, D. (2012). Beyond school spirit: The effects of youth-led participatory action research in two urban high schools. *Journal of Research on Adolescence, 22*(2), 267–283. https://doi.org/10.1111/j.1532-7795.2012.00780.

Voight, A. (2015). Student voice for school climate improvement: A case study of an urban middle school. *Journal of Community & Applied Social Psychology, 25*(4), 310–326. https://doi.org/10.1002/casp.2216

Voight, A. & Velez, V. (2018). Youth participatory action research in the high school curriculum: Education outcomes for student participants in a district-wide initiative. *Journal of Research on Educational Effectiveness, 11*(3), 433–451. https://doi.org/10.1080/19345747.2018.1431345

Index

About the Editors

Lakisha Odlum is an assistant professor of English education at CUNY Queens College, where she teaches undergraduate and graduate preservice and inservice teachers. Her research interests include racial literacy and teacher preparation, the intersection of racial and digital literacies, diversifying the teaching profession, and the teaching of Black girls.

Nicole Mirra is an associate professor in the Graduate School of Education at Rutgers University. Her research utilizes participatory design methods in classroom, community, and digital spaces to collaboratively create civic learning environments with youth and educators that disrupt discourses and structures of racial injustice and creatively compose liberatory social futures.

Antero Garcia is an associate professor in the Graduate School of Education at Stanford University. His research explores the possibilities of speculative imagination and healing in educational research.

About the Authors

Karmel Abutaleb, who hails originally from Palestine but was born and raised in Jordan, is a secondary math educator at Natividad Pagan International Newcomers Academy. She takes pride in being a bilingual role model deeply committed to fostering integrity and resourcefulness within the dynamic backdrop of diversity. She has implemented YPAR in her classes for the past three years with a focus on social justice. Hoping for a more equitable world for all humanity, she helps students find their voices and challenge the system through research and actions. She believes in the invaluable tool of YPAR to pursue her research interests: social justice in education, student engagement and motivation, and school attendance and its impact on performance.

Erin Ashcraft is a former K–5 classroom teacher. In her time in the classroom, she taught kindergarten, second-grade, and fifth-grade ELA. She is currently a doctoral fellow pursuing her PhD in the Department of Curriculum and Instruction at the University of North Texas, focusing on language and literacy. She is also a preservice teacher field supervisor for a residency program. She enjoys coaching and mentoring preservice teachers through collaborative, validating, affirming, and reflective dialogue and practices. Her research interests include social justice-oriented preservice teacher preparation programs, culturally sustaining pedagogies, critical literacy practices, and critical discourse analysis surrounding book censorship and read-alouds.

Andrea Avery, EdD, is a disabled writer, teacher, and unaffiliated scholar. She is the author of *Sonata: A Memoir of Pain and the Piano* (2017) and the forthcoming novella *Visiting Composer*. Her work has appeared in the *Harvard Educational Review*, *Radical Teacher*, and *The Politics of Women's Bodies: Sexuality, Appearance, and Behavior* (Third Edition).

Dr. Mónica Baldonado-Ruiz is an assistant professor of literacy at San Diego State University who believes that the power of stories connects us to others around us. She has used her own voice as an advocate for students and to celebrate the communities of those students. Her research interests include literacy education, culturally sustaining pedagogy, equitable practices of teaching writing, and Lat-Crit theory of education, specifically testimonio. Her most recent publications, *Stories of Self, Stories of Us: Bearing Witness and Writing Testimonios* and *From Silence to Testimonio: Adolescent Latinas Agency in Writing,* highlight the importance of personal, community writing, testimonio, and oral history in the secondary writing curriculum. Her work with the National Writing Project as a co-director of the Central Arizona Writing Project, which resulted in her establishment of the *Cuentos* writing workshops as well as the *Pláticas* reading and writing group, has prepared her to develop and implement professional development opportunities that highlight the teacher-teaching-teachers model.

Dr. Sarah A. Bonner is an assistant professor at the University of North Carolina at Wilmington.

Mary Frances (Molly) Buckley-Marudas, PhD, is an associate professor in the Levin College of Public Affairs & Education at Cleveland State University and faculty-in-residence at Campus International High School in the Cleveland Metropolitan School District. She received her PhD in reading/writing/literacy at the University of Pennsylvania. She is the cofounder and co-director of the Cleveland Teaching Collaborative (www.cleteaching.org) and co-producer of the podcast, *ChalkTalk with CLE Teaching.* Her research interests include youth-led research, adolescent literacies, digital literacy, and English education.

Nathaniel Cha is currently a doctoral candidate in Literacy, Language, and Culture at the University of Illinois at Chicago. As a former middle school teacher, his research focuses on critical pedagogy, civic literacies, and healing-centered education.

Mike P. Cook is an associate professor of English language arts education at Auburn University. His research and teaching draw on justice, equity, and antiracism in English language arts teacher education and utilize a critical lens to explore teachers as agents of change. Specifically, his work explores the ways ELA teacher educators prepare antiracist 6–12 grade ELA teachers and how activism is taken up as part of ELA teaching and learning at all levels. His work has been published in the *Journal of Teacher Education*, *English Education*, *Journal of Adolescent & Adult Literacy*, and other scholarly outlets.

Nicholas DePascal is currently a doctoral student in the Department of Language, Literacy, and Sociocultural Studies at the University of New Mexico, as well as a high school English teacher.

Dr. Kristian Blake Douglas, a 2022 UNCF Faculty Fellow and 2024 RISER Fellow, is director of undergraduate teacher education and an assistant professor in the School of Education at Clark Atlanta University, where he teaches courses centered on early childhood education, educational foundations, and literacy. He holds a master of arts in bilingual and bicultural education from Columbia University and a bachelor of arts in foreign languages (Spanish) from the University of Alabama at Birmingham. He completed his PhD in curriculum and instruction with a concentration in literacy education. Dr. Douglas is a member of the Literacy Research Association, American Council of the Teaching of Foreign Languages, National Council of Teachers of English, and Georgia Association for Educators. He also serves on the ELA Advisory Council for the Georgia State Department of Education, on numerous committees with the Georgia Professional Standards Commission, and as a literacy consultant with the New York State Department of Education.

Demetrius Dove is a senior elementary education major student at Clark Atlanta University, hailing from Tacoma, Washington. Passionate about shaping young minds and fostering positive change in generations to come, he has emerged as a leading force in the field of education. Throughout his academic journey, he has actively engaged in various leadership roles, leaving a lasting impact on educational organizations at the local, state, and national levels. He served as the 2022–2023 membership chair for the Georgia Association of Educators Aspiring Educators program, where he played a crucial role in fostering a strong community of aspiring educators. In addition, he took on the responsibilities of Secretary for the 2022–2023 GAE, CAU Chapter, showing immense dedication to the chapter's success, even chartering it himself. At the national level, Dove has made significant contributions, being elected to serve on the NEA Board of Directors for a two-year term. His journey of service and dedication is anchored in the sentiments of Clark Atlanta University, as he continues to embody its motto, "A Culture for Service."

Alexia Enriquez is a humanities and ethnic studies teacher at High Tech High Chula Vista and will be one of the K–12 educator leaders in this project. She identifies as a *transfronteriza*, having grown up in the San Diego-Tijuana border region in which she now teaches. For the last seven years, she has dedicated her teaching career to creating equitable learning environments for all students. Additionally, her work in building community-based writing instruction curriculum that reflects the communities of her students makes her uniquely qualified to share her expertise through professional development opportunities with teachers.

Rosalinda Godinez, PhD, is a postdoctoral fellow at the Center for Urban Education at Cleveland State University. She received her PhD in social and cultural studies from the University of California, Berkeley, and a bachelor's degree in sociology from Washington State University. As an education ethnographer, Godinez is committed to establishing collaborative and action-based partnerships that document and honor people's everyday life and community, movement, and education practices.

Kevin "Kei" Ho (he/they) is a fifth-year English teacher in Chicago Public Schools. Their teaching strives to empower students by centering inclusivity, culturally sustaining pedagogy, and humanizing forms of assessment. Ho is a Stanford Hollyhock fellow and a founding member of the Alternative Assessment Collective. They recently received their master of education degree from Loyola University Chicago, and previously they taught in Vietnam through the Fulbright ETA program.

Dr. Mariah Kornbluh is an assistant professor in community psychology in the Department of Psychology at the University of Oregon. Her current research is funded through the William T. Grant Scholars Program. This work focuses on supporting educators in utilizing research as a tool to identify, vet, and use high-impact civics curriculum. **Dr. Sherry Bell** is a postdoctoral scholar in the Psychology Department at the University of Oregon. **Raquel Amador** is a second-year clinical/developmental doctoral student in the Psychology Department at the University of Oregon. All three authors are part of the Oregon Youth Empowerment Project, an applied research group working in partnership with communities to develop applied research, interventions, and policy change that promotes positive and equitable youth development. Lastly, **Dr. Audrey Lucero** is an associate professor of language and literacy education in the Department of Education Studies at the University of Oregon.

Daniel P. Moore (he/him) is a doctoral candidate at Stanford University's Graduate School of Education in the Curriculum & Teacher Education and Race, Inequality & Language in Education programs. His research interests include literacy education, English education, culturally sustaining pedagogy, assessment, teacher education, and issues of educational equity. He was previously a secondary English teacher for ten years, mostly in New York City. He is also an experienced teacher educator and instructional coach.

Jessica Murdter-Atkinson, PhD, is a former K–5 classroom teacher and instructional coach. Currently, she is an assistant professor of literacy education at the University of North Texas. Her research focuses on the intersections of early literacy, coaching and mentoring preservice teachers, and culturally sustaining approaches to literacy instruction. She earned her bachelor's and master's degrees from the University of Texas at Austin and earned her PhD in curriculum and instruction, language and literacy studies, also from the University of Texas at Austin. Her scholarly work has been published in *Reading Research Quarterly, Urban Education, Literacy, Research, and Instruction*, and the *Teacher Educator*.

Mary Rose O'Shea, NBCT, is a Chicago Public Schools secondary English language arts teacher and reading specialist, labor activist and former union delegate, and doctoral candidate in Literacy, Language, and Culture at the University of Illinois at Chicago. Her research focuses on critical literacy pedagogy, teacher preparation and mentorship, and self-study of teacher practices. She is also the founder of Tutoring by ChiPraxis, an organization dedicated to providing literacy support to people of all ages and backgrounds. In addition to her work in education, she is part of an interdisciplinary sibling research team examining the maintenance and development of Irish American identity in mid-twentieth-century Chicago, specifically through the role of dance halls as social centers.

Dr. Reshma Ramkellawan-Arteaga has the crux of her expertise nested in secondary literacy instruction. But she has also supported math and science teachers with their pedagogy and curriculum planning. Her interests and expertise include digital and media literacy, curriculum development, staff and leadership coaching, and education research. She has served as an assistant principal for a prominent New York City charter network. She has over twelve years of experience in the educational field, serving in the roles of teacher, mentor, team leader, and staff developer. During the 2012 to 2013 school year, she participated in the National Academy of Advanced Teacher Education (NAATE) program to refine her skills as a teacher leader. In 2016, she worked in the New York City Department of Teaching and Leadership, helping to redesign the Principal Candidate Pool assessment. She received her undergraduate degree in secondary English language arts education from the University of Central Florida. In 2009 and 2011, respectively, she earned her master of arts in curriculum and teaching and master in education in the teaching of English from Teachers College, Columbia University. Dr. Ramkellawan also earned her EdD in English education from Teachers College, Columbia University.

Rachel Ranschaert, PhD, is an assistant professor of literacy education at the University of North Texas. Her research focuses on literacy teacher preparation and its intersections with sociopolitical discourses, news media, community contexts, and school partnerships. She earned both her bachelor's and master's degrees from the University of Notre Dame before beginning her career as an English language arts teacher in Arizona and Texas. She earned her PhD in educational theory and practice, along with a certificate in interdisciplinary qualitative research, from the University of Georgia. Her scholarly work also extends to writing pedagogies, middle grades education, teaching residencies, and qualitative methodologies. Her work has been published in leading journals, including the *Journal of Teacher Education*, *Educational Studies*, and *Middle School Journal.*

Drew Retherford is a secondary social studies teacher at Lincoln-West School of Science and Health. He is deeply committed to serving the people of Cleveland through ensuring their children receive a high-quality public education. He has implemented YPAR for the past four years in both classroom and student club settings. He has a background in labor and antiwar organizing and sees YPAR as a method of empowering students and passing organizing skills on to younger generations.

Mary Rice is an associate professor in the Department of Language, Literacy, and Sociocultural Studies at the University of New Mexico. Prior to earning her PhD, she taught English language arts, reading, and English as a second language at the middle school level.

Celina Rodriguez is a humanities and ethnic studies teacher at High Tech High Chula Vista, With a background in Chicanx studies, international relations, and a masters in education with a focus on Chicano art curriculum, she is also a lifelong resident of the San Diego-Tijuana border region. The high school ethnic studies movement pulled her back into the classroom after a fourteen-year career in education and community-based nonprofits across California and Tijuana. She is dedicated to a humanities curriculum that integrates culturally sustaining and decolonial pedagogies.

Brandon L. Sams teaches in the Department of English at Iowa State University. He works with undergraduates studying English education and still can't believe he gets to teach for a living.

Dr. Robyn Seglem is a professor in the School of Teaching and Learning at Illinois State University in Normal, Illinois.

Kate Sjostrom is a senior lecturer and associate director of English education at the University of Illinois at Chicago whose research and teaching focus on writing pedagogy. Her creative and scholarly work has appeared in *RHINO*, *English Journal*, *Teaching/Writing*, and elsewhere. She is the coeditor of the collection *Unsettling Education: Searching for Ethical Footing in a Time of Reform.*

Andrea Vaughan is a researcher, organizational leader, and educator devoted to understanding and deepening learners' experiences across in- and out-of-school contexts. She is the interim director of the Center for Literacy (CFL) and a visiting research assistant professor in the College of Education at the University of Illinois at Chicago. She serves as a co-director of the Chicago Area Writing Project.

María Luisa García Underwood has accumulated over three decades of experience in education. Underwood has held positions as a classroom teacher, instructional coach/staff developer, and program/district administrator. She served as the director of the Multicultural Education Center, where she developed and supervised diversity education. She has worked as an administrator in various institutions of higher education, including Teachers College, Columbia University's Institute for Urban and Minority Education (IUME). She works with K–12 educators in the areas of literacy, second language acquisition, and special education. She has created culturally responsive curricula to help K–12 teachers transform and root literacy instruction with antiracist pedagogy and social justice standards. She has made many presentations for the National Council of Teachers of English (NCTE), the Association for Supervision and Curriculum Development (ASCD), and the National Association for Bilingual Education (NABE). Underwood earned a bachelor of arts in early childhood and elementary education from Fairleigh Dickinson University and a master of science in education in learning sciences from the University of Pennsylvania, an education master in reading and bilingual education from Teachers College, Columbia University, and a master of arts in special education with a specialization in learning disabilities from the same institution. She is currently a doctoral candidate at the University of Pennsylvania, focusing on antiracist pedagogy and learning design in teacher preparation programs.

Kristine Wilber is a doctoral candidate in the Language, Literacy, and Culture program at the University of Illinois at Chicago. Her research includes arts-based and post-qualitative methodologies and writing pedagogies. She is a high school teacher/librarian in Chicago Public Schools and serves as a co-director of the Chicago Area Writing Project.

Rebecca Woodard is an associate professor of curriculum and instruction at the University of Illinois at Chicago and is a coeditor of the journal *Language Arts*. Her research on writing and writing pedagogy is grounded in sociocultural and critical theories that recognize teaching and learning as social, cultural, and historically and politically situated. Dr. Woodard's recent research has focused on climate justice; embodied learning and theater-informed pedagogies; and culturally sustaining writing pedagogies. She teaches courses on elementary literacy methods, disciplinary literacy, and writing/composition.

This book was typeset in PT Sans, PT Sans Narrow, and Alternate Gothic No3 by Cynthia Gomez.

The typefaces used on the cover include Franklin Gothic Medium and Avenir Black.

The book was printed on 50 lb., white, offset paper.